DUE PROCESS OF LAW BEYOND THE STATE

Due Process of Law Beyond the State

Requirements of Administrative Procedure

GIACINTO DELLA CANANEA

OXFORD
UNIVERSITY PRESS

OXFORD
UNIVERSITY PRESS

Great Clarendon Street, Oxford, OX2 6DP,
United Kingdom

Oxford University Press is a department of the University of Oxford. It furthers the University's objective of excellence in research, scholarship, and education by publishing worldwide. Oxford is a registered trade mark of Oxford University Press in the UK and in certain other countries

First edition published in 2016

Published in the United States of America by Oxford University Press
198 Madison Avenue, New York, NY 10016, United States of America

British Library Cataloguing in Publication Data
Data available

Library of Congress Control Number: 2016945127

ISBN 978–0–19–878838–6

To Simonetta; *fidelitas et amor*

Foreword

The current stage of globalization has increased legal relations between individuals, social groups, and firms with governments other than their own, either from another nation or from an international or supranational organization, with the consequence that questions concerning exercises of power by public authorities have increased. These questions are differentiated in nature. In several nations of the world such questions are traditionally conceptualized in terms of procedural fairness. In the day-to-day working of government in the twentieth century sound administration has assumed equally prominent importance. In one sense, this latter way of looking at administrative procedure might be represented as being in conflict with the former. I have tried, therefore, both to illustrate the variety of legal institutions that are inspired by these instrumental and non-instrumental rationales, and to discuss the problems raised by exercises of administrative powers from the viewpoint of general principles of law. In contrast to the opinion that general principles are increasingly more difficult to discern in our differentiated world, I argue that it is precisely at the level of general principles that we can find the instruments for understanding, and possibly solving, some such problems. In studying and teaching transnational law I have found that the works of administrative and constitutional lawyers on the one hand and those of lawyers working in the vast realm of international law, and in particular in the fields of world trade and of foreign investment, leave a gap that is sometimes hard to bridge. This book is an attempt to bridge that gap.

I have been studying and writing on aspects of this topic for longer than it might have been expected initially. The idea came to my mind almost fifteen years ago, during a series of seminars held in my old University ('La Sapienza', Rome), in the context of the problems raised by regional and global authorities, such as the European Union and the World Trade Organization, in relation to administrative action. Those problems were not wholly new, but to a degree they had a more profound sense of novelty that required a shift in perspective. I thus attempted to think about administrative due process in terms of the demands that adjudication and regulation must meet in an increasingly globalized world. This shift in perspective has led me to reconsider some received ideas about administrative law, still conceived by some as a sort of national enclave, and more particularly to look at the parallel developments and external influences that characterize an important trend of our epoch, the codification of administrative procedure. Together with a renewed interest in legal comparison, this academic work has been characterized by a growing attention to the standards set out by regulatory regimes and the rulings of international courts and tribunals. It is trite wisdom, but still wisdom that confronting one's views about certain legal institutions with those who work in other areas is not always easy, but can be very helpful. I have not retracted my former views that the global diffusion of ideas and thoughts about the law is much more complex than the one-way processes on which some critics of globalization tend to focus, and that looking beyond the borders of the State, of each State, is sometimes the only way to fully understand its particularities in terms of both concepts and principles. However, I have had the chance to come across a lot of new information and argument about the role of public authorities and to refine the views expressed initially. Even a quick look at the shorter book published some years ago (*Al di là dei confini statuali. Principi di diritto pubblico globale* (Il Mulino, 2009)) shows profound differences, empirical and normative, to that which is presented here. Readers will judge whether I have been successful in proposing an integration, rather than a mere juxtaposition, of legal realities that are too often considered only from a particular point of view.

Whatever the success of the enterprise, it has been made possible by the contribution of many. The Italian Ministry for Research and Universities has granted funds for empirical work and some younger scholars have helped me in collecting legal materials and literature. Two Italian universities ('Federico II', Naples and 'Tor Vergata', Rome) have allowed me to spend several periods of research abroad over the course of the last decade. Two French universities (Bordeaux and Science-Po, Paris) and the Max Planck Institute for Comparative and International Law (Heidelberg) have generously hosted me more than once. The Duke Law School and the Yale Law School, where I have had the chance to teach, have provided not only the resources of their libraries but also an environment that stimulated a gradual refinement of my arguments. Several colleagues (among them, Jean-Bernard Auby, Armin von Bogdandy, Mauro Bussani, Edoardo Chiti, Bernardo Mattarella, Ralf Michaels, Gregory Shaffer, Stephan Schill, and Jacques Ziller) have provided helpful comments on earlier versions of some chapters of this book. Their support is gratefully acknowledged, together with that of two anonymous reviewers. For criticism and most valuable suggestions for improving (and purging) the manuscript I am greatly indebted to two good friends and distinguished colleagues, Paul Craig and Alec Stone Sweet. For what remains, I only am culpable.

Last but by no means least, I want to express my gratitude to my wife Simonetta and to our kids—Isabella, Alfonso, and Federico—for their invaluable support during all these years.

Rome, 1 February 2016

Table of Contents

Table of Cases xiii
Table of Treaties xvii
Table of Legislation xix
List of Abbreviations xxi

1. Administrative Justice: A Transnational Perspective 1

PART I—REQUIREMENTS OF ADMINISTRATIVE DUE PROCESS

2. The Requirement to Carry Out a Procedure 17
3. *Audi Alteram Partem* 35
4. The Giving Reasons Requirement 61

PART II—RATIONALES FOR DUE PROCESS REQUIREMENTS

5. Variety of Rationales for Due Process Requirements 85
6. Dignity and Participation 103
7. Sound Administration and Cooperation 121

PART III—A THEORY OF ADMINISTRATIVE DUE PROCESS BEYOND THE STATE

8. Administrative Due Process: A Conceptual Analysis 139
9. Administrative Due Process as a General Principle of Public Law 155
10. Administrative Due Process as a Global Principle of Public Law 179

Index 207

Detailed Table of Contents

Table of Cases xiii
Table of Treaties xvii
Table of Legislation xix
List of Abbreviations xxi

1. Administrative Justice: A Transnational Perspective 1
1. Old and New Transnational Situations and Standards 1
2. Limits to the Inquiry 7
3. Structure of the Inquiry 13

PART I—REQUIREMENTS OF ADMINISTRATIVE DUE PROCESS

2. The Requirement to Carry Out a Procedure 17
1. The Legal Importance of Administrative Procedure 17
2. Codification of Administrative Procedure 23
3. National Procedures Under External Influence 27
4. Procedural Requirements for Non-State Authorities 31
5. The Intrinsic Value of a Procedure 33

3. *Audi Alteram Partem* 35
1. The Closest Thing to an Invariant: Due Process for Civil Servants 35
2. A Minimum Standard: Hearing Adversely Affected Parties 40
3. A Transnational Minimum Standard 47
4. A Minimum Standard for Non-State Authorities 53
5. Conclusions 59

4. The Giving Reasons Requirement 61
1. Origins and Variety of Giving Reasons Requirements 61
2. A Minimum Standard for State Authorities: Justifying Disadvantageous Distinctions 65
3. A Transnational Minimum Standard 70
4. A Minimum Standard for Non-State Authorities 75
5. The Global Diffusion of Due Process Requirements: Two Caveats 78

PART II—RATIONALES FOR DUE PROCESS REQUIREMENTS

5. Variety of Rationales for Due Process Requirements 85
1. The Concept of 'Rationales' 85
2. Rationales of Due Process Within the State 91
3. Rationales of Due Process Beyond the State 94
4. A First Cut at the Argument 101

6. Dignity and Participation 103
1. The Right of Defence 103
2. From the Right of Defence to the Protection of Dignity 105
3. From the Right of Defence to Collaboration and Participation 110
4. Conclusions 118

7. Sound Administration and Cooperation 121
1. Sound Administration 121
2. Cooperation Between Public Authorities 126
3. Conflicting Rationales of Due Process 132
4. The Next Steps 136

PART III—A THEORY OF ADMINISTRATIVE DUE PROCESS BEYOND THE STATE

8. Administrative Due Process: A Conceptual Analysis 139
1. Conceptual Clarity and Operational Standards 139
2. Beyond Non-arbitrariness 140
3. Due Process and Legality: A Distinction 146
4. Due Process of Law as Distinct from Denial of Justice 149
5. Two Lines of a Theory of Due Process 153

9. Administrative Due Process as a General Principle of Public Law 155
1. General Principles of Law in the National and Transnational Arenas 155
2. Due Process as a General Principle 163
3. A Complementary and Corrective Role 170
4. A Foundational Role 173
5. From the Generality of Due Process to its Global Reach 178

10. Administrative Due Process as a Global Principle of Public Law 179
1. Variety of Views About Invariable Laws 179
2. Due Process of Law as the Closest Thing to an Invariant 184
3. Two Objections Refuted 198
4. Implications for Legal Interpretation 204

Index 207

Table of Cases

A) NATIONAL COURTS

Belgian Constitutional Court

Judgment n 91/2013 of 13 June 2013. 24
Judgment n 2014/74 of 8 May 2014 68

France

Conseil d'État
5 May 1944, *Dame Veuve Trompier-Gravier* 41
26 October 1945, *Aramu*. 41
10 April 1992, *M. Aykan*. 66
Conseil Constitutionnel, decision n 2011–183/184 QPC of 14 October 2011 46

Indian Supreme Court

AK Gopalan v The State of Madras (1950) SCR 88 (India) 38
State of Orissa v Dr. (Miss) Binapani Dei & Ors., (1967) 2 SCR 625 (India) 39
Maneka Gandhi v Union Of India (1978) 2 SCR 621 (India). 39

Italy

Consiglio di Stato IV, *Chiantera* (1895). 37
IV, Judgment of 3 April 1997, n 333 43
VI, Judgment of 20 January 2004 n 1559 . . . . . 153, 177
Regional Administrative Court for the Regione Campania, decision of 12 June 2007, n 6075 51
Tribunal of Rome, Judgment n 3906/1953 (1954) 48 Am J Int'l L 259 148

Peruvian Constitutional Court, judgment of 26 May 2011
(Application no 02638/2010) 67

South Africa, Constitutional Court, *Minister of Health v New Clicks South Africa (Pty) Ltd*,
2006 (2) SA 311 (CC). 67

Spanish Constitutional Court

Judgment n 82/2009 of 23 March 2009 67
Judgment n 186/2013 of 4 November 2013 67

UK courts

King's Bench, *James Bagg's* case 35–36
Queen's Bench, *R v Knightsbridge Crown Court, ex p International Sporting Club*
[1982] 1 QB 304. 62

House of Lords

Ridge v Baldwin (1964) AC 40. 37
Bushell v Secretary of State for the Environment [1980] 2 All ER 608 46
R v Secretary of State ex parte Doody [1994] 1 AC 53. 66

US Supreme Court

FCC v Pottsville Broadcasting Co, 309 US 134 (1940). 151
Goldberg v Kelly, 397 US 254, 90 (1970) 23

Palmer v Thompson, 403 US 217 (1971). 69
Citizens to Preserve Overton Park v Volpe, 401 US 402 (1971) 91, 97
Roe v Wade, 410 US, 113, 164 (1973) 106
Mathews v Eldridge, 424 US 319, 334–5 (1976) 92
Vermont Yankee Nuclear Power Corp v Natural Resources Defense Council Inc., 435 US 519 (1978) 92

B) INTERNATIONAL AND SUPRANATIONAL COURTS AND TRIBUNALS

Ad hoc arbitral tribunals

Arbitral Tribunal (Great Britain–United States), Award, (1912) 6 Reports of International Arbitral Awards 114. 157
Arbitral Tribunal *Southern Bluefin Tuna Case between Australia and Japan and between New Zealand and Japan*, Award on Jurisdiction and Admissibility, 4 August 2000 (2000) 23 Rep Int Arb Awards, 1. 125

ICSID Arbitral Tribunals

Klochner industry v Republic of Cameroon, ICSID Case No ARB/81/2, Award of 21 October 1983. 170
Amco Asia Corporation and others v Republic of Indonesia (ICSID Case No ARB/81/1), Award of 20 November 1984. . . . . 51, 165–66, 171
Maffezini v Spain (ICSID Case No ARB/97/7), Award (13 November 2000). 8
Metalclad Corporation v United Mexican States, ICSID Case No ARB(AF)/97/1, Award of 30 August 2000 . . . . . 30, 32, 52, 72
Alex Genin and others v Republic of Estonia (*Genin*), ICSID Case No ARB/99/2, Award of 25 June 2001 52
Middle East Cement Shipping and Handling Co. S.A. v Arab Republic of Egypt (*Middle East*), ICSID Case No ARB/99/6, Award of 12 April 2002 . . . . . 72, 140, 160
Técnicas Medioambientales Tecmed S.A. v United Mexican States (ICSID Case NoARB (AF)/00/2), Award of 29 May 2003. 196
The Loewen Group, Inc. and Raymond L. Loewen v United States of America (Case No ARB(AF)/98/3), Award of 26 June 2003 151
Waste Management Inc. v United Mexican States (ICSID Case No ARB(AF)/00/3), Award of 30 April 2004. 142
AES, Corporation v Argentina, ICSID Case No. ARB/02/17, Decision on jurisdiction (April 26, 2005) 167
ADC Affiliate Limited and ADC & ADMC Management Limited v Republic of Hungary (*ADC*), ICSID Case No ARB/03/16, Award of 2 October 2006. 52
PSEG Global Inc. v Republic of Turkey (ICSID Case No ARB/02/05), Award of 19 January 2007. 143
OKO Pankki Oyj and others v Republic of Estonia (ICSID Case No ARB/04/6), Award of 19 November 2007. 143
Bywater Gauff v Tanzania (ICSID Case No ARB/05/ 22), Award of 24 July 2008 140
Merrill & Ring Forestry v Canada (UNCITRAL, ICSID Administered Case), Award of 31 March 2010) 140
Helnan International Hotels A/S v Arab Republic of Egypt, ICSID Case No ARB/05/19, Award of 14 June 2010 . . . . . 151, 159
Joseph Charles Lemire v Ukraine (Lemire), ICSID Case No ARB/06/18, Award of 28 March 2011. . . . . 30, 197
Unglaube v Republic of Costa Rica (*Unglaube*) (ICSID Case No ARB/08/1), Award of 16 May 2012 . . . . . 142, 197

Bosh International, Inc and B&P Ltd Foreign Investments Enterprise v Ukraine, ICSID Case No. ARB/08/11, Award of 25 October 2012 152
ICSID Ad Hoc annulment committee on *Klockner*, Committee's Decision of 3 May 1985 on Annulment of the Award of 21 October 1983 171

UNCITRAL arbitral tribunals:

Pope & Talbot v Canada, Award in respect of damages of 31 May 2002 143
Thunderbird Gaming Corporation v United Mexican States, UNCITRAL Award of 26 January 2006 . . . . 153, 160
Saluka Investments B.V. v The Czech Republic, Award (partial) of 17 May 2006 166

Administrative Tribunal of the International Labour Organization

Judgment n 203 of 14 May 1973, *Ferrecchia v International Centre for Advanced Technical and Vocational Training* 55, 165
Judgment n 1355, of 14 July 1994, *Suprapto v UPU* 75
Judgment n 2232 of 17 July 2003, *Bustani v OPCW* 55–56
Judgment n 2355, of 1 February 2006, *J.F. v the International Atomic Energy Agency (IAEA)*. 76

EU Court of First Instance (now General Court)

Joined Cases T-79/89 et al, *BASF* et al. *v Commission* [1992] ECR II, 315 168
Case T-148/99, *Tréfilunion v Commission* [1995] ECR II-1063 104
Case T-315/01 *Kadi v Council and Commission* [2005] ECR II-3649. . . . . 57, 144, 189, 202
Case T-306/01 *Yusuf and Al Barakaat International Foundation v Council and Commission* [2005] ECR II-3533 57
Case T-228/02, *Organisation de Modjahedins du Peuple de l'Iran v Council* [2006] ECR-II, 4674. . . . . 77, 110

European Court of Justice (now Court of Justice of the EU)

Joined Cases 43, 45, and 48/59, *von Lachmuller* et al. *v Commission* [1960] ECR 453 77
Case 33/62, *Maurice Alvis v Council of the EEC* [1962] ECR 109. 54
Case 17/74, *Transocean Marine Paint Association v Commission* [1974] ECR 1063 . . . . 55, 105, 176
Case 222/86, *Unectef v Heylens and Others* [1987] ECR I-1987, 4097 73
Joined Cases 46/87 and 227/88, *Hoechst AG v Commission* [1988] ECR 2859. 104–05
Case C-212/91, *Angelopharm v Freie Hansestadt Hamburg* [1994] ECR I-171 115
Case C-367/95, *Commission v Sytraval* [1998] ECR-I, 1719 64
Case C-149/96, *Portugal v Council* [1999] ECR I-8396. 133
C-93/02, *Biret International v Council* [2003] ECR I-10487 133
Case C-27/04, *Commission v Council* [2004] ECR-I 6679 33
C-377/02, *Léon Van Parys NV v Belgisch Interventie- en Restitutiebureau (BIRB)* [2005] ECR I-1465. 133
Joined Cases C-402/05 and 415/05, *Kadi v Council and Al Barakaat v Council and Commission* [2008] I-06351 . . . . 57–58, 144, 202
Case C-297/08, *Commission v Italy* [2010] ECR I, 1749 50
Case C-605/13 P, *Anbouba v Council* (2015) 5

European Court of Human Rights

Niemietz v Germany (Application no 13710/88) Series A, No 251–B, 33 105
Pellegrin v France (Application no 28541/95) 31 Eur Ct HR 651 (1999) 37–38
Fogarty v United Kingdom (Application no 37112/97), judgment of 21 November 2001, Reports, 2001, IX–157 152
Tysiac v Poland (Application no 5410/03) 20 March 2007, [2007] ECHR 219 . . . . 106–07, 149

Taskin and others v Turkey (Case no 46117/99) [2004] ECHR, X. 123–24, 201
Lombardi Vallauri v Italy (Application no 39128/05) 20 October 2009 74

WTO Dispute Resolution Bodies

Panel Report, United States - *Import Prohibition of Certain Shrimp and Shrimp Products* WT/DS58R, 15 May 1998 53

Appellate Body

United States - Import Prohibition of Certain Shrimp and Shrimp Products, WT/DS58/AB/R, 12 October 1998 . . . . 53, 71, 99, 175
United States—Imposition of Countervailing Duties on Certain Hot-Rolled Lead and Bismuth-Carbon Steel Products Originating in the United Kingdom (AB Report WT/DS138/AB/ R, 10 May 2000). 116–17
European Communities—Trade Description of Sardines, WT/DS231/AB/R, adopted 23 October 2002 117
Appellate Body, United States - *Import Prohibition of Certain Shrimp and Shrimp Products* WT/DS587AB7RW, 22 October 2001 . . . . 53, 99, 116, 130, 144
Appellate Body, *United States—Definitive Safeguard Measures on Imports of Certain Steel Products,* WT/7DS248–254 and 258, 259/AB/R, adopted 10 December 2003 71
United States—Measures Affecting the Cross-Border Supply of Gambling and Betting Services WT/DS285/AB/R, 20 April 2005 132

Other International Rulings

International Court of Justice (Arbitral Chamber), *Elettronica Sicula Spa (ELSI), United States v Italy* [1989] ICJ Reports 15 . . . . 2, 130
International Court of Justice, *Advisory Opinion on the Threat or Use of Nuclear Weapons* (1996) ICJ Rep 323. 173
International Tribunal for the Law of the Sea
Juno Trader (*Saint Vincent and the Grenadines v Guinea Bissau*), Prompt Release, Judgment (2004) ITLOS Reports 17 . . . . 96, 104
Southern Bluefin Tuna Cases (New Zealand v Japan; Australia v Japan), Provisional Measures, ITLOS Reports, 23, 1 125
Permanent Court of International Justice, *Mavrommatis Palestine Concession* case (*Greece v UK*) [1924] Court Reports, A—No 2 2

Table of Treaties

1) BILATERAL INTERNATIONAL TREATIES

A) Treaties of Friendship, Commerce and Navigation

Italy - US Treaty of Friendship, Commerce and Navigation (1948) 141, 148

B) Bilateral Investment Treaties

Argentina – Ecuador BIT (1994). 147
Argentina – Italy BIT (1990). 147
Argentina – Mexico BIT (1996) 147
Argentina – US BIT (1991). 48
Association of Southeast Asian Nations – Australia – New Zealand BIT 48
Canada Model BIT 194
China – Botswana BIT (2000). 147
China – Cameroon BIT (1997). 147
China – Myanmar BIT (2001) 147
China – North Korea BIT (2005) 147
China – Poland BIT (1988). 147
China – Syria BIT (1996) 147
Egypt – Russia BIT (1997) 147
German Model BIT 147, 194
Indian Model Text of Bilateral Investment Promotion and Protection Agreement 194
Italy – Albania BIT (1991) 147
Italy – Egypt BIT (1989). 147
Italy – Libya BIT (2000) 147
Italy – Lithuania BIT (1994). 147
Italy – Saudi Arabia BIT (1996). 147
Italy – Tunisia BIT (1985). 147
Italy – Turkey BIT (1995) 147
Mexico – Germany BIT (1998). 147
Mexico – South Korea BIT (1996) 147
Mexico – UK BIT (2006) 147
Mexico – Uruguay (2010) 147
US – Congo BIT (1990) 147
US – Croatia BIT (1996). 147
US – Estonia BIT (1994) 147
US – Georgia BIT (1994) 147
US – Jamaica BIT (1994) 147
US – Jordan BIT (1997) 147
US – Lithuania BIT (1998). 147
US – Mongolia BIT (1994). 147
US – Ukraine BIT (1994) 147
US – Uruguay BIT (2005). 28, 48
US Model BIT (2004). 147
US Model BIT (2012). 194

2) REGIONAL TREATIES

Central America Free Trade Agreement (2004). 48
EU Treaties
  Charter of Fundamental Rights 44, 56, 77, 159
  Treaty of Maastricht, establishing the European Union (1992). 86
  TEU, as amended in (2007) 56, 86
  Treaty of Paris, establishing the European Coal and Steel Community (1952) 4
  Treaty of Rome, establishing the European Economic Community 55, 168
  Treaty on the Functioning of the European Union (2007). 32
European Convention for the Protection of Human Rights and Fundamental Freedoms (1950). 73–74, 92, 104, 106, 108, 193, 196
North American Free Trade Agreement (1992) 72, 205

3) GLOBAL TREATIES

Treaties related to the World Trade Organization (1994)
  Agreement on Subsidies and Countervailing Measures. 70
  Agreement on the Application of Sanitary and Phytosanitary Measures 125
  Government Procurement Agreement. 27–8, 48
  Treaty Establishing the World Trade Organization 27
  Trade-Related Aspects of Intellectual Property Rights Agreement 48, 193

Other Multilateral International Treaties
Aarhus Convention on Access, Public Participation in Decision-Making and Access to Justice in Environmental Matters (1998) 48, 70, 113, 123
American Convention on Human Rights (1969) 106, 192
Convention for the conservation of Southern Bluefin Tuna (1993) 128
Convention establishing the International Centre for Settlement of Investment Disputes (1968). 30, 161, 171
General Agreement on Tariffs and Trade (GATT 1994) 133, 144
ILO Convention concerning Indigenous and Tribal Peoples in Independent Countries, n 169 (1989) 97
Patent Cooperation Treaty (1970) 59
Statute of the International Court of Justice (1945) 150, 160–1, 184, 188, 195
Statute of the International Criminal Court (2000). 159, 188
Statute of the Permanent Court of International Justice (1920). 157
Universal Declaration of Human Rights. 106
United Nations Convention on the Law of the Sea (1994) 96
Vienna Convention on the Law of Treaties (1969). 161, 189

Table of Legislation

A) NATIONAL CONSTITUTIONS

Argentina 70
Brazil 62
Germany (*Grundgesetz*) 108
India 38, 191
Netherlands 62
Peru 62, 70
Portugal 65, 79
South Africa 44, 69
South Korea 70
Turkey 70
United States 2, 69, 164, 191

B) NATIONAL LEGISLATION*

Argentina

Civil Code (1896) 156
Administrative Procedure Act (1972) 67

Austria

Civil Code (1811) 156
Administrative Procedure Act (1925) 18, 23

Belgium

Law of 29 July 1991 68

Chile

Civil Code (1855) 156

Colombia

Civil Code (1887) 156

France

Civil Code (1804) 41, 156
Act. n 79–587 of 11 July 1979 66
Code of Relations Between Public Administrations and the Public (2015) 25

Germany

Administrative Procedure Act (1976) 17, 24, 44, 66

Hungary

Code of Administrative Procedure (1957) 19, 20

Italy

Civil Code (1865; 1942) 156
Administrative Procedure Act (1990) 24, 66–67

Japan

Administrative Procedure Act (1993) 26, 44

Netherlands

General Law of Administrative Procedure (1994) 24, 44, 70

Peru

Civil Code (1894) 156
Law n 27444 (2001) 67

Poland

Code of Administrative Procedure (1960) 20, 26

Portugal

Civil Code (1867) 156

South Africa

Promotion of Administrative Justice Act (2000) 25, 44

Spain

Civil Code (1888) 156
Administrative Procedure Act (1958) 18, 24
Administrative Procedure Act (1992) 67

Sweden

Administrative Procedure Act (1986) 46

Switzerland

Civil Code (1907) 156

Taiwan

Administrative Procedure Act, of 3 February 1999 25

United States

International Organizations Immunities Act (1945). 75

Administrative Procedure Act, of 11 June 1946. . . . . 19, 23, 42, 67

Endangered Species Act (1973) 52

Venezuela

Administrative Procedure Act (1981). . . . 44, 67

Yugoslavia

Code of Administrative Procedure, of 8 December 1956. 19

* Generally, the date is that in which the statute has been adopted, while in two cases it is that of publication or that in which the statute entered into force, respectively

COUNCIL OF EUROPE

Committee of Ministers, Resolution (77) 31 on the protection of the individual in relation to the acts of administrative authorities 3, 47, 169

Organisation for Economic Co-operation and Development, *Revised Recommendation of the Council Concerning Co-operation between Member Countries on Anticompetitive Practices Affecting International Trade* (1995) 129

EUROPEAN UNION

Directive n 97/11 of 3 March 1997, [1997] OJ L/73, 5. 123

Directive n 98/5, of 16 February 1998, [1998] OJ L/77, 36. 73

Regulation n 659/1999 of 22 March 1999 [1999] OJ L/83, 1. 114

Directive n 22/2002 on universal service [2002] OJ L/108, 51. 113

Directive 2009/50, of 25 May 2009, [2009] OJ L/155, 17

Directive n 2006/12, of 5 April 2006,[2006] OJ L/114, 9 50

Directive n 2009/140, of 25 November 2009, [2009] OJ L/68, 3. 48

Directive 2014/24/EU of 26 February 2014 on public procurement, [2014] OJ L/94, 65. 29

INTERNATIONAL AUTHORITIES

Internet Corporation for Assigned Names and Numbers, Bylaws 59

United Nations

Financial Regulation (2013) 31

Guidelines of the Sanctions Committee (2007) 58

List of Abbreviations

AB	Appellate Body
APA	Administrative Procedure Act
ASEAN	Association of Southeast Asian Nations
BIPA	Bilateral Investment Promotion and Protection Agreement
BIT	Bilateral Investment Treaty
CAFTA	Central America Free Trade Agreement
CAO	Compliance Advisor Ombudsman
CFI	Court of First Instance
CJEU	Court of Justice of the European Union
EC	European Community
ECHR	European Convention on Human Rights
ECJ	European Court of Justice
ECtHR	European Court of Human Rights
FET	Fair and equitable treatment
GALA	Dutch General Law of Administrative Procedure
GATS	General Agreement on Trade in Services
GATT	General Agreement on Tariffs and Trade
GPA	Government Procurement Agreement
ICANN	Internet Corporation for Assigned Names and Numbers
ICC	International Criminal Court
ICJ	International Court of Justice
ICSID	International Centre for Settlement of Investment Disputes
IFC	International Finance Corporation
ILO	International Labour Organization
ITLOS	International Tribunal for the Law of the Sea
NAFTA	North American Free Trade Agreement
NGO	Non-governmental organization
NRA	National regulatory authority
OCSE	Organization for Security and Co-operation in Europe
OECD	Organization for Economic Cooperation and Development
OPCW	Organisation for the Prohibition of Chemical Weapons
PCT	Patent Cooperation Treaty
SPS	Agreement on the Application of Sanitary and Phytosanitary Measures
TFEU	Treaty on the Functioning of the European Union
TRIPS	Agreement on Trade-Related Aspects of Intellectual Property Rights
UN	United Nations
UNCLOS	UN Convention on the Law of the Sea
US	United States
WTO	World Trade Organization

1

Administrative Justice

A Transnational Perspective

The subject to which this book is addressed is that of the due process requirements that are applicable to administrative procedure beyond State borders. More precisely, three themes will be considered throughout the chapters. First, the fact that some of the requirements that 'regional' and global regulatory regimes—such as the European Union (EU) and the World Trade Organization (WTO) respectively—impose on States' administrative procedures have striking similarities with those set out by the most developed legal systems of the world. Secondly, the fact that, beyond State borders, such requirements of administrative procedure are not justified only by the traditional concerns for the protection of individual interests against misuses of power by public authorities, but also by other values, such as good governance and cooperation between public authorities. Thirdly, that such requirements can be conceptualized in terms of administrative due process of law and, precisely because they are legal requirements, arbitral tribunals and other agencies should follow them when interpreting standards of justice.

1. Old and New Transnational Situations and Standards

As a first step, it is helpful to explain in more detail what this book is concerned with, that is to say, the exercise of administrative powers by public authorities. Since the focus is on the exercising of powers, there is no reason to exclude situations in which they are conferred upon private bodies charged with the performance of certain public functions. Similarly, by using the word 'administrative', while we exclude the work of legislators and the courts,[1] I include a variety of exercises of power that take place through rule-making and adjudication, and therefore a much broader range of procedures. While the focus is on issues of procedure, substantive issues concerning the way in which discretion is exercised will not be addressed, a

[1] On the duties that apply to legislators and the courts, see Susan Rose-Ackerman, Stefanie Egidy, and James Fawkes, *Due Process of Lawmaking. The United States, South Africa, Germany and the European Union* (Cambridge University Press, 2015) and Jan Paulsson, *Denial of Justice in International Law* (Cambridge University Press, 2005).

Due Process of Law Beyond the State. First Edition. Giacinto della Cananea. © Giacinto della Cananea 2016.
Published 2016 by Oxford University Press.

point to which we will return later (Section 2). Last but not least, precisely because the objective of this inquiry is to provide some general guidance about how the issues of fair procedure are dealt with in a variety of contexts, it is helpful to clarify why such issues may no longer be regarded as being a sort of reserved domain of the States.

Beyond national procedural exclusivity

Until a few decades ago, the issues concerning the exercise of administrative powers by public authorities were considered as a sort of national *enclave*. The sovereign enjoyed absolute powers with regard to its citizens, with few limits: the 'inviolable' rights such as property.[2] Although more recent limits to sovereign powers have stemmed from constitutions and statutes, the underlying institutional model has remained unchanged. The essence of this model is that the valid basis for government intrusion into individuals' primary goods is exclusively the consent of the governed, because only this ensures that all citizens are treated as 'free and equal'. Adequate procedural safeguards serve precisely to prevent any undue interference with those primary goods.[3] Within this model, the powers of the sovereign are no less significant with regard to aliens. In the middle of the eighteenth century, in his treatise about *jus gentium*, Emmerich de Vattel argued that any injury caused to the citizen of another State constituted an injury to that State, which had to protect its citizen and seek to ensure that the general prohibition of injury was enforced.[4]

As a result, if an alien suffered from a confiscation of property without compensation or arbitrary imprisonment, it was the home State that could present an international claim against the other State.[5] But it could also choose not to do so, preferring to use diplomatic instruments, or simply deciding to do nothing. Moreover, if the home State intervened 'on behalf of its citizen', this became an interstate dispute and was subject to the rules of international law. With regard to our subject, that is to say, due process of law, if the due process clause of the US Constitution is 'very abstract',[6] the international minimum standard was even more abstract. For example, in an oft-cited ruling which will be considered later in more detail, *Elettronica Sicula*, the Arbitral Chamber of the International Court of Justice held that protection of the foreign investor was based on such standard, which was infringed only in the case of a 'wilful disregard of due process of law, an act which shocks, or at least surprises a sense of judicial propriety'.[7]

[2] Emmerich de Vattel, *Le droit des gens* (first published 1758; Liberlog, 2011) t I, Chapter II, paragraph 109.

[3] Richard B Stewart, 'The Reformation of American Administrative Law' (1975) 88 Harvard LR 1675, 1724.

[4] Emmerich de Vattel, *Le droit des gens*, t I, Chapter VI, paragraph 71.

[5] As the Permanent Court of International Justice held in 1924 in the *Mavrommatis Palestine Concession* case (*Greece v UK*) [1924] Court Reports, A—No 2, 'by taking up the case of one of its subjects ... a State is in reality reasserting its own rights'.

[6] Ronald Dworkin, *Freedom's Law* (Harvard University Press, 1986) 148.

[7] ICJ, *Elettronica Sicula Spa (ELSI), United States v Italy* [1989] ICJ Reports 15.

Today, not only would the same dispute be regarded in a different way, but the requirements of procedural due process of law would be invoked in other types of transnational situations involving individuals, corporations, and public entities.[8] Consider, first, the standard of procedures (a decision "is normally preceded by a series of activities and acts, a sequence of steps that is called 'procedure'") which private parties may invoke. Two countries may reach an agreement in respect of certain requirements of procedural fairness in the context of a bilateral investment treaty (BIT), for example, a due process clause concerning expropriation. Although an agreement of this kind may be considered a mere self-limitation of national sovereignty, it would inevitably imply an erosion of the doctrine that the State is 'absolute master in its own house'.[9] A further move away from national procedural exclusivity occurs if such clause also refers either to the law of a third country (eg, that which previously was the motherland of those countries or that which had occupied them) or to a certain set of international rules. While in this case national law has to be interpreted in the light of another body of procedural law, the increasing cooperation between the States that are members of a regulatory regime may suggest that national particularities should be attenuated or even severely limited. It is from this perspective that within the Council of Europe a broad consensus has emerged concerning the 'fundamental principles which should guide' administrative procedure, and also, in view of the increasing movement of persons, it has been affirmed that it is 'desirable to promote a common standard of protection'.[10]

Consider, secondly, the enforcement of procedural requirements. In our first example, national judicial sovereignty would thus be retained, but the State's courts would be entrusted with the task of ensuring the implementation of such a clause. However, the contracting parties may also agree that disputes between a foreign investor and the host State can be brought before an arbitral tribunal, which would imply a limitation of that State's monopoly in the administration of justice and a direct protection, as opposed to the indirect protection that rests on the will of the home State to intervene.[11] A variation of this situation occurs if, despite the fact that a dispute resolution mechanism can be activated only by the public entities that signed the agreement, the dispute resolution body allows the intervention of a third party, such as an environmental association. In such a circumstance, both State and non-State entities equally participate in transnational public law litigation.[12] Finally, an individual, for example a refugee seeking asylum or requesting that the rest of his or her family joins him or her in the host State, may bring a case not only before national courts, but also before a non-judicial body, such as the

[8] See Philip C Jessup, *Transnational Law* (Yale University Press, 1953) 53; Harold H Koh, 'Transnational Legal Process' (1996) 75 Nebraska L Rev 181, 184.

[9] Philip C Jessup, *Transnational Law*, 53; Alfred C Aman, *The Democracy Deficit. Taming Globalization through Law Reform* (New York University Press, 2004) 125.

[10] Council of Europe, Committee of Ministers, Preamble of Resolution (77) 31 on the protection of the individual in relation to the acts of administrative authorities, available at the website http://www.coe.int.

[11] See W Michael Reisman and Robert D Sloane, 'Indirect Expropriation and its Valuation in the BIT Generation' (2004) 74 British Ybk Int'l L 115.

[12] Harold H Koh, 'Transnational Public Law Litigation' (1990) 100 Yale LJ 2373.

United Nations Human Rights Committee, or before a fully-fledged international court, such as the European Court of Human Rights. Both this Court and the Inter-American Court of Human Rights may hear the case of a group alleging that its right to be consulted was infringed by government.

What is new, and particularly significant from a legal perspective, therefore, is not only the reach of modern regulatory regimes into aspects of life traditionally governed by national rules or even left to private rules of conduct, but also the gradual erosion of national procedural exclusivity. A related, though distinct, development is the fact that other canons of conduct—principles and rules of law—exist and their implementation can be ensured directly, not indirectly.[13] This development interacts with a growth of due process litigation before supranational courts, such as the two 'regional' courts of human rights or the Court of Justice of the European Union (CJEU). This is not, in itself, a problem; it may simply be a consequence of the accession of new Member States. But such increased litigation reveals a more profound transition from one structure of government to another, in which traditional bodies of authority are no longer the only ones that exercise powers over individuals and businesses.[14]

The requirements of due process of law are not invoked only against some States, as happened when citizens and corporations from the richer countries of the world lamented the infringement of their rights abroad, but against all of them. Nor are such requirements invoked only against the authorities of a State, in whatever form, but also against the new *pouvoirs publics*, such as the EU and the United Nations (UN), although until recently legal scholarship has been reluctant to acknowledge this development.

Due process claims against international and supranational authorities

Part of the difficulty in analysing this issue derives from the reluctance of legal scholars to accept that the exercise of power by 'external' authorities may affect the rights and interests of citizens and other individuals, as well as of social groups and corporations, within the territory of the State. Another part of the difficulty is related to the impact on national safeguards against misuses and abuses of power.

The State is still the public administration par excellence, but no longer that by definition. This becomes clear when considering the European Community (EC). Its administration—centred on the High Authority—was instituted in 1952 and was entrusted with powers affecting the conduct of private undertakings.

[13] Jan Paulsson, *Denial of Justice in International Law*, 3.

[14] See Benedict Kingsbury, Nico Krisch, and Richard B Stewart, 'The Emergence of Global Administrative Law' (2005) 68 Law & Contemp Problems 15 (arguing that such developments cannot be understood in terms of classical international law); Nico Krisch and Benedict Kingsbury, 'Introduction: Global Governance and Global Administrative Law in the International Legal Order' (2006) 17 Eur J Int L 1 (same thesis).

A system of remedies was deemed necessary, in order to prevent misuses of those powers. The Court of Justice was thus the first international tribunal hearing claims against administrative decisions and it contributed to the development of some of the requirements of due process. More than six decades later, the exercise of power by the EU administration does not affect only public institutions, citizens, and businesses within the European legal space, but also externally. Indirect effects derive, for example, from the decision to prohibit a merger between two US corporations, if the Commission reaches the conclusion that it is susceptible of producing negative effects on the Single Market. Direct effects derive from measures restricting the free movement of senior officers of regimes that oppress human rights.[15]

The significance of these facts can be appreciated in various ways. They could be regarded as undermining the traditional legal doctrine according to which international law cannot confer rights or impose duties directly on individuals.[16] Alternatively, this doctrine could be retained, at the cost of a reduction in its scope of application, by excluding EC law from the field of international law. Orthodoxy would thus be preserved, although the heuristic value of the traditional doctrine would be reduced.

At the beginning of the twenty-first century, however, even those who still adhered to the traditional doctrine had to admit a further and important limit.[17] After the terrorist attacks on US territory in 2001 the UN Security Council passed measures distinct from those having general effects, such as an economic embargo. The new measures included, in particular, 'the freezing of funds'. Functionally, such measures are not sanctions, because they are issued against physical and legal persons and other legal entities suspected of giving material or financial aid to terrorist organizations. But the relevant points for present purposes are, first, that these measures do not affect only States, but also persons and, second, that a 'mixed' procedure has been envisaged for their issuing, with national officers providing information and participating in the meetings of an auxiliary body of the UN Security Council, which includes both legal and physical persons on a 'black list', while the measures are applied locally by national governments. In this particular field a sort of 'world system of governance established at three levels' has thus emerged.[18]

These measures have raised complex and challenging issues concerning conflicting needs, perceived by the courts, to ensure collective security and, at the same

[15] See the ruling of the CJEU in Case C-605/13 P, *Anbouba v Council* (2015) nyr.

[16] Philip Jessup, *Transnational Law*, 7.

[17] See José Alvarez, 'Hegemonic International Law Revisited' (2003) 97 Am J Int'l L 873, 875 (arguing that such measures are a 'rare phenomenon in international law').

[18] Christian Tomuschat, *Comment* to CFI, Case T-360/01, *Ahmed Ali Yusuf and Al Barakaat International Foundation v Council and Commission*; Case T-315/01 *Yassin Abdullah Kadi v Council and Commission* (2005) 43 Common Mkt L Rev 537. Similarly, Paul Craig, *UK, EU and Global Administrative Law. Foundations and Challenges* (Cambridge University Press, 2015) 3, points out the 'vertical interaction' between the global level and the regional and national levels that emerges in *Kadi* and other disputes.

time, protect the process rights of targeted individuals and groups. Several substantive and procedural aspects of UN measures have thus been rectified, a consequence of criticism expressed by political and judicial institutions. But, in one sense, such changes do not affect the essence of the new paradigm that is emerging in the field of public law. Measures adversely affecting citizens and businesses are no longer issued only by the States, but also by non-State authorities, which administer them in conjunction with national governments. It is for this reason that the procedures used for listing and de-listing individuals and bodies must respect certain requirements of due process of law.

This brings us to the second part of the problem. The procedural guarantees to which the decisions of national authorities are subject are lost if such decisions are taken elsewhere, without any comparable constraint on exercises of power, in terms of both fairness and transparency.[19] This problem is worsened by another fact, which has been raised by discontents of globalization. Although members of global regulatory regimes have an equal status, sometimes decision-making procedures fail to respect their equality. For example, according to critics, the decisions of the WTO are often predetermined at meetings where only a limited circle of negotiators is present.[20] There is no need to subscribe to some sort of ideology opposed to globalization to realize that the procedure used by an international authority is a key instrument for ensuring its legitimacy, in the sense that the binding character of a decision can more easily be accepted if it is the outcome of an institutionalized process and procedural rules are respected.[21] The concern for procedural propriety and fairness is even stronger if one thinks that fair procedures can balance the limited legitimacy of international institutions.[22]

The findings made signal the growing transnational effects of decisions taken and rules made by domestic and international or supranational authorities and, thus, the growing concern for administrative justice. Old and new issues of legitimacy therefore arise beyond 'state-centric approaches and habits of mind'.[23]

[19] See Richard B Stewart, 'Administrative Law in the XXI century' (2003) 78 NYU Un L R 437. On the treatment of States within international organizations, see C Wilfred Jenks, 'Due Process of Law in International Organizations' (1965) 19 Int Org 163.

[20] Joseph Stiglitz, *Globalization and its Discontents* (Penguin, 2002) 50. See also Alfred C Aman, *The Democracy Deficit*, 4 (criticizing the impulse to harmonize domestic law through rules that have 'a rubberstamp quality').

[21] For this approach, see Niklas Luhmann, *Legitimation durch Verfahren* (2nd edn, Suhrkamp, 1975).

[22] Robert Howse, 'The Legitimacy of the World Trade Organization' in Jean-Marc Coicaud and Veikko Heiskanen (eds), *The Legitimacy of International Organizations* (Free Press, 2001) 397. See also Michael Zurn, 'Global Governance and Legitimacy Problems' (2004) 39 Government and Opposition 260.

[23] Alfred C Aman, *The Democracy Deficit*, 5. See also, for the same remark, Jean-Bernard Auby, *La globalisation, le droit et l'Etat* (2nd edn, LGDJ, 2012) 11 and Ebherard Schmidt-Assmann, 'The Internationalization of Administrative Relations as a Challenge for Administrative Law Scholarship' (2008) 9 German L J, 2061; Matthias Ruffert, 'The Transformation of Administrative Law as a Transnational Methodological Project' in Matthias Ruffert (ed), *The Transformation of Administrative Law in Europe* (Sellier, 2007) 3, 11.

2. Limits to the Inquiry

Before discussing the issues arising from transnational legal relations, let us note some limits to our inquiry. The first limit, as was indicated at the beginning, is that the inquiry focuses on procedural due process of law. The second limit is that due process is regarded as a legal principle, not as a moral requirement. A third limit regards the legal materials selected.

Process and substance

The distinction between process and substance may look 'natural' on the basis of some theory of justice.[24] It is consolidated in studies about public law too.[25] However, it is not undisputed. The first argument against such a distinction is of a functional nature. As an American expert of due process, Jerry Mashaw, has observed, the attempt to separate questions of substance and process is unlikely to be wholly successful because such questions are 'functionally inseparable', in the sense that procedures determine outcomes;[26] on the other hand, procedures are often challenged by the discontents of the outcomes. A second argument—which will be considered later—is that procedures and the principles governing them are not at all neutral or value-free, but embody values and beliefs.

Although the first argument highlights a real problem, it may prove too much and miss something that is evident in the machinery of the law. In all fields of law it is important to evaluate not only the *results* of a process, but the *process* itself, either to prevent errors or to ensure the impartiality of the decision-maker.[27] This is, of course, important where a public authority exercises authoritative powers, that is to say, *imperium*, which may unilaterally and adversely affect the exercise of rights, for example, the immigration officer's refusal to let a foreigner enter. An agency's decision either to expropriate a foreign investor or to withdraw a licence for building and managing a hotel provides another example. The procedures through which public authorities act are of crucial importance also when they either dispense money or some other sort of government largess or impose burdens. For example, a decision to allocate scarce resources such as a licence to use or exploit a natural (gas or oil)

[24] See Raoul C van Caenegem, *European Law in the Past and the Future. Unity and Diversity over Two Millennia* (Cambridge University Press, 2002) 49.

[25] Paul Craig, 'Procedures and Administrative Decisionmaking: A Common Law Perspective' (1993) 3 Eur Rev Public L 56.

[26] Jerry Mashaw, *Due Process in the Administrative State* (Yale University Press, 1985) 5; Lawrence H Tribe, 'The Puzzling Persistence of Process-Based Constitutional Theories' (1979) 89 Yale L J 1065 (pointing out the 'substantive roots of procedural norms'); Paul Ricoeur, 'Une théorie purement procédurale de la justice est-elle possible? À propos de la théorie de la justice de Rawls', in *Le Juste* (Esprit, 1995) 73 (discussing Rawls' theory of justice).

[27] See Robert S Summers, 'Evaluating and Improving Legal Processes—a Plea for 'Process Values' (1974) 60 Cornell L Rev 1; Jeffrey Lever, 'Why Procedure is More Important than Substantive Law' (1989) 48 Int'l & Comp LQ 285; Michael D Bayles, *Procedural Justice. Allocating to Individuals* (Kluwer, 1990) 4.

or an artificial resource (frequencies for electronic communications) raises issues of distributive justice in the Aristotlean sense.[28] Far from being merely abstract, such issues emerge, for example, when individuals and groups contest the programmes for distributing social entitlements not simply because they wish to obtain higher benefits, but because they argue for fair procedures to determine the benefits that are distributed.[29] Three consequences follow from this: there is a need to ensure that the exercise of discretionary powers by public authorities does not degrade into arbitrariness;[30] public authorities are thus subject to duties of fairness and transparency that are not simply more intense than those governing private transactions, but different in nature; such duties, however, are often procedural in nature.

This brings into question the practical importance of procedural due process. For example, a giving reasons requirement may be acceptable for policymakers because it is a procedural constraint and a loose constraint.[31] Similarly, the more international arbitrators and judges are requested to solve disputes concerning regulatory acts where policy choices are expressed, the more they must take the autonomy of national policymakers into account. A duty to hear an investor who would be adversely affected by a new decision or to disclose its reasons does not undermine the States' prerogative to revise or withdraw an authorization or a licence. Arbitrators and judges thus do not have to tell a public authority that the policy choices it has made are wrong. If the public authority has missed a procedural step, what is at issue is 'the failure to perform a required course of action, not ... the badness of the action performed'.[32] In this sense, several scholars in a variety of contexts have argued that administrative law is eminently procedural.[33] Similarly, international law literature regarding denial of justice points out that it is 'always procedural'.[34] An inquiry into due process requirements is, thus, not only timely, but also fully justified.

Due process as a legal principle

The other argument against the distinction between process and substance, which calls into question its underlying values, also concerns the second limit of this inquiry, that is to say, its method.

[28] Aristotle, *Nicomachean Ethics*, Book 5.

[29] Jeffrey Jowell, 'The Rule of Law Today', in Jeffrey Jowell and Dawn Oliver (eds), *The Changing Constitution* (2nd edn, Oxford University Press, 1996) 62.

[30] Kenneth C Davis, *Discretionary Justice. A Preliminary Inquiry* (Greenwood Press, 1969).

[31] Martin Shapiro, 'The Giving Reasons Requirement' (1992) 7 Un Chi Legal Forum 179.

[32] See *Maffezini v Spain* (ICSID Case No ARB/97/7), Award (13 November 2000) § 64 ('ICSID tribunals cannot pass judgment on whether such policies are right or wrong') available at the website http://www.icsid.org; W Michael Reisman, *The Quest for World Order and Human Dignity in the Twenty-first century* (The Hague Academy of International Law, 2012) 454; James Crawford, *State Responsibility. The General Part* (Cambridge University Press, 2013) 343 (distinguishing between the obligation to do something and doing it in a timely manner).

[33] See Martin Shapiro, *The Supreme Court and Administrative Agencies* (The Free Press, 1968) 106; Jean Rivero, *Droit administratif* (12th edn, LGDJ, 1987) 35.

[34] Jan Paulsson, *Denial of Justice in International Law*, 98.

It ought to be stated at the outset that the argument based on values is not simply a different argument, but one that operates at another level, that is to say, normatively. It is also particularly challenging for due process of law on moral grounds.[35] This may support the idea that due process should be studied from a deductive perspective, *à la* Kant or *à la* Fuller, that is to say, founding justice on moral premises and drawing all consequences from the postulate.[36] An approach of this type is followed by studies that ask what process standards would suit a good or just society.[37] However, for all the importance of the ideal of justice or the ethical aspiration underlying the very idea of law,[38] this approach is problematic both in general and specific terms.

In general terms, it underestimates the difficulty of finding a procedure that is sure to reach the desired outcome.[39] It also underestimates the difficulty that any attempt to solve conflicts between different ideas and interests is likely to meet, even in the context of a community that has a framework of shared beliefs and values.[40] *A fortiori*, it fails to provide a satisfactory account of how conflicts between competing visions of the world can be accommodated in modern secularized and differentiated societies.

In more specific terms, as we move beyond the borders of the State, the notions of 'justice' and 'fairness' may, and do, differ not only between Western countries and other countries of the world, but also between these groups of countries. This suggests, first, the necessity of caution when considering values[41] and, second, the opportunity of an empirical approach,[42] rooted in the realities of government and law, which is neither based on an aprioristic model of justice nor on the undemonstrated assumption that it is 'universally' recognized that all persons must be afforded some procedural protections.[43]

[35] See J Roland Pennock and James W Chapman (eds), *Due Process: Nomos XVIII* (New York University Press, 1977).

[36] For Kant, this meant beginning with the supreme principle of the doctrine of morals ('Act on a maxim which can also hold as a universal law!'): see the *Grundlegung der Metaphisik der Sitten* (first published 1785; de Gruyter, 1978), particularly the Preface, where the distinction between 'metaphysic' and practical rules (*praktische regeln*) is drawn; Lon Fuller, *The Morality of Law* (2nd edn, Yale University Press, 1967) 81.

[37] See Richard A Cass, 'Review of Jerry Mashaw, Due Process in the Administrative State' (1986) 3 Constitutional Commentary 525.

[38] See R Alexy, *The Argument from Injustice* (Stanley L Paulson and Bonnie Litschewski Paulson (trs), Oxford University Press, 2002) (criticizing the idea that, below a certain threshold, a 'rule of law' exists as such).

[39] See John Rawls, *A Theory of Justice* (Harvard University Press, 1971) 85–6. For further discussion, see Amartya Sen, *The Idea of Justice* (Allen, 2009) 43.

[40] Isaiah Berlin, *Two Concepts of Liberty* (Clarendon Press, 1958) 1; Stuart Hampshire, *Justice is Conflict* (Princeton University Press, 2000) 5; Alasdair MacIntyre, *After Virtue. A Study in Moral Theory* (2nd edn, University of Notre Dame Press, 2007), especially Chapter 6 (noting that there is no self-evident truth).

[41] Bruno Simma and Andreas Paulus, 'The Responsibility of Individuals for Human Rights Abuses in Internal Conflicts: A Positivist View' (1999) 93 Am J Int'l L 302.

[42] For a similar line of reasoning, see Gregory Shaffer and Tom Ginsburg, 'The Empirical Turn in International Legal Scholarship' (2012) 106 Am J Int'l L 1.

[43] See, for instance, Michael D Bayles, *Procedural Justice*, 39.

What might be suggested, then, is a sort of 'Burkean' approach. For Burke, society was not based on logic, but on evolution:[44] it was the outcome of a prolonged process of cumulative growth. And this process gave rise to limits on the exercise of power by the sovereign. In particular, nobody but a tyrant 'could think of seizing on the property of men … unheard'.[45] In a similar vein, it might be said that it is precisely from a process of growth, resulting from the standards agreed by policy-makers and applied by courts and other agencies, that due process of law requirements have emerged, not from an architect's design. However, to the modern mind, a Burkean approach is hardly acceptable, because it makes the mere existence of a certain practice an argument for its legitimacy.[46] In fact, the legitimacy of public authorities depends not only on the benefits that they are capable of providing to the citizenry; it depends also on respect for the rules of conduct that have been previously set out and disseminated, as well as from the openness and transparency of their procedures.

The defects in traditional theories have induced other commentators to argue for a rights-based approach. This is based upon certain views of legality and is designed to prevent misuses and abuses of power. In particular, if this approach is based on the protection of fundamental rights, it is a substitute for considering certain background ideas of justice or, in our case, the concept of due process of law and its related requirements, even though it should not be assumed that concerns about due process or fair procedures will necessarily be absent from this theoretical framework. However, there are two problems with this approach, empirically and normatively. Empirically, many would agree that 'prior to the constitutional recognition of human rights, theories of justice tended to focus on procedural justice'.[47] But the following assertion, that the legitimacy of international authorities is defined in terms of rights held by individuals, is questionable, for in the transnational arena different rationales for procedural requirements exist.[48] Equally questionable is the

[44] Edmund Burke, *Considerations on the French Revolution* (first published 1793; Liberty Fund, 1999).

[45] Burke, *Considerations*, 203.

[46] See Jerry Mashaw, *Due Process in the Administrative State*, 101 (criticizing 'Burkean obscurantism'); Cass R Sunstein, 'Due Process Traditionalism' (2008) 106 Mich L Rev 1543, 1545 (holding that traditionalist views emphasize 'longstanding practices').

[47] Ernst-Ulrich Petersmann, 'Justice as Conflict Resolution: Proliferation, Fragmentation and Decentralization of Dispute Settlement in World Trade' (2006) 27 Pa J Int'l Econ L 275, 277; 'Time for a United Nations "Global Compact" for Integrating Human Rights in the Law of Worldwide Organizations: Lessons from European Integration' (2002) 13 Eur J Int'l L 621, 624 (proposing a 'change from international functionalism to constitutionalism'). On the contrast between this approach and the opposite views of the New Haven School, see Armin von Bogdandy, 'Constitutionalism in International Law: Comment on a Proposal from Germany' (2006) 47 Harvard Int'l LJ 222, 224. See also Sidney A Shapiro and Richard E Levy, *Government Benefits and the Rule of Law: Toward a Standards-Based Theory of Due Process*, 57 Admin L Rev 107, 135 (2005) (stressing the advantages of an approach based on standards, as opposed to rights) and Neil MacCormick, *Legal Reasoning and Legal Theory* (Oxford University Press, 1978) (discussing the role of principles, as distinct from rights); Martti Koskenniemi, *The Politics of International Law* (Hart, 2001) 137 (highlighting the difficulties that are met by attempts to translate different normative demands into rights–duties relationships).

[48] See Chapter 5. For a partially different view, see Sabino Cassese, 'A Global Due Process of Law?', in Gordon Anthony et al (eds), *Values in Global Administrative Law* (Hart, 2011) 69 (holding that in global law participation is often viewed as a human right).

assertion—on normative grounds—that this is necessary. Even among those who support a rights-based approach, there is considerable diversity of opinion as to its foundations. Moreover, all rights-based views of public law rest on important institutional premises that may not be, and are not, shared by other legal cultures. By contrast, there is some common ground between rights-based views and those that are based on the preoccupation that sound administration is assured.[49] This approach does not exclude the importance of rights, but it argues that courts and other bodies (arbitral tribunals, supervisory boards) should, in addition, develop standards of review. A somewhat similar conclusion is reached by yet another approach, which builds on theories of adjudication and holds that the courts must elaborate and follow standards of fairness and due process in order to ensure their integrity.[50]

The law to be observed and the law breached

While this is not the place for a detailed examination of these theories, their relevance for our present purposes cannot be neglected and has an important implication as to grounds of methodology, also in light of what was suggested before regarding the limits of a 'Burkean approach'. It is not sufficient to consider the practice of government and the decisions of courts, arbitral tribunals, and other public agencies. Two reasons justify this conclusion.

First, if we want to understand the ordinary course of the law, that is to say, the rules that must be respected and in fact usually are respected, we cannot focus only on the rules that are breached and the remedies provided by the legal system.[51] Of course, there are always rules of law that are not, or are no longer, applied. Even so, however, such rules may continue to retain some legal value. As observed by Hart, even extreme 'realists', who emphasize judge-made law, recognize that courts need a 'verbal covering for the exercise of an unfettered discretion'.[52] *A fortiori*, a shift in administrative or judicial practice can be more easily justified by referring to pre-existing rules, also in view of concerns regarding judicial activism.

Second, the analysis of arbitral and judicial practice is not sufficient.[53] Arbitral tribunals and fully-fledged courts judge only a limited number of cases and often focus on the same types of disputes. As a result, much of the business of government goes relatively unnoticed. Moreover, a practice, though relatively stable, is not sufficient to indicate the law, without the support of the belief that it is lawful. Too often, instead, the literature on transnational legal relations appears to adopt the conception of law

49 See, for instance, Stefano Battini, 'The Procedural Side of Legal Globalization: The Case of the World Heritage Convention' (2011) 9 I-CON 340.

50 For further discussion, see Paul Craig, *Administrative Law* (5th edn, Sweet & Maxwell, 2003) 23.

51 This distinction is drawn from Laura Nader, 'Introduction', in Karl Llewellyn and Edward Adamson Hoebel, *The Cheyenne Way: Conflict and Case Law in Primitive Jurisprudence* (first published 1941; University of Oklahoma Press, 1992) 11.

52 For a critical appraisal of the emphasis put on cases in US legal scholarship, see Jerry Mashaw, *Creating the American Constitution* (Yale University Press, 2012) 3; Mark Tushnet, 'Truth, Justice and the American Way: An Interpretation of Public Law Scholarship in the Seventies' (1979) 57 Texas Law Rev 1307, 1335.

53 Herbert L Hart, *The Concept of Law* (3rd edn, Clarendon Press, 1994) 147.

that is typical of common law countries, though with a few reservations, in order to accommodate certain distinctive traits. As a consequence of this, the attempts made to describe the law as it is reflect a particular idea as to what the law ought to be, in other words a 'certain' conception of the legal order, as observed by Santi Romano.[54] In sum, the overemphasis on arbitral and judicial decisions is not only an obstacle to the development of an adequate doctrine of due process, but is also a major hindrance to accurate observation of the legal realities that characterize the current stage of globalization.

A selective analysis

A third limit to our inquiry can be better appreciated in the light of another issue of method. This issue, which regards the scope of comparative analysis, becomes clearer when considering what Martin Shapiro, one of the main experts of comparative law in this field, observed twenty years ago:

> when we speak of the globalization of law, we must be conscious that we are speaking of an extremely narrow, limited, and specialized set of legal phenomena … We will almost always discover that we are really taking about North America, Europe, Australia, and New Zealand. Japan will sometimes be on and sometimes off this globe. The rest of Asia and Africa will almost never be seen and, for most of us, Latin America south of Mexico will be irrelevant.[55]

In short, frequently an approach to legal globalization turns out to be focused on the US and Western Europe, while limited attention is devoted to other regions of the world. An approach of this type has two major weaknesses, empirical and normative. Empirically, it neglects many important legal developments concerning administrative procedure. Examples include the constitutional and legislative provisions of South Africa, the codes issued by Latin American countries, and the interpretation given by Indian courts to the constitutional provision imposing the respect of procedures. Normatively, an approach that focuses only on the US and Western Europe worsens the doubt raised earlier; that is, whether a focus on procedures is appropriate only in some parts of the world. That said, it is important to add that, logically, the same line of reasoning that warns us that we cannot take for granted that similar requirements of due process exist elsewhere implies that their existence cannot be denied. This confirms the necessity for analysis that considers legal systems of several regions of the world.

This raises, however, another issue of method. In the abstract, one may think that a rigorously empirical approach must not be influenced by received ideas that would prevent us from discovering the infinite variety of existing rules and customs. But practically one needs to have some sort of preconception of the object of the research. Since there is potentially an infinite variety of rules and customs, it is virtually impossible to give an exhaustive picture of it. Jorge Luis Borges' novel of the

[54] Santi Romano, *L'ordinamento giuridico* (1946, 2nd edn), (French tr. Pierre Gothot, *L'ordre juridique*, 1975, Dalloz).

[55] Martin Shapiro, 'The Globalization of Law' (1993) 1 Indiana J Glob Leg St 37. See also Richard D Glensy, 'Which Countries Count? Lawrence v. Texas and the Selection of Foreign Persuasive Authority' (2005) 45 Va J Int'l L 358; Jeffrey Jowell, 'The Universality of Administrative Justice?', in Matthias Ruffert (ed), *The Transformation of Administrative Law in Europe*, 55.

geographers who were ordered by the Chinese Emperor to draw an accurate map of his Empire, and who eventually drew a map having the same dimensions of the Empire,[56] provides an illuminating example of this difficulty. Even if knowing and describing all the situations in which 'the obligation to abide by due process of law has been questioned in varying degrees in the name of natural justice' were possible, 'it would be tedious, it is unnecessary, and it would not be appropriate to try to recapitulate' all of them,[57] simply because, though facts have an autonomous existence, they receive meaning from their observers.[58] This explains why this inquiry can be regarded as an attempt to draw a map which does not arbitrarily exclude any part of the globe, but which is limited to some aspects of the reality.

To say that this is a mapping exercise also has a further implication. Although there is evidence that due process litigation is increasing in some fields of international law and within 'regional' organizations such as the Council of Europe and the EU, what will follow is a qualitative analysis of cases that are regarded as particularly important.[59]

3. Structure of the Inquiry

After clarifying the subject and method of this inquiry, it is easier to illustrate its structure. There is, first, an empirical part, which serves to ensure that the analysis of legal arrangements is rooted in the realities of government. However, it is important not to lose sight of the basic categories of legal analysis. For this purpose, Part II discusses the various rationales of due process requirements, while in Part III the various interpretations of current legal realities will be subject to critical scrutiny in respect of their internal coherence, as well as of empirical findings and normative standards.

In our journey into the requirements of due process, separate treatment will be helpful in connection with three of the major developments that emerge comparatively and transnationally: the requirement to carry out a procedure (Chapter 2), the right to be heard within that procedure (Chapter 3), and the giving reasons requirement, with regard to the final step of the procedure (Chapter 4). Each of these chapters has a similar structure, in that they begin by exploring the 'first and most obvious source of administrative law principles: national administrative law system'[60] and then analyse the requirements of procedural due process that regulatory regimes set out for their founders, the States, or for their own institutions. As far as the latter are concerned, particular attention is devoted to the vast province of

[56] Jorge L Borges, *Del Rigor en la Ciencia*, in *El Hacedor* (Aleanza Editorial, 1972).

[57] C Wilfred Jenks, *Due Process of Law in International Organizations*, 165.

[58] Alasdair MacIntyre, *After Virtue*, Chapter 7 (emphasizing the importance of interpretation).

[59] It is the method qualified as the 'crucial case study' by Martin Shapiro and Alec Stone Sweet, *On Law, Politics and Judicialization* (Oxford University Press, 2002) 209.

[60] Carol Harlow, 'Global Administrative Law: The Quest for Principles and Values' (2006) 17 Eur J Int L 187, 188; Martin Shapiro, 'Administrative Law Unbounded: Reflections on Government and Governance' (2001) 8 Indiana J Global Legal St 369.

UN agencies and to the EU, which is regarded as a case of supranational 'administration beyond the State'.[61]

For an adequate understanding of such requirements, it is important to understand the common and distinctive traits that connote not only their functioning, but also their underlying rationales. The reason is that, though procedural requirements can be found more or less everywhere and may thus be regarded as a constant of modern administrative systems, this does not exclude the need to justify their existence. Their purpose must not be delineated only for intellectual clarity, but also for practical reasons.[62] Clarifying the rationale that underlies a procedural norm will permit a better understanding of the type of requirement that it sets out. It will also allow us to understand whether the same type of requirement is justified by different rationales and, if so, whether any consequences follow from it.

In this respect, Part II points out that the procedural requirements examined in the previous chapters may, and do, have a variety of rationales, which only partially coincide with those that are traditionally highlighted by accounts of administrative due process in the national arena; in order words, in the transnational arena there is a distinct set of rationales for due process requirements (Chapter 5). A distinction is drawn between non-instrumental and instrumental rationales. While the former focus on dignity and participation (Chapter 6), the latter are centred on good administration, seen from several points of view, as well as on cooperation between public authorities (Chapter 7).

If the requirements of due process of law can be approached from several directions and can be meaningful in different, even contrasting ways, the further question that arises is how these findings can be taken into account in the conceptual structures that explicitly or implicitly shape our views about the subject. As we have noted earlier, there is not only a variety of legal realities, but also a variety of interpretations of those realities, that is to say, rival legal theories. In Part III, these theories will be subject to critical scrutiny in respect of their internal coherence, as well as of empirical findings and normative foundations. As a first step, administrative due process of law will be considered from a conceptual point of view, in order to distinguish it from other notions with which it is often associated, including the principle of legality and the prohibition of arbitrariness (Chapter 8). The next step will be to look at administrative due process of law in order to see whether it works as a variable or non-variable standard and whether its legal importance is limited to the gap-filling function identified by traditional scholarship or it has a foundational value (Chapter 9). Finally, the view that due process can be regarded as being a principle of law in the current global legal environment will be asserted in both normative and empirical terms and the objections to such a view that emerge from legal scholarship will be subject to critical scrutiny (Chapter 10).

[61] For a similar approach, see Carol Harlow and Richard Rawlings, *Process and Procedure in EU Administration* (Hart, 2014) 5; Susan Rose-Ackerman and Peter L Lindseth, 'Comparative Administrative Law: An Introduction', in Susan Rose-Ackerman and Peter L Lindseth (eds), *Comparative Administrative Law* (Edward Elgar, 2010) 17; George A Bermann, 'A Restatement of European Administrative Law: Problems and Prospects', in Susan Rose-Ackerman and Peter L Lindseth (eds), *Comparative Administrative Law* (Edward Elgar, 2010) 595.

[62] Paul Craig, *Procedures and Administrative Decisionmaking*, 56.

PART I

REQUIREMENTS OF ADMINISTRATIVE DUE PROCESS

2

The Requirement to Carry Out a Procedure

In our journey into the requirements of procedural due process of law, the starting point is the concept of administrative procedure, for which three facts will be examined: procedures are more important from a legal point of view, they are often codified, and they are increasingly subject to the standards set out by international regulatory regimes.

1. The Legal Importance of Administrative Procedure

From administrative acts to procedures

The concept of administrative procedure is increasingly important in modern public law. It is through procedures that the law plays a key role in both facilitating and constraining exercises of power by public authorities, and in thus promoting public goals and protecting individual interests. However, this concept emerged relatively late because early doctrines of public law focused on the acts and measures taken by public authorities. In particular, Otto Mayer, a German public lawyer who had a profound knowledge of French administrative law and was in academic terms the leading academic figure of his generation, defined the administrative act (*Verwaltungsakt*) as the act 'which establishes the law for an individual or a certain group of individuals'.[1] This definition was at the root of the attempt made to conceptualize in terms of a 'complex act' (*Gesammakt*) the activities that precede the issuing of a decision and determine its content.[2] The influence of Mayer's emphasis on acts is still visible in the German administrative procedure act of 1976, where the central concept is the administrative act, defined as an 'order, decision or other sovereign measure taken by an authority to regulate an individual case in the sphere of public law and intended to have a direct, external legal effect'.[3] It would be easy to say that this view was defective, but this critique would miss the mark both

[1] Otto Mayer, *Droit administratif allemand* (French translation by the author, 1904; CPSA, 2011) 29.

[2] For critical remarks, see Maurice Hauriou, *Principes de droit public* (Dalloz, 1910) 145.

[3] German APA of 25 May 1976, Article 35. For further discussion, see Hermann Pünder, 'Administrative Procedure—Mere Facilitator of Material Law versus Cooperative Realization of Common Welfare', in Hermann Pünder and Christian Waldhoff (eds), *Debates in German Public Law* (Hart, 2014) 214.

Due Process of Law Beyond the State. First Edition. Giacinto della Cananea.
Published 2016 by Oxford University Press.

historically and conceptually. Historically, the fact that a particular view might now be regarded as defective does not exclude the fact that it succeeded in formulating the dominant method by which administrative law was conceived at that time; the reasons underlying that view, therefore, should be considered. Conceptually, it is important to discuss the reasons why that view is less suitable for making sense of the reality of our time.

The focus on acts, as distinct from procedures, had three main causes: the influence played by private law scholarship, the peculiarities that characterized some measures taken by public authorities, and the resulting necessity to protect citizens. Since administrative law emerged relatively recently, it was almost inevitable that it would take into account the ideas and thoughts about the law elaborated by private lawyers, such as the doctrine of contract. But although many acts carried out by public authorities were largely similar to those of private parties, other acts were carried out in the exercise of powers that did not 'have direct parallels' in private relationships.[4] Not only were public authorities empowered to determine that a certain right (of using goods, in a requisition; of ownership, in an expropriation; of credit, if subject to taxation) be transferred to someone else, but they were also authorized by law to use coercion to enforce their decision (Hauriou).[5] Precisely because a legal command was 'backed by force',[6] there was a much greater necessity to elaborate and justify limits to exercises of power. Judicial control was thus conceived as a safeguard against an otherwise unlimited power and, in practice, was carried out by reviewing administrative acts, as distinct from procedures. As government largess grew, and relationships between citizens and the State proliferated, this approach was extended to *dominium*.

However, since the end of the nineteenth century several legal systems have moved from considerations of judicial protection against the acts and measures that affect the rights and interests of individuals to considerations of procedural form. Administrators, referring to a sequence of activities and acts functionally and legally connected, such as the measure taken by a public authority after consulting a technical body or receiving a legal opinion, increasingly used the notion of 'procedure'.[7] At the same time, courts began to review the process followed by a public authority, particularly from the viewpoint of respecting certain requisites of form.

An important impulse came from the first legislative codification of administrative procedure, which was achieved in Austria. The law of 21 July 1925 benefited from both the case law of the administrative court established in 1875 and the legal theories elaborated by the School of Wien. It was seen as a model by some nations profoundly influenced by the Austrian tradition, such as Czechoslovakia, which

[4] Dawn Oliver, *Common Values and the Public-Private Divide* (Cambridge University Press, 1999) 33; Yves Gaudemet, *Droit administratif* (19th edn, LGDJ, 2012) 321.

[5] Maurice Hauriou, *Principes de droit public*, 138.

[6] Terence Daintith, 'The Techniques of Government', in Jeffrey Jowell and Dawn Oliver (eds), *The Changing Constitution* (2nd edn, Oxford University Press, 1996) 211.

[7] Maurice Hauriou, *Principes de droit public*, 145; Guy Isaac, *La procédure administrative non contentieuse* (LGDJ, 1968) 73. An example of the approach that focuses on the sequence of acts is Article 29.V.1 of the Spanish law of 17 July 1958.

passed legislation before 1945 and partially kept it when they fell under Soviet Rule, while other nations defined their rules in the 1950s.[8] Meanwhile, the US approved the Administrative Procedure Act (1946). Though enacted in a particular institutional context and as a reaction to the unprecedented governmental activism that followed the Great Depression,[9] this Act had an increasing resonance abroad. After 1989 the shift from acts to procedures increasingly emerged in legislation and sometimes in new constitutional provisions.[10]

Advantages and costs of procedures

Several advantages can be secured by requesting that power is not exercised as a 'one shot', but after a certain procedure has been carried out. First, the necessity to carry out a procedure can be regarded as a sort of shield against arbitrariness. From a slightly different viewpoint, a requirement of this type can facilitate the courts in exercising their supervisory function. Secondly, an obligation to perform a certain course of action can be a powerful instrument in ensuring that the will of political authorities is correctly implemented. Thirdly, the performance of a procedure—as opposed to an isolated decision—can be of real significance in ensuring that a variety of interests are considered and adequately weighed by the public authority.[11]

The first vision of administrative procedure gradually emerged at the end of the nineteenth century, as public authorities increasingly interfered with property and the conduct of business, as well as with civil rights.[12] A reaction against what was perceived as an excess of discretionary powers gradually took place. If citizens had an obligation to obey the law, the authority's decision had to be made in accordance with established procedures. New safeguards against misuses and abuses of governmental power were thus requested, not simply through judicial review of an administrative action, but during the course of the action. The French *Conseil d'État* was the first court in Continental Europe to develop a doctrine of invalidity on grounds of form (*vices de forme*), as distinct from substance, in two main respects. First, the specific rules defining procedures sometimes provided that the individuals who could be adversely affected by the final decision should be heard. Second, when a decision adversely affecting them was taken, the administration had a duty to give reasons for its choices. This approach has been followed not only by the higher courts of other jurisdictions, but also by legislators in their attempts to limit and structure the discretionary powers enjoyed by public administrations.

[8] Yugoslav code of 8 December 1956 and Hungarian code of 1 October 1957.

[9] See Paul R Verkuil, 'The Emerging Concept of Administrative Procedure' (1978) 78 Colum LR 258, 268.

[10] See, for example, the Spanish Constitution (1978), Article 105.

[11] See John Bell, 'Comparative Administrative Law', in Mathias Reimann and Reinhard Zimmermann (eds), *The Oxford Handbook of Comparative Law* (Oxford University Press, 2006) 1277 (focusing on safeguards, accountability, and efficiency).

[12] See Ernst Freund, *Administrative Powers Over Persons and Property* (The University of Chicago Press, 1928) 578.

While, in the approach to administrative procedures just considered, formalism can be regarded as an instrument for protecting rights and liberties, controlling the order and details of procedures can serve a very different purpose, the political control of bureaucracies.[13] Precisely for this reason, although Hungary fell under Soviet rule after 1945 and foreign domination became even stronger after 1956, legislation was enacted in order to regulate administrative procedures.[14] A legislative regulation of administrative procedures was adopted also by authoritarian regimes such as that which ruled Spain in 1958 and Poland in 1960.[15] The Polish act not only laid down a giving reasons requirement, but it also emphasized citizens' participation in procedures. These statutes may be explained in different ways. Administrative procedures can be effective as instruments for limiting and structuring the exercise of power only if there are independent judges willing to enforce them, which certainly was not the case, while the obligation to respect predefined procedures helps to attain the objectives of government. Another explanation is that an authoritarian political regime found it useful to leave some space to discontents.

Finally, administrative procedure can be considered an instrument of government, from a managerial (or Weberian) perspective. Especially after 1945 the positive State is increasingly viewed as an organization that is entrusted with the task of achieving a variety of goals in the interest of society.[16] If the machinery of government is not something against us, but something working in the interest of all, then the citizenry has as much interest in its efficiency and effectiveness as in its fairness. In other words, the tasks of government must be carried out quickly and well. From this viewpoint, administrative procedure is not only an instrument of government, but also of good governance.

A focus on administrative procedure serves to understand the potential tension between its uses, as well as its costs. Procedures are said to have a sort of Janus face, in the sense that they can be regarded as 'an adjunct to and a reaction against' the new role of the State.[17] Moreover, though procedures permit modern government to gain in fairness, there is a price to be paid. The disadvantages of procedures are said to be that they impose unnecessary constraints on the exercise of discretion, thus favouring the excesses of formalism and increasing the costs for agencies and

[13] Matthew McCubbins, Roger Noll, and Barry Weingast, 'Administrative Procedures as Instruments of Political Control' (1987) 33 J Law & Org 257, 261 (arguing that 'much of administrative law … is written for the purposes of helping … politicians retain control of policymaking'); Louise S Bressmann, 'Procedures as Politics in Administrative Law' (2007) 107 Columbia L Rev 1749.

[14] For further analysis, see Andràs Jakàb et al (eds), *The Transformation of the Hungarian Legal Order 1985–2005* (Kluwer, 2008).

[15] Marek Wierzborski and Stephen C McCaffrey, 'Judicial Control of Administrative Authorities: A New Development in Eastern Europe' (1984) 18 Int'l Lawyer 645.

[16] See Jerry Mashaw, 'The Management Side of Due Process' (1973–74) 59 Cornell Law Review 772; Nicholas Parrillo, 'Testing Weber: Compensation for Public Services, Bureaucratisation, and the Development of Positive Law in the United States', in Susan Rose-Ackerman and Peter L Lindseth (eds), *Comparative Administrative Law* (Edward Elgar, 2010) 47.

[17] See Paul R Verkuil, 'The Emerging Concept of Administrative Procedure', 258.

the length of policy formation processes.[18] Consider again our example concerning the issuing of licences for electronic communications. If there is a plurality of applications for a single licence, which implies that most of them will receive a denial, an elementary sense of justice requires that a hearing be held before the decision is taken and several legal systems conform to this, sometimes even providing comparative hearings. However, this not only makes a deadline for presenting applications necessary, but it also raises a question of time from another viewpoint, that of the length of the procedure. For this reason, some legal systems opt for online consultation, while in others the use of informal rulemaking procedures is said to have many practical advantages. Openness and participation are also said to favour the influence of special interests. Although all too often overemphasized, the risk that regulators may be 'captured' by regulated companies is not merely theoretical. Finally, administrative procedure can be a victim of its own success. In particular, when US courts widened the scope for public comments, administrative procedure became a surrogate of the political process, not without some drawbacks.[19] This might explain why in other cases the movement away from more formal procedures takes a more radical form, when legislators exclude any general notice and comment requirement from their codes.

The concept of administrative procedure

I have pointed out the legal relevance of administrative procedures to emphasize that in a field such as administrative law, where there is no general codification of the type that historically characterizes private law in many countries of Europe and Latin America, scholarly and judicial doctrines are particularly important. If theorization means that we seek to understand the institutions and practices of public law, then no characterization of administrative action should fail to acknowledge the increasing importance of the concept of administrative procedure. It is 'a concept at the heart of administrative law',[20] though administrative action also includes a much greater variety of sequences of activities than legislation or the judicial process.[21] The consequence of such greater variety is that generalization in description is much harder and generalization in prescription is still harder. Nevertheless, the concept of administrative procedure is no longer used only by theorists and judges, but also by legislators.

[18] See Jim Rossi, 'Participation Run Amok: The Costs of Mass Participation for Deliberative Agency Decisionmaking' (1997) 2 Northwestern Un L Rev 173. On economic costs, see Richard Posner, 'An Economic Approach to Legal Procedure and Judicial Administration' (1973) 2 J Legal Studies 399, but see also Jerry Mashaw, *Due Process in the Administrative State* (Yale University Press, 1985) 47 (criticizing the idea that the costs incurred by government can be measured in the same currency as the costs for dignity).

[19] Richard B Stewart, 'The Reformation of American Administrative Law' (1974–75) 88 Harvard L Rev 1795.

[20] Neil Walker, 'Review of Dennis J. Galligan, Due Process and Fair Procedures: A Study of Administrative Procedures' (1999) 62 Modern L Rev 962.

[21] Michel Fromont, 'Les types des procedures administratives', in Michel Fromont (ed), *La procédure administrative non contentieuse en droit français* (Esperia, 2000) 11.

More importantly for present purposes, the term 'administrative procedure' is not simply a surrogate for 'administrative process' or other such terms, but it possesses specific qualities. First, unlike that of a private body, the decision (and the same applies to administrative rulemaking) of a public authority is normally preceded by a series of activities and acts, a sequence of steps that is called 'procedure'. In short, as Sabino Cassese has observed, an administrative decision cannot be taken as a 'one shot'.[22] Secondly, all the phases must be duly carried out with respect to a pre-established order[23] that cannot be altered by the decision-maker unless the conditions provided by the law are satisfied or the public officer in charge of carrying out the procedure deems it necessary—under his or her responsibility—to add a phase, for example, to consult a scientific body. In other words, a procedure is a sort of code, which prescribes how things are to be done,[24] thus permitting certain types of conduct and prohibiting others. Thirdly, and consequently, an obligation to act consistently arises. The final decision is 'validly' taken only if, and to the extent to that, the rules that govern the procedure have been respected. Otherwise, the decision is either invalid[25] or irregular if it is affected by minor deviations from the pre-established order. If it is invalid, and if the same public authority that has issued the decision does not correct or withdraw it, the courts can quash it. Additionally, or alternatively, a duty of compensation for damage may arise.

The underlying reason is not just that the conduct of a public authority must respect the standards governing such conduct but, more substantially, that an administrative procedure serves to protect and balance a variety of interests. An example may clarify this. Suppose that legislation allows the building of a nuclear plant by undertakings that apply for an authorization or licence and meet certain requisites. The department or agency that is empowered to take the final decision cannot proceed *ex officio*, autonomously from the receipt of applications. Moreover, if the agency is required by law to consult a specialized scientific body, it cannot take the final decision until the opinion is formulated or the deadline for formulating it expires. The same applies if the agency is requested to provide participation through hearings with individuals or groups. These may bring a claim, either to court or to an ombudsman, if participation is non-existent. A twofold implication, practical and theoretical, follows from this. Practically, the process is no less legally relevant than the substance of the decision taken by a public authority. Theoretically, the concept of administrative procedure cannot be regarded as being equivalent to 'process'.

[22] Sabino Cassese, *Le basi del diritto amministrativo* (3rd edn, Einaudi, 2005) 307.

[23] Maurice Hauriou, *Principes de droit public*, 143; Ebherard Schmidt-Assmann, 'Sobre el objeto del procedimiento administrative en la dogmàtica administrative alemana', in Javier Barnès (ed), *El procedimiento administrativo en el Derecho comparado* (Civitas, Madrid) 320.

[24] W Michael Reisman, *The Quest for World Order and Human Dignity in the Twenty-first Century* (The Hague Academy of International Law, 2012) 100.

[25] Édouard Laferrière, *Traité de la juridiction administrative et des recours contentieux* (Berger-Levrault, 1888) II, 494 (arguing that, unlike in private law, in public law there is no need for legislation to clarify that a deviation from the norm entails invalidity).

2. Codification of Administrative Procedure

Codification of administrative procedure is an increasingly important legal phenomenon. As George Bermann has observed in a recent comparative survey, 'only a minority of States, it would appear, lack administrative procedure codes of one kind or another at the present time'.[26] A quick retrospective can be helpful to illustrate this growing trend.

Legislative regulation in the 1970s

Until a few decades ago, codification of administrative procedures was very limited, even considering the countries that are members of the Organization for Economic Cooperation and Development (OECD), a sort of club of the world's most advanced economies. It ought to be stated at the outset that in the OECD there is no such thing as a 'uniform administrative law'.[27] However, the members of this exclusive club share common standards and the club does not only include more or less all the countries that are members of the EU and the North American Free Trade Agreement (NAFTA), but also Turkey, Japan, and South Korea. It is, therefore, interesting to see whether these legal orders follow common principles, or at least some common guidelines, in order to introduce some elements of procedural due process of law. In the mid-1970s, a group picture showed that only in a few countries was administrative procedure codified. Interestingly, neither the UK nor France had any code of this kind.

The two main codes of administrative procedures were the Austrian (1925) and the American (1946). These codes are so different that one could place them at the two extremes of a continuum.[28] The Austrian legislation is based on the model of the judicial process. Administrative procedures had to provide citizens with a first protection against the administration.[29] Citizens thus enjoy certain process rights, such as the *audi alteram partem* maxim, the right to require an authority to state its reasons and the existing legal remedies. At the other extreme, it is not so much the US Administrative Procedure Act, but the complex of procedural requirements crafted by the courts. Judicial interpretation not only eroded the distinction between rights and privileges,[30] but also widely used doctrines of standing

[26] George A Bermann, 'Foreword', in Jean-Bernard Auby (ed), *Codification of Administrative Procedure* (Bruylant, 2014) v. For a distinction between types of codes, see Javier Barnès, 'Towards a Third Generation of Administrative Procedure', in Susan Rose-Ackerman and Peter L Lindseth (eds), *Comparative Administrative Law* (Edward Elgar, 2010) 336.

[27] James Salzman, 'Decentralized Administrative Law in the Organization for Economic Cooperation and Development' (2005) 68 Law & Cont Probl 181.

[28] On less recent codes, see Giorgio Pastori, *La procedura amministrativa* (Neri Pozza, 1964) and Celine Wiener, *Vers une codification de la procédure administrative* (PUF, 1975).

[29] Guy Isaac, *La procédure administrative non contentieuse*, 110; Heinz Schaffer, 'Administrative Procedure in Austria. 80 Years of Codified Procedure Law' (2005) 17 Eur Rev Public L 871.

[30] US Supreme Court, *Goldberg v Kelly*, 397 US 254, 90 (1970).

and intervention, producing an expansion of the class of interests entitled to seek judicial review.

The Spanish law of 1958 was in a somewhat intermediate position. It drew its inspiration from the doctrine of *Rechtsstaat*, that is to say, a thin version of the Rule of Law, and was thus acceptable to the authoritarian political regime of the time. Probably this was a crucial reason, in addition to cultural homogeneity, why the Spanish legislation was regarded as a model by the legislators of Latin American countries such as Argentina and Venezuela.[31] The doctrine of *Rechtsstaat* was also at the heart of a codification that took place in a very different institutional context, in Germany. Its legislative framework that regulates procedures (1976) has been considered a sort of model, whether to follow it or to deviate from it, by other countries. It is an act that contains numerous provisions. Although it focuses on the enactment of an administrative act, it regulates process rights, seen as a manifestation of the fundamental instances of *Rechtsstaat*. It also provides an interesting solution for the division of competence between the Federation and its components. Since these (*Länder*) enjoy a wide-reaching autonomy, the federal law does not preclude further *Land* legislation being enacted for the purposes of regulating the *Länder*'s own administrative procedures.[32] As a result, although federal law serves as a framework, it leaves room for a certain degree of diversity.

The new wave of codification

A solution similar to that of Germany was used by the procedural legislation adopted in Italy (1990) and Spain (1992). In particular, the Italian APA provided that the general provisions of the Act would be binding for the regions, though regional legislation could adopt higher standards. Also, in Belgium neither the regions nor the communities may limit the procedural protections provided by the federal law on administrative procedures.[33] There is, however, an important difference between the German APA and those of the other countries just mentioned. While the former is a comprehensive codification of procedures, the latter lay down only some general rules relating to process rights concerning administrative procedures and other rights, including access to files.[34]

In the following years, codification of administrative procedure spread throughout the OECD countries—for example, in the Netherlands[35]—and elsewhere. In

[31] For an analysis of the Venezuelan APA, see Allan R Brewer Carias et al, *Ley organica de procedimientos administrativos* (Editorial Juridica, 1989).

[32] See Diana U Galetta, 'Legislative Regulation of Administrative Procedures: The Role of the Bund and the Lander' (2010) 2 Italian J Public L 352.

[33] Belgian Constitutional Court, Judgment n 91/2013 of 13 June 2013, available at the website http://www.const-court.be/.

[34] For further analysis, see Mario P Chiti (ed), *General Principles of Administrative Action* (Bononia University Press, 2006).

[35] See the Dutch General Law of Administrative Procedure (GALA) of 1994.

Europe, a new wave of laws regulating administrative procedures followed the fall of the Berlin Wall in 1989. For example, Hungary modified its legislation in 1994 and Bulgaria and Croatia in 1991, while Latvia and Bulgaria issued their APA in 2003. There are, of course, several distinctive traits among these codes. Some of them only concern administrative adjudication, others deal also with rulemaking, and there is still another group of codes that regulate both administrative procedures and the judicial process, for instance, in Austria. However, there is clearly a common trend.[36] This is confirmed by the fact that the French Parliament, after enacting general rules governing the relationship between citizens and public administrations,[37] authorized the executive branch to introduce a codification by the end of 2015.

In the same period, new rules governing administrative procedures were enacted by some nations in Latin America, including Peru, where civil and political rights were re-established after years of dictatorship. Codes of administrative procedures have also been issued by Far East countries that are members of the OECD, such as South Korea and Japan. In both cases, the political decision to introduce a legal framework for the economy was followed by the adoption of guarantees concerning administrative procedures.[38] In 2001 a code of administrative procedure was issued in Taiwan. It regulates adjudication, rulemaking and contracts, aims at achieving the goal of protecting individual rights and promoting administrative efficiency, and, finally, affirms that all administrative acts shall be governed by the general principles of law.[39] Similarly, one year earlier, South Africa enacted the Promotion of Administrative Justice Act (2000) that aims at giving effect to the 'right to administrative action that is lawful, reasonable and procedurally fair'. The Act thus establishes a range of due process requirements, including the right to be heard and the duty to give reasons.

A period of twenty years is not much in the life of legislation. Many legislative provisions sleep for years before their implications begin to be felt. However, they stand as potentially helpful. Moreover, these codes appear to do two things. First, they show a general trend towards the adoption of important statutes governing administrative procedures. Second, these codes reveal important similarities in their contents. Of course, the contents are not exactly the same. It would be strange if they were, given the persistent and significant diversities between the countries that have codified administrative procedures.

[36] Sabino Cassese, 'Legislative Regulation of Adjudicative Procedures: an Introduction' (1993) 5 Eur Rev of Publ Law 15.

[37] See Jean-François Brisson, 'Les principes de la procédure administrative en droit français', in Michel Fromont (ed), *La procédure administrative non contentieuse en droit français*, 75.

[38] See Bin Takada, 'El procedimiento administrativo en Japón', in Javier Barnès (ed), *El Procedimiento Administrativo en el Derecho Comparado*, 318. See also, for a comparison with Korea, Tom Ginsborg, *Comparative Administrative Procedure: Evidence from Northeast Asia* (2002) 13 Const Pol Econ 256.

[39] Taiwan APA (Presidential Decree of 3 February 1999), Articles 1 and 4.

Learning from our neighbours

In the light of the diversities between national systems of public law, which derive from history and culture, it is interesting to seek to understand the reasons for the similarities just mentioned. This task may appear to be easier where there are old and strong ties between nations, for example, between Britain and Australia, that have been part of the same political system and are now included in the Commonwealth.[40] Where there are no political ties of this type, do similarities concerning administrative procedure derive either from functional needs, that are more or less the same, or from political choices and, if so, to what extent are such choices autonomous or influenced by external forces?

Consider, first, central European countries. As noted earlier, Austria took the first step in regulating its procedures in 1925, with a set of statutes. Other countries followed suit shortly afterwards: Czechoslovakia and Poland in 1928 and Yugoslavia in 1930.[41] The reasons for this were various and included the desire to strengthen democracy and the need to simplify administrative procedures in composite polities. Interestingly, the radical changes in the political regime after 1945 did not imply the demise of procedural legislation, as noted earlier with regard to Hungary. Similarly, the Polish legislative framework regulating administrative procedures of 1960 was amended in 1980, although the country was still subject to Soviet influence. This may be explained by referring again to the use of administrative procedures as instruments of political control. However, the resilience of public law structures, despite sudden political changes, and the cultural influence of neighbouring countries (*vicinitas*) should not be neglected.

Consider also Japan. It has been suggested that soon after 1945 American influence carried 'great weight' regarding the whole project of Constitution, which incidentally had a certain importance in the Indian 'avoidance of due process language'.[42] Whether or not 'influence' is a more appropriate representation than coercion, it is still an external factor. However, it provides only a partial explanation of subsequent events. It does not explain why, if the due process clause was regarded as being 'foreign' to national culture and unnecessary for the practical needs of the country, it has not been abrogated or substantially changed later. Quite the contrary—rules governing administrative procedure have been defined and refined. Similar steps have been taken by another OECD member, South Korea, as well as by the more authoritarian government of Taipei.[43] A local custom has thus emerged in that part of East Asia.

[40] See Edward I Sykes et al, *General Principles of Administrative Law* (3rd edn, Butterworths, 2006) (discussing the rules of natural justice in Australia).

[41] See Guy Isaac, *La procédure administrative non contentieuse*, 111.

[42] Wallace Mendelson, 'Foreign Reactions to American Experience with "Due Process of Law"' (1955) 41 Va L Rev 493, 501.

[43] John Ohnesorge, 'Administrative Law in East Asia: A Comparative-Historical Analysis', in Susan Rose-Ackerman and Peter L Lindseth (eds), *Comparative Administrative Law* (Edward Elgar, 2010) 86 (seeing changes that have occurred after 1990 as partly due to the democratization processes).

Consider, finally, Latin American countries. While the Spanish influence has already been mentioned, the possibility of cross-fertilization should not be ruled out. For example, the Argentinian, Chilean, and Peruvian codes of administrative procedure define administrative acts in the same way and place a duty on administrative agencies, in respect of their functions of adjudication, to state the reasons for their decisions and publish them. Undoubtedly, neither legislative requirement ensures real improvement in agencies' discharge of such duties; nor can the necessity of further improvements in other respects be neglected. Finally, it can be expected that the practice of these countries will not be uniform, given their constitutional and administrative diversities. However, all these codes stand as potentially useful for improving the conduct of public authorities and reveal significant similarities that cannot be explained by coercion or harmonization.

3. National Procedures Under External Influence

While comparative analysis shows that there are growing similarities in national procedural laws (public authorities must carry out a procedure, instead of making a 'one off' decision, and procedures are increasingly codified), as a result of both imitation and mutual learning, a different development derives from the growing influence exerted by regional and global organizations, such as the EU and the World Trade Organization (WTO) respectively.[44] It is, more precisely, a twofold development: on the one hand, such organizations lay down principles and rules governing administrative procedures, with more or less binding effects for national authorities; on the other hand, non-State bodies follow existing procedural requirements. In both respects, the States are no longer the absolute masters of their own procedures.

Procedural requirements for national authorities

The external influence on national administrative procedures can be considered from different points of view. For example, the provisions laid down by the WTO have a very wide scope of application and have binding effects on the contracting parties. However, some of the provisions that are more relevant for present purposes only concern the partners which have agreed to submit themselves to such provisions: this is the case with the Government Procurement Agreement (GPA).[45]

[44] On the concept of influence, see Robert A Dahl, *Modern Political Analysis* (5th edn, Prentice Hall, 1991) 28. On the influence of a variety of non-State entities, see Giacinto della Cananea, *Beyond the State: The Europeanization and Globalization of Procedural Administrative Law* (2003) 9 Eur Publ L 563, 573.

[45] At present, the GPA binds forty-four WTO members, while another eleven are in the process of acceding to the agreement. For an early analysis of membership, see Bernard Hoekman and Petros Mavroidis, 'The WTO's Agreement on Government Procurement: Expanding Disciplines, Declining Membership?' (1995) 4 Public Proc 63.

The recommendations issued by the OECD, instead, have a more limited scope of application and lack any binding effect, though they are taken into account by most, if not all, OECD members, at least because respecting them can be an important factor in the choices of foreign investors. Foreign investors' concern for the host State's procedures is even more relevant in BITs, some of which have recently laid down specific provisions governing administrative procedures. Finally, the EU has a marked impact on national procedural laws because of the twin pillars of EU law, supremacy and direct effect. These procedural requirements will now be examined in turn.

Let us begin with a typical manifestation of autonomy: freedom of contract. A private undertaking is fundamentally free to choose where it purchases labour or other services. By contrast, neither a public authority nor a private body charged with some public function is free to choose its counterparts in the same way, but must follow a certain procedure or set of procedures. Traditionally, this choice was taken by legislators and was motivated by concerns for legality and value for money, since governments spend large sums on procuring the goods and services they need. But in the last decade of the twentieth century government procurement was characterized by a 'global revolution':[46] global standards were introduced and were aimed at ensuring transparency and, thus, competition. Consider the provisions of the GPA. They require that governments ensure open, fair, and transparent conditions of competition in their procurement procedures. More specifically, 'a procuring entity shall publish a notice of intended procurement' and such notice 'shall remain readily accessible to the public'.[47]

BITs, too, lay down duties of fairness and transparency. Consider, for example, the US–Uruguay BIT. Some of its provisions are typical manifestations of general standards of conduct, to the extent that the contracting parties 'shall accord to covered investments treatment in accordance with customary international law, including fair and equitable treatment and full protection and security' and accept that their expropriation procedures are subject to 'due process of law'.[48] By contrast, another provision requires each party to ensure that its 'laws, regulations, procedures and administrative rulings of general application' are 'promptly published or otherwise made publicly available'.[49]

This is a mild requirement because it simply implies that the host State's procedures must be made known; yet, it presupposes that the design of a certain administrative procedure has been established before such procedure is carried out. This is not an irrelevant legal development because one of the great and admitted defects in many national systems of administrative justice is a generalized lack of information

[46] Sue Arrowsmith and Anne Davies (eds), *Public Procurement: Global Revolution* (Kluwer, 1998).

[47] GPA, Article VII(1). For further remarks, see Sabino Cassese, 'The Globalization of Law' (2005) 37 NYU J Int'l L & Pol 973, 975.

[48] See the US–Uruguay BIT, Articles 5(1) and 6(1)(d) respectively. See also Article 11 concerning more broadly issues of transparency. This BIT and the others have been consulted on the World Bank's Database of Bilateral Investment Treaties, available at https://icsid.worldbank.org.

[49] US–Uruguay BIT, Article 10(1).

as to their procedures of adjudication and rulemaking. Moreover, because the design of a procedure must be previously established and be made publicly available, it facilitates national courts and arbitral bodies in their supervisory function.[50]

EU rules have a much more marked impact on national procedures. As regards government procurements, EU directives do not simply lay down general principles of transparency and openness, but place a more stringent duty on all 'public' procurement bodies because they establish a *numerus clausus* of procedures. They include: (i) the open procedure, in which all providers may take part; (ii) the restricted procedure, in which all providers may participate, but only those that have been selected may present an offer; (iii) the negotiated procedure, where the procurement agency must invite at least three providers with whom it negotiates the terms of the contract; (iv) and the so-called 'open dialogue', which is used for complex contracts such as large infrastructure projects. The solution envisaged by EU law, therefore, is not always to impose a public call to tender, excluding any possibility of direct procurement. Indeed, experts are well aware of how a tender can be won without real competition between operators, and a direct award is sometimes the only solution possible.[51]

It is helpful to pause a little in order to reflect on the consequences of the trends just illustrated. There is, first, a growing body of rules imposing specific requirements of procedural propriety or fairness, seen as dictates of 'good governance', on the States. Secondly, these rules inevitably limit the procedural autonomy of national authorities, particularly in the case of the EU. Even with the best will in the world, there will be clashes between these external general rules and the exceptions that a national authority deems reasonable in a specific case. There will also be cases in which a national authority may be tempted to break a single procurement into several parts in order to escape from those general rules. However, any violation of external procedural rules not only exposes public administrators to the risk of litigation and of seeing their acts and transactions annulled by national courts, but also grants the right to compensation for damage to economic operators. It may induce them, when EU law is applicable, to seek the intervention of the European Commission. In this case, their individual interest can be combined with that of the public concerning the protection of the level playing field. Our discussion thus shifts to the instruments that can be used in order to ensure the enforcement of procedural rules.

Enforcing transnational standards: Foreign investment

Although other regulatory regimes lack a centralized enforcement mechanism such as that of the EU, they do not rely only on the good will of the contracting parties;

[50] Article 24(1) of the US–Uruguay BIT allows foreign investors to submit a claim under the ICSID Convention, the UNCITRAL Arbitration Rules, or, if both parties agree, 'any other arbitration rules'.

[51] Directive 2014/24/EU of the European Parliament and of the Council of 26 February 2014 on public procurement, [2014] OJ L 94, 65; Sue Arrowsmith, 'The Purposes of the EU Procurement Directives, Ends, Means and the Implications for National Regulatory Space for Commercial and Horizontal Procurement Policies' (2012) 14 Cambridge Ybk Eur Legal St 1.

nor are they simply based on amiable or diplomatic procedures. Non-centralized and non-judicial procedures will be exemplified by referring to arbitration in the field of direct foreign investment, with specific regard to the ICSID Convention. The reasons that justify this choice are, first, that over time the exclusivity of its arbitral tribunals was established, due to direct actions against the host State, restrictions on State immunity, the absence of a duty to exhaust local remedies, and the direct enforceability of awards;[52] second, that arbitration in the field of foreign investment guards the problematic boundary between a specific type of plaintiffs, foreign investors, and the host States. It is, therefore, a sort of judicial review of administrative action and has important elements in common with the principles that govern the exercise of power by public authorities in national legal systems.[53]

Consider one of the most cited and controversial arbitral awards, *Metalclad*. What was at stake was that Mexican federal authorities initially looked inclined to allow a US waste disposal company to create a subsidiary in Mexico, with a view to carrying out the same activity abroad. They hoped to attract foreign investments. However, eventually the Mexican local authority refused to permit the subsidiary to open and operate a hazardous waste facility. The tribunal put the issue of procedural fairness and propriety neatly. It found that not only had the permit not been issued, but also that no procedure was in place for dealing with building permits. It then found that an indirect expropriation had taken place because the conduct of the local authority caused the cessation of work on the project and thus damaged the foreign investors' interests.[54]

A 2011 award, *Lemire*, followed the same line of reasoning.[55] A US citizen claimed that Ukraine had infringed the BIT. Although a prior award had already been obtained in 2000, the claimant argued that the State had violated the fair and equitable standard. The tribunal dismissed Ukraine's objections to its jurisdiction and upheld the claim. It held that the process of awarding broadcasting frequencies was unfair because they had been awarded using non-public and non-transparent procedures. It added that the Ukrainian executive had acted without complying 'with the requirements or applying the procedures established in the law'.[56] What emerges from this award is that the conduct of the State not only violated basic

[52] See Rudolf Dolzer and Christian Schreur, *Principles of International Investment Law* (2nd edn, Oxford University Press, 2012) 20.

[53] Thomas W Wälde, 'The BIT Experience', in Federico Ortino et al (eds), *Investment Treaty Law—Current Issues*, II (BIICL, 2007) 141 (seeing investment arbitration as 'a form of international administrative law'); Martin Loughlin and Gus Van Harten, 'Investment Treaty Arbitration as a Species of Global Administrative Law', 17 Eur J Int'l L 121 (2006) ('international investment arbitration … provides … a singularly important and under-appreciated manifestation of an evolving system of global administrative law').

[54] *Metalclad Corporation v United Mexican States*, ICSID Case No ARB(AF)/97/1, Award of 30 August 2000, paragraph 108. This award and the following awards are published on the ICSID website: https://icsid.worldbank.org/.

[55] *Joseph Charles Lemire v Ukraine (Lemire)*, ICSID Case No ARB/06/18, Award of 28 March 2011, paragraph 99.

[56] *Lemire*, paragraph 178 (pointing out that 'more than 80 licences for radio broadcasting were issued directly by the executive … without meeting the requirements of or following the procedures established').

standards of adjudicatory fairness, especially when scarce resources are allocated to a few, but also, or primarily, showed the necessity for a procedure.

The standard applied by arbitrators is not a standard that is particularly high in terms of procedural protections for investors, a standard focusing on the impossibility to present evidence or to cross-examine the evidence and arguments on which the public authority relied. It is, rather, a lower standard: an orderly procedure is viewed essentially as an instrument of rational conduct, which may ensure consistency, prevent errors, and attenuate the risk of arbitrariness, though of course not eradicate it. In this sense and within these limits we can see arbitral tribunals in a way familiar to domestic courts, that is to say, as bodies engaged in producing acceptable rules for agency decision-making for the purpose of controlling it and making it accountable. In so doing, arbitral tribunals have matched the practical way in which agencies operate with a normative theory about how they should operate in a legal environment based on the assumption that respect for the rules of law is necessary to ensure that the conduct of the States is consistent with the commitments they take on when entering into BITs.

4. Procedural Requirements for Non-State Authorities

Thus far we have considered the procedural requirements imposed by international regulatory regimes on national authorities. We have seen that such requirements, in particular that to carry out the procedure previously established, broadly correspond to those that are shared by most, though not all, national legal systems. It is now time to see whether this requirement is also relevant, and if so with what legal consequences, for international and supranational authorities.

The procurements of international authorities

Until a few decades ago, international authorities enjoyed broad discretion in procuring the goods and services they needed,[57] a discretion that has been limited by the 'global revolution' mentioned earlier. There are now rules and general guidelines, as exemplified by the UN financial regulations and guidance respectively.[58] Their general guiding principle is that transparency and value for money must be assured.[59] Both goods and services must, therefore, be acquired through competition unless there are solid reasons that justify an exception.

What is more relevant for present purposes is that there is guidance in relation to procedures. A different procedure must be followed for a different type

[57] The amount of money involved is not irrelevant: in 2012 the UN alone has spent almost 3 billion dollars. For further details, see Elisabetta Morlino, 'Cosmopolitan Democracy or Administrative Rights? International Organizations as Public Contractors' (2014) 3 Cambridge J Int'l & Comp L 1.

[58] See UN Financial Regulation (last updated 2013, available on the UN's website).

[59] UN Financial Regulation, Section 5(12); UN *Procurement Manual*, § 1(a), available at https://www.un.org/Depts/ptd/about-us/procurement-manual.

of procurement. Formal and informal methods of solicitation are available. With regard to the former, open procedures are, in principle, to be followed, though a request for proposals and even the solicitation of a single vendor can be allowed in some cases.[60] Electronic auctions are provided for by the guidelines too. There are also detailed prescriptions concerning the commencement, management, and termination of a contract. A standardized form of procedure thus predominates.[61] This can save costs and reduce time for the contracting authority, although flexibility is needed in order to take account of the needs of a particular contract.

Although some commentators think that the procurements of institutions such as the UN and the EU would be improved by enshrining their procedures in a specific body of law, there are clearly advantages to the present system, which is based on soft law. However, two elements of the present system should not be underestimated. First, they are subject to the procedures they have issued, following the logic *tu patere legem tuam quam fecisti*. Second, the standards governing such procedures are fundamentally the same as those they suggest to national authorities, or impose on them, in the case of the EU.

The EU procedure concerning excessive government deficits

The following of a pre-defined procedure is even more important when the decision to be taken may adversely affect the interests of the contracting parties to an international agreement.

The ECJ's ruling in the dispute that saw the Commission opposed to the Council with regard to a government's excessive deficit furnishes a good example of this. The division of powers established by the Treaty was very simple: the Commission proposed, the Council disposed. On the procedural side, the Treaty made three choices. First, a particular procedure was established, with the consequence that the rules concerning the infringement procedure did not apply.[62] Secondly, after the Commission made its recommendation to the Member State whose deficit was examined, the maxim *audi alteram partem* was applied. The Member State could thus present its 'observations' and could produce data, extrapolating trends from them, or suggest a course of action different from that proposed by the Commission. Finally, following the other maxim of natural justice, *nemo judex in causa propria*, the Member State could not take part in the Council's final decision. This procedure could thus be regarded as trying to provide accuracy and fairness on one side and a consistent margin of appreciation on the other.

However, while the Commission's proposals (in the form of recommendations) were substantially followed with regard to several Member States, when it came to

60 UN *Procurement Manual*, paragraph 9(10) ('the UN may solicit only a single Vendor for a particular procurement action provided that' there has been a determination that using formal methods 'is not in the best interest of the Organization').

61 UN *Procurement Manual*, paragraph 9(9).

62 See Article 125(11) TFEU. For further analysis, see Jean-Victor Louis, 'The Economic and Monetary Union: Law and Institutions' (2004) 41 Common Mkt L Rev 575, 586.

assessing the deficits run up by France and Germany, a twofold problem emerged. There was a problem of substance because the Commission did not succeed in convincing the required majority of Member States that in both cases an excessive government deficit existed and the Council had, therefore, to impose specific obligations on France and Germany. There was also a problem regarding process because the Council did not follow the procedure prescribed by the Treaty, but a different one. As a result, the excessive deficit procedure was put in abeyance.

Not surprisingly, the Commission reacted against what it perceived as a misuse of powers and an abuse of procedure. Advocate General Antonio Tizzano suggested to the Court of Justice that a distinction had to be made between process and substance. On grounds of substance, he observed, the Council 'may obviously depart from the Commission's recommendation if it so decides'.[63] But, he added, on grounds of process the Council could not 'abstain from assessing the measures taken by the Member State concerned'. The reason was, according to Tizzano, that 'such an assessment constitutes an important step in order to enable the Community institutions to react speedily to any inadequacy of the measures prescribed for the Member State concerned'.[64] Following this opinion, the Court found that the Council had held the excessive deficit procedure in abeyance and, therefore, that this had to be regarded as a breach of its obligations stemming from the Treaty.[65] In sum, if a procedure exists, it must be followed.

5. The Intrinsic Value of a Procedure

In modern legal systems there is an increasing focus on procedures in two respects. First, if a procedure exists, but the decision-maker does not follow it, there is a *prima facie* case for arguing that the decision-making process followed by that authority is against the law. To the extent that there is a specific course of action, prescribed by law or by the internal rules of that authority, that thus limits and structures its own powers, a procedure cannot differ considerably from one case to another. Otherwise, the general principle to treat like cases alike would be infringed. Second, if a procedure does not exist at all, courts and other reviewing bodies focus on the necessity of organizing administrative decision-making in a way that makes it consistent with precedents,[66] as well as with the expectations of affected parties.[67]

The term 'administrative procedure', therefore, is not simply a surrogate for 'administrative process' or other such terms, but it possesses some specific qualities.

[63] Opinion of Advocate General Tizzano of 19 May 2004, Case C-27/04, *Commission v Council* [2004] ECR-I 6653, paragraph 99.

[64] Opinion of Advocate General Tizzano, paragraphs 100–101.

[65] Court of Justice, Case C-27/04, *Commission v Council* [2004] ECR-I 6679. For further remarks, see Paul Craig, *EU Administrative Law* (Oxford University Press, 2006) 195.

[66] Nils Herlitz, 'Swedish Administrative Law' (1953) 2 Int'l & Comp LQ 231.

[67] *Metalclad v United Mexican States*, ICSID Case No ARB(AF)/97/1, Award of 30 August 2000, paragraph 108 ('no procedure was in place for dealing with building permit applications').

Precisely because a certain procedure exists and must be followed, thus assuring a certain order in the exercise of power,[68] it is a limit not so much on discretion, which is an inevitable feature of modern government, but on arbitrariness. Concerns about the fairness and propriety of procedures should not, therefore, be equated with formalism.[69]

The analysis carried out also shows that, although there is no such thing as a conscious process of harmonization, procedural requirements are increasingly characterized by analogies. Though processes of mutual learning and even legal transplants were not unknown in the first half of the twentieth century, by the end of it they had become more frequent. A process of cross-fertilization, probably unavoidable in the current phase of globalization, has thus emerged. In this context, the regulatory regimes created by the States are developing some procedural requirements of their own, partly to impose them on national authorities and partly to afford due process to individuals and other legal entities potentially affected by their measures. Which requirements of due process must be afforded and in what circumstances are the crucial questions that will be addressed in the next two chapters.

[68] Maurice Hauriou, *Précis de droit administrative et de droit public general* (4th edn, Sirey, 1901) 507.

[69] Denis J Galligan, *Due Process and Fair Procedures. A Study of Administrative Procedures* (Clarendon Press, 1996) (noting the increasing importance of procedural fairness).

3

Audi Alteram Partem

The development of the requirement to carry out a procedure illustrated in the previous chapter is not isolated. It has been preceded and accompanied by another development, whose significance for legal systems can hardly be exaggerated. It regards one of the two traditional requirements of procedural justice, expressed by the maxim *audi alteram partem* (the other being the rule against bias, expressed by the maxim *nemo judex in causa propria*). For a long period of time this requirement has mainly been the product of case law and has been constructed beyond the borders of individual legal systems. A quick historical digression can be helpful to understand both these features.

1. The Closest Thing to an Invariant: Due Process for Civil Servants

Variations on a given theme: *Medea*'s argument

That the development of due process of law, and more specifically of the maxim *audi alteram partem*, is a manifestation neither of bounded legal systems nor of strict positivism is demonstrated by a story that is four centuries old and 'has the ring of a Shakespearean comedy':[1] *Bagg*'s case.

James Bagg, a civil servant (Chief Burgess), was dismissed on the grounds of his misconduct without permitting him to make his case. He thus brought his case to the King's Bench. The court, presided over by sir Edward Coke, found that the dismissal was unjustified on two grounds, related but distinct. Substantially, it found that Bagg's removal was not based on any just cause. Procedurally, the King's Bench held that administrators had 'proceeded without hearing him answer to what was objected'. A removal, the court continued, 'without hearing the party removed, is bad'.[2] Of particular interest for present purposes is not only the court's conclusion, but also its reasoning. Coke referred to the administrative process that was required 'by the law of the land', an expression that was regarded as synonymous with the

[1] Dawn Oliver, *Common Values and the Public-Private Divide* (Cambridge University Press, 1999) 45.

[2] See *The Reports of Sir Edward Coke* (The Lawbook Exchange, 2002) II, 174.

Due Process of Law Beyond the State. First Edition. Giacinto della Cananea.
Published 2016 by Oxford University Press.

old expression *per legem terrae*. But Coke was not simply applying the legal document he referred to. Indeed, he relied on Seneca's *Medea*, when he affirmed that, without a hearing, the removal was 'against justice and right'.[3] Writing one century after Cook's dicta, William Blackstone was perfectly aware of this. In expounding his critical remarks about the summary proceedings before the justices of the peace, Blackstone underlined the necessity to summon the party accused before a decision was taken. He underlined that this was an 'indispensable' requisite, emphasizing that it constituted a 'rule of natural reason expressed by Seneca',[4] although, he noted, justices had forgotten it.

At the basis of this concept of due process clause there were, however, two profoundly distinct elements. One is the quest for a rule of (natural) reason or *recta ratio*;[5] the other is pragmatism. Coke's attitude was pragmatist, if not instrumentalist, in that he perceived the incompleteness of existing rules of law and integrated them with an unwritten norm of 'natural justice'. In so doing, however, he interpreted *Medea*'s maxim in a way that differed from its original meaning. A closer look at Seneca's *Medea* reveals that the maxim worked differently regarding what may be called today the judicial and administrative functions of the State. The sense of this distinction is that a public authority acting as a judge is in breach of natural justice if the affected party—including an alien, such as Medea—is not provided with a reasonable opportunity to be heard, while if the same authority acts administratively, natural justice would not apply, at least not necessarily.[6] In this respect, *Bagg*'s case does not only show how the court was concerned with protecting an individual from what was perceived as an arbitrary decision, but also that in doing justice it extended—having 'nothing to do with legislative intent'[7]—the principles of natural justice from the judicial to the administrative function. This has been, during the following centuries, the justification for treating judicial and quasi-judicial decisions alike in common law countries.[8] By contrast, at the end of the nineteenth century under German administrative law the right to be heard was still considered an exclusive feature of the judicial process, as opposed to administrative procedures, although Otto Mayer concedes that things were different as far as disciplinary procedures were concerned.[9] It is interesting, therefore, to look at our issue comparatively, by way of a quick journey through the world.

[3] See Seneca's *Medea* (paragraphs 190–202): 'He who decides an issue without hearing one side has not been just, however just the decision' (the original text, quoted by Coke, is the source of the maxim *Qui statuit aliquid parte inaudita altera, aequum licet statuerit, haud aequus fuerit*).

[4] William Blackstone, *Commentaries on the Laws of England* (1765; Clarendon Press, 1966) IV, Chapter 20.

[5] James AC Grant, 'The Natural Law Background of Due Process' (1931) 31 Colum L Rev 56.

[6] This distinction is evident in Medea's words to King Creon: 'If you are acting as judge, investigate the case; if as king, give orders' (*Si iudicas, cognosce, si regnas, iube*).

[7] Dawn Oliver, *Common Values*, 47; Paul Craig, *UK, EU and Global Administrative Law* (Cambridge University Press, 2015) 35.

[8] William Wade, '"Quasi-Judicial" and Its Background' (1949) 10 Cambridge LJ 216.

[9] Otto Mayer, *Droit administratif allemand* (1904; CPSA, 2011) 29.

Parallel developments in civil law and common law countries: Italy and the UK

Our journey begins with a comparison between the conceptions of administrative due process that emerged in cases concerned with deprivation of offices in two European legal systems, those of Italy and the UK, which are based on different ideas and thoughts about administrative justice, particularly with regard to the question as to whether the State must be subject to a special judge or to the ordinary courts of the land. We will focus later on India, which is particularly interesting also for showing that theories of constitutional interpretation that emphasize legislative intent do not reflect reality.

Consider, first, the ruling of the Italian *Consiglio di Stato*, an administrative court created in 1890, in the *Chiantera* case (1895). One of the first claims brought before the court regarded a deprivation of office in a municipality. *Chiantera*, a civil servant who served as a secretary, had been dismissed without receiving any notification of the charge against him or enjoying any opportunity to be heard before his dismissal. The municipality argued that such an opportunity existed only when legislation specifically imposed it upon a public authority, as in criminal proceedings. The court rejected this positivist conception of the right to be heard. It affirmed, somewhat emphatically, that 'it is an eternal principle of justice that no punishment may be imposed without giving the interested party the opportunity to be heard and to defend himself'.[10] If this essential legal requirement had not been observed, it reasoned, then the final decision had to be annulled.

The right to be heard before the administration takes the final decision is a principle of eternal law, and had been upheld by English courts for a long time before, as noted earlier. Without repudiating this principle, the courts have subsequently attenuated its importance. A change, however, occurred in the landmark decision taken by the House of Lords in *Ridge v Baldwin*.[11] Also in this case a civil servant, a chief constable of local police, had been dismissed without being entitled to notification of the charges against him and an opportunity to be heard before being dismissed. The House of Lords revived the principles of natural justice to affirm that the lack of a hearing can justify the quashing of an administrative decision, though this is neither a judicial nor a quasi-judicial decision. This revival of the natural justice doctrine and the courts' following of this precedent justified the assertion by Sir William Wade, a key figure in English public law, that the ruling was a 'historic turning point'.[12]

The existence of a set of procedural safeguards for civil servants is confirmed by the jurisprudence of the European Court of Human Rights. In *Pellegrin v France*,

[10] The decision is published in Aldo Sandulli and Gabriele Pasquini (eds), *Le grandi decisioni del giudice amministrativo* (Giuffrè, 2001) 53. The translation is mine.

[11] *Ridge v Baldwin* (1964) AC 40.

[12] William Wade, 'Administrative Justice in Great Britain', in Aldo Piras (ed), *Administrative Law. The Problem of Justice* (Giuffrè, 1994) I, 174. See also Carol Harlow and Richard Rawlings, *Law and Administration* (3rd edn, Cambridge University Press, 2010) 617 (according to whom this was a 'watershed case').

the Court decided on the applicability of Article 6(1) of the European Convention on Human Rights to disputes between States and their servants. It applied a 'functional' criterion based on the nature of the employee's duties and responsibilities. It thus held that Article 6 does apply to such disputes, unless the public servant is acting as the depositary of public authority responsible for protecting the general interests of the State or other public authorities.[13]

An evolving constitutional interpretation: The case of India

It is interesting to compare the English and Italian cases, where the courts have enforced due process of law without any formal constitutional basis, with India, where excluding due process of law—in the way it was conceived in the US—was the original intent of the framers of the Constitution.

Article 21 of the Indian Constitution provides: 'No person shall be deprived of his life or personal liberty except according to *procedure established by law*.' There are similarities to the Fifth Amendment of the US Constitution, but at the same time there are evident differences between the two provisions. Unlike the Fifth Amendment, in Article 21 of the Indian Constitution only life and liberty are mentioned, while property is not, due to the majoritarian collectivist views that dominated the Constituent Assembly. Nor, more importantly for our purposes, is there any requirement of 'due process'. There is, rather, a more modest obligation to follow the procedure established by law.

This is neither a modest difference nor an unintended one. By design, the framers expressly rejected including a provision akin to the Due Process Clause of the Fifth Amendment. They chose a more modest obligation, in the sense that the administration is under a duty to follow legislative procedures whenever it impinges on fundamental rights. They did so, in part, for procedural reasons. The advocates of a due process clause argued that the best way to protect the principles of natural justice, as affirmed in English law, was to follow the practice of earlier colonies that had gained independence from the British Empire. Others objected on the ground that to do so would unduly limit the powers of the legislative and executive branches of government. US Justice Felix Frankfurter had warned as much in consultations with an Indian expert who had travelled to Washington to meet him.[14] As a consequence of all this, it can be argued that, absent any specific procedural requirement, the administration may impinge on fundamental rights outside the safeguards ensured by the traditional principles of natural justice. This is, in substance, what the Indian Supreme Court held in the first 'hard case' it had to decide, the *Gupalan* case.[15]

[13] *Pellegrin v France*, App No 28541/95, 31 Eur Ct HR 651 (1999). For further remarks, see Paul Craig, 'The Human Rights Act, Article 6 and Procedural Rights' (2003) 47 Public L 753.

[14] Manoj Mate, 'The Origins of Due Process in India: The Role of Borrowing in Personal Liberty and Preventive Detention Cases' (2010) 28 Berkeley J Int'l L 216, 220. For further remarks on Frankfurter's theses, see Alfred C Aman, *The Democracy Deficit* (New York University Press, 2004) 17.

[15] *AK Gopalan v The State of Madras* (1950) SCR 88 (India). This ruling and the other referred to in the following footnotes are available at http://supremecourtofindia.nic.in/.

The Court subsequently reversed course in a 1967 ruling involving the involuntary retirement of a civil servant on grounds that her date of birth had been incorrectly reported.[16] The public authority making the decision neither disclosed its findings nor gave her an opportunity to respond. The seriousness of these procedural deficiencies led the High Court to grant a writ, which the Supreme Court confirmed on appeal, after distinguishing the case from the *Gupalan* precedent. The Court further held that an administrative procedure of this kind is very similar to a judicial proceeding. It must, therefore, 'be made consistently with the rules of natural justice'. As a result, the Court continued, the civil servant 'must be informed of the case of the State and the evidence in support thereof and must be given a fair opportunity to meet the case before an adverse decision is taken'. This case shows how the courts were concerned with the impact of government decisions on individuals. It also shows the importance of the assimilation between judicial and quasi-judicial decisions.[17]

The courts' predisposition to go beyond legislative intent was consolidated ten years later in *Maneka Gandhi*.[18] That case involved a government order to deprive a citizen of his passport, and therefore his right to travel. Among other things, the government argued that the right claimed by the individual was trumped by the superior, collective interest being protected by the public authority, namely ensuring that public order was respected and, thus, the security of all. The Supreme Court insisted that the claimant should have been granted a better opportunity to make his case, that the government had not given a 'good enough reason … for impounding [his] passport', and that 'the public interest [could] be better served in some other manner'. This conception of procedural fairness thus went well beyond the 'procedure established by law', even pointing to proportionality. For Judge Bhagwati, evaluating extra-judicially the significance of the ruling, it is never enough that a statute authorizes an interference with personal liberty; instead, it 'should prescribe a procedure for so doing and such procedure must be reasonable, fair and just'.[19]

The Indian case confirms the courts' willingness to go beyond legislative intent in order to impose on decision-makers duties of procedural propriety and fairness as far as the exercise of their powers is concerned. It also confirms that such duties cannot be seen simply as a peculiarity or a legacy of Western countries. Finally, it suggests that the justification for those duties of procedural propriety and fairness is not only the need to ensure that the servants of the State do not suffer from an arbitrary deprivation of office. Their justification is, rather, the necessity of limiting and structuring power in order to ensure that

[16] *State of Orissa v Dr. (Miss) Binapani Dei & Ors.* (1967) 2 SCR 625 (India). Government held an enquiry into the date of birth of the civil servant, did not disclose the report, did not give her any opportunity to meet the evidence used against her, and dismissed her.

[17] Mangal Chandra Kagzi, *The Indian Administrative Law* (5th edn, Anmol Publications, 1991) 134.

[18] *Maneka Gandhi v Union Of India* (1978) 2 SCR 621 (India).

[19] Judge Prafullachandra N Bhagwati, *Foreword*, in Anand N Chaturvedi, *Rights of Accused Under Indian Constitution* (Deep & Deep, 1984) 6–7.

justice is also done in cases concerning other citizens. This raises the question whether the line of reasoning followed by Coke—a decision taken without hearing the other party may be just, but is unfair—can be extended to all types of procedure.

2. A Minimum Standard: Hearing Adversely Affected Parties

Our journey thus proceeds, with the intent of seeking to understand whether similar developments occurred not merely in other fields of public law, but generally, as well as whether they occurred in other legal systems. As a first step, we will focus on the French system of administrative law, which can be regarded as a paradigmatic case of judicial development of general principles of administrative procedure. Next, a distinction will be made between two great types of administrative procedures, dealing with adjudication and rulemaking.

The right to be heard as a general principle of law: The French case

The French and Italian legal systems are similar in many respects, in particular with regard to the fundamental choice of a dualist system of judicial review of administrative action, with a strong role for the administrative judge. They have differed, however, for a long period of time as far as recognizing the general principles of law are concerned. In Italy—as noted earlier—the administrative judge did not hesitate to enforce certain requirements of procedural due process of law, with more than an assonance with theories of natural law. By contrast, in France, although early writers such as Édouard Laferrière had already indicated that the *Conseil d'État* based its decisions, in the absence of legislative rules, upon the general principles of administrative and public law, it rejected even the expression 'general principles of law'.[20] It could be said, therefore, that it discretely applied them without recognizing them formally. Whatever the influence played by positivist theories of the law, a shift occurred immediately after the fall of the Vichy regime.[21] In two famous cases, *Aramu* and *Dame Veuve Trompier-Gravier*, the *Conseil d'État* abandoned its previous reluctance.

Three aspects of this *revirement* are particularly relevant for our purposes. First of all, both cases concerned the right of defence against the executive branch, more specifically against an administrative sanction in *Aramu* and the withdrawal of a licence in *Dame Veuve Trompier-Gravier*. In neither case did existing rules provide

[20] Roland Drago, 'The General Principles of Law in the Jurisprudence of the French Conseil d'Etat' (1962) 11 Am UL Rev 126. Eduard Laferrière referred in particular to 'formal' aspects such as the omission of a hearing and the lack of reasons: *Traité de la juridiction administrative et du recours contentieux*, II, 493.

[21] That there was not only a temporal relationship, but also a causal one, was affirmed by Jean Rivero, 'Les principes generaux du droit dans la jurisprudence du Conseil d'Etat' [1951] Etudes et Documents 7.

that the decision-making authority had the duty to inform the addressee of the measure that it was going to take.[22]

Secondly, despite this absence of a specific requirement of due process, in *Dame Veuve Trompier-Gravier* the *Conseil d'État* affirmed that a measure seriously and adversely affecting the interests of the claimant could not 'legally' be taken without providing her with an opportunity to contest the measure, which in turn required the administration to send her a notice.[23] The same doctrine was applied in *Aramu*. In this case the *Conseil d'État* went even further, to the extent to that it argued that an act of the executive branch is illegal if it violates the 'general principles of law applicable even in the absence of a text'.[24] Although the administrative judge has refrained from generalizing this rule, it has extended it to other decisions affecting individual interests, such as inspections and sanctions.[25]

Thirdly, and very important for our discussion, when trying to give an explanation for the *revirement*, Maxime Letourner and Roland Drago used a very well-known *topos*, that of *non liquet*, which was widely referred to also by international lawyers during the same period. They observed that, unlike in the *Ancien Régime*, Article 4 of the French Civil Code prohibits any denial of justice by providing: '[T]he judge who shall refuse to judge, on the pretext of the silence, the obscurity, or the adequacy of the law, may be prosecuted as one guilty of denial of justice.' They argued that this applied 'especially' to an administrative judge,[26] who is called upon to fill the lacunae in a context which is not characterized by a comprehensive code, with the ensuing axiom of the completeness of the legal system. Letourner and Drago somewhat delimited the role of the administrative judge by specifying that 'when the judge applies general principles, he interprets the presumed will of the legislator and does not create law'.[27] This was clearly one of those fictions which lawyers use when they are aware that existing paradigms, in this case the positivist theory, are simply unfit to assure the adherence to minimum requirements of justice, in this case in the context of administrative adjudication. Whatever the formal respect paid to such a theory, the jurisprudence of the French administrative judge represents a move away from the institutional context in which that theory was developed.

[22] See Conseil d'État, 26 October 1945, *Aramu*. Both this case and the following are included among the most significant rulings of the Court and are available at http://www.conseil-etat.fr/.

[23] Conseil d'État, 5 May 1944, *Dame Veuve Trompier-Gravier*.

[24] See Conseil d'État, *Aramu* (referring to unwritten principles: 'principes généraux du droit applicables même en l'absence de texte').

[25] Pascale Idoux, *La contradiction en droit administratif français* (Faculté de droit de Montpellier, 2005).

[26] Maxim Letourner and Roland Drago, 'The Rule of Law as Understood in France' (1958) 7 Am J Comp L 147.

[27] Maxim Letourner and Roland Drago, *The Rule of Law as Understood in France*, 149. On the distinction between obscurity of the law and lacunae, see Lucien Siorat, *Le problème des lacunes en droit international. Contribution à l'étude des sources du droit et de la fonction judiciaire* (LGDJ, 1959) 63–85.

Adjudication v regulation

The French case raises a further point of interest from a comparative viewpoint. Despite the traditional differentiation between the public law systems of England and France, seen as the paradigmatic examples of common law and civil law, a closer look at their judicial doctrines reveals 'striking' similarities.[28] The question that thus arises is whether all can invoke due process in all cases.

In this respect, some important points should be borne in mind. First, in the vast field of adjudication,[29] the content of natural justice that should be applicable, absent any particular procedural requirement, may well vary depending on a number of relevant factors. The reason is that procedures are based on interests, which inevitably differ, with the consequence that the former must be fashioned in ways that are better suited to the particular needs of the latter.

Secondly, the principles and rules governing adjudication often reflect an adversarial conception of process rights. But process rights can, and often do, reflect a different conception. Mirjan Damaska, a specialist of the judicial process, masterfully clarified this point. He observed the diversity of arrangements and institutions through which justice is administered and noted that sometimes such arrangements and institutions are characterized by variation within two broad models of justice.[30] Such models, each with several variants, are the adversarial and the inquisitorial. While the adversarial model maximizes the contest, and thus the conflict solving type of process, in the inquisitorial model what really matters is the achievement of certain policy goals. For all these reasons, there is no such thing as a 'model' of administrative adjudication.

Thirdly, we should be prepared to think more broadly about what connotes procedural protection because an increasing number of administrative procedures are devoted to rulemaking. In both cases, administrative procedures can be used to promote the policies and values of government as opposed to individual rights. But administrative procedures are structured differently in adjudication and regulation. While the former is used to announce what citizens or businesses should do in individual cases, the latter is used to lay down rules affecting them directly (binding precepts) or indirectly (policy guidelines for administrators). As a result, at one end of the spectrum there are the adjudicative procedures that are regarded as being quasi-judicial and are thus heavily influenced by the requirement to hear the other side. At the other end of the spectrum, there are rulemaking and planning procedures that are sometimes open to all those who have something to say about how

[28] Anthony Lefas, 'A Comparison of the Concept of Natural Justice in English Administrative Law with the Corresponding General Principles of Law and Rules of Procedure in French Administrative Law' (1978) 4 Queen's LJ 197.

[29] In the US APA, 5 USC § 551(7), 'adjudication' refers to 'agency process for the formulation of an order'. The definition thus shifts from the action to the final act or measure. Article 35 of the German APA, instead, regulates administrative action aiming at adopting an act affecting an individual or a group of individuals, defined or definable.

[30] Mirjan Damaska, *The Faces of Justice and State Authority. A Comparative Approach to the Legal Process* (Yale University Press, 1986) 1–2.

a collective interest should be weighed. Procedural requirements developed against a backdrop of adjudication can be less appropriate in these circumstances, which require separate treatment.[31]

The right to be heard in administrative adjudication

With these caveats in mind, two main trends can be identified with regard to administrative adjudication. First, while the scope of application of the *audi alteram partem* maxim was limited in a number of ways, several limitations have been lifted. Second, while this maxim was regarded as a shield for citizens against the authority of their State, it is increasingly applied to all.

In civil law and common law systems it is evident from the late nineteenth century cases and scholarly literature on the right to a hearing that a gradual change has emerged. Initially, this right was regarded as being a typical trait of the judicial function. Consequently, whenever a State activity was qualified as judicial, the right to be heard automatically applied. According to the authoritative treatise of Otto Mayer, for example, such a right characterized the activity of the new administrative judges created in some parts of Germany.[32] In a similar way, in the UK the courts distinguished administrative and judicial decisions, taking a narrower view of the latter and affirming that only these decisions had to be preceded by a reasonable opportunity for the affected individual to be heard. However, this limitation was attenuated by the predisposition of the courts to go beyond the dichotomy between administrative and judicial decisions. In some cases, the courts found that, though in the abstract a public authority was exercising administrative powers, it was in fact acting quasi-judicially because the decision it was empowered to take affected a relationship between two parties, a situation very similar to that of a trial.[33] Following this line of reasoning, for instance, the Italian administrative judge has affirmed that, in a procedure concerning a popular referendum, its proponents must be provided with a fair opportunity to be heard before the court that decides on the admissibility of such referendum.[34] Another judicial technique to reduce the scope of limitation of the *audi alteram partem* maxim was to overcome the traditional distinction between rights and privileges. In other words, not only rights, but also privileges, such as welfare entitlements, received procedural due process protection.

While these doctrines of due process were developed by the courts, during the second half of the century State legislation produced a twofold change. Statutes specified certain aspects of procedural rights as they applied in specific areas, such as confiscation and expropriation, implementing constitutional provisions protecting private property. More recently, codes of administrative procedure have introduced a general framework for adjudication, which includes the right to be heard and

[31] Paul Craig, 'Procedures and Administrative Decisionmaking', 56.
[32] Otto Mayer, *Droit administratif allemand*, 28.
[33] Paul Craig, *Administrative Law*, 409.
[34] Consiglio di Stato, IV, judgment of 3 April 1997, n 333 (available at https://www.giustizia-amministrativa.it).

the right to have access to the documents held by public authorities. Parliaments have sometimes passed legislation governing administrative procedures in order to enhance economic reforms; also in the context of membership of international regulatory regimes. For instance, in South Korea the political decision to introduce a legal framework for the economy was followed by the adoption of guarantees concerning administrative procedures. Another interesting case is that of Japan, where the APA of 1993 (as revised in 2005) requires the hearing of individuals adversely affected by administrative decisions and provides for their intervention.[35]

Generally, the maxim *audi alteram partem* implies that notice must be given of the beginning of a procedure that may lead to the issuing of a decision adversely affecting someone and that 'some kind of hearing' must be provided. The two requisites are, logically and legally, strictly connected. It is because the decision-making authority is requested to give notice to 'all interested parties' that such parties may have access to the files, submit evidence and arguments, and take part in a hearing. This includes, in most national legislations, the right to be given 'an opportunity of commenting on the facts relevant to the decision'.[36]

However, legislators are afraid of opening the floodgates regarding administrative action and, therefore, often distinguish between formal and informal procedures.[37] They also exclude any duty to provide a hearing if the objection raised by a private party is either manifestly ill-founded[38] or a vexation for the administration. More importantly, legislators require not only that an interest, although not presently held, exists but also that such interest is negatively affected by the decision or measure that the public authority is empowered to take. A clear example of this is Article 41(2) of the Charter of Fundamental Rights of the EU, which is applicable also to its Member States when implementing European Union (EU) law. It provides that the right to good administration includes, among other things, 'the right of every person to be heard, before any individual measure which would affect him or her adversely is taken'. Similarly, the principle of 'just administration' laid down by the Constitution of South Africa has been implemented by a legislative provision establishing that 'administrative action which materially and adversely affects the rights or legitimate expectations of any person must be procedurally fair'.[39] There is of course discussion about what the word 'adversely' means, but it certainly implies that the holders of a right or an interest must receive notice in due time and be provided with a reasonable opportunity to be heard. Thus, if, for example, a public authority intends to expropriate real property, this requires some form of process rights before the measure is taken. This is equally the case if the public authority intends either to refuse the renewal of a licence or to withdraw it.

[35] See the Japanese APA, Article 13(1)(a) and (b), providing for hearings in the case of measures that 'rescind some permission' or deprive the parties of qualification or status.

[36] German APA, Article 28; Venezuelan APA (1981), Article 8.

[37] See, for example, the German APA, Article 66(1).

[38] See, for example, Dutch APA (GALA), Section 7.3.

[39] Promotion of Administrative Justice Act (2000), Article 3(1).

There is thus a growing sense that the more an administrative decision affects some individuals and impinges on their substantive rights, the greater the care that must be taken to guarantee their procedural rights. This sense is strengthened by the fact that the right to a hearing is not limited to citizens, but is increasingly recognized as being available to all. Not only aliens but legal residents who are subject to antiterrorism measures affecting their liberty and property and also 'enemy combatants' are regarded as being entitled to exercise the right to a fair hearing. However, the importance of such a trend must not be overestimated because it does not concern all administrative procedures, but only those relating to adjudication.[40] Moreover, what the right to a hearing concretely means varies from one country to another. For example, in common law countries a hearing is often provided for by law, a specific hearing officer is in charge of it, the hearing is open, and a record must be made and kept. In other countries, including Sweden, a private party can be afforded an opportunity to be heard.[41] But there are still other countries where there is no such thing as a general rule requesting public authorities to carry out hearings. As a result, there is simply an exchange of evidence and opinions between the parties and the public authority. All this suggests that, instead of a harmonization of procedural requirements, there is a sort of ladder, with a minimum requirement and higher standards.[42]

Rulemaking: A differentiated legal framework

Citizens and businesses are affected by administrative action not only through individualized adjudication, but also through the adoption of rules, either directly or indirectly, that is to say, when such rules impose or prohibit a certain conduct on administrators. A detailed study waits to be written on the way in which the various State norms set forth procedures for administrative rulemaking. Comparative studies,[43] however, reveal that while with adjudication it is perhaps possible to locate unity within variety, rulemaking and planning procedures are characterized by extreme variety.

In OECD countries, the principle of openness is regarded as a hallmark of democratic government, whilst at the same time providing decision-makers with the information provided by citizens.[44] Rules aiming at ensuring transparency have long been issued by most, though not all, its members.[45] For some procedures

[40] Sabino Cassese, 'Legislative Regulation of Adjudicative Procedures: An Introduction' (1993) 5 Eur Rev of Publ Law 15.

[41] See the 1986 *Administrative Procedure Act*, Section 15. On earlier rules, see Nils Herlitz, 'Legal Remedies in Nordic Administrative Law' (1967) 15 Am J Comp L 687.

[42] For this metaphor, see Pascale Idoux, *La contradiction en droit administratif français*.

[43] See Theodora Ziamou, *Rulemaking, Participation and the Limits of Public Law in the USA and Europe* (Ashgate, 2001).

[44] OECD, *Recommendations of the Council on Regulatory Policy and Governance* (Paris, OECD, 2012) § 2 (urging governments to provide 'meaningful opportunities (including online) for the public to contribute to the process of preparing draft regulatory proposals and to the quality of the supporting analysis').

[45] This is the case, for instance, with Turkey: *OECD Reviews of Regulatory Reform OECD Reviews of Regulatory Reform: Turkey* (OECD, 2002) 62.

affecting a large number of persons, such as those aiming at adopting urban plans or tariffs for public utilities, there is a common tendency to oblige decision-makers to seek more accurate information and to consult stakeholders. In some national systems, additional procedural requirements are imposed on public authorities. They are obliged to hear the voices of all those whose interests are affected by the final outcome of the procedure in a hearing, as happens in France with public enquiries, as well with regulations affecting the environment.[46] But in other national systems there is no similar legal instrument. As a result, confrontation and cooperation between citizens and public authorities take place without a formal hearing.

If we move away from particular norms to those having a broader scope of application, two basic models emerge: pluralist democracy and representative democracy.[47] They can be exemplified using the US legal framework and that of some European countries. In the US, the fundamental choice made by the APA is that, whether the rulemaking procedure be formal or informal, it must always assure the receipt and consideration of public comments. An agency that intends to formulate, amend, or repeal a rule must, therefore, provide general notice through publication in the Federal Register and must give interested persons an opportunity to participate in the rulemaking process, either in written form or through a hearing.[48] By contrast, some European codes of administrative procedure exclude regulation as being subject to the same requirements established for adjudication (Italy, for example). Elsewhere, for example in France and the UK, the receipt and consideration of public comments is ensured only in specific cases, notably for urban planning. The courts, moreover, show a certain degree of cautiousness when dealing with demands for participation in administrative procedures.[49]

Precisely because national legal frameworks are more differentiated than in the case of adjudication, the policies adopted by international regulatory regimes are even more important. Sometimes, they simply adopt recommendations, such as OECD reports on regulation. Sometimes, more binding legal precepts are enacted. For example, EU directives on electronic communications impose notice and comment requirements on national regulators when setting standards and tariffs. Interestingly, similar requirements have also been imposed not by the World Trade Organization (WTO) political institutions, but by its dispute resolution bodies. It is time, therefore, to turn to the standards issued by international and supranational bodies.

[46] French Conseil Constitutionnel, decision n 2011–183/184 QPC of 14 October 2011, available at http://www.conseil-constitutionnel.fr.

[47] For this distinction, see Carol Harlow, 'Interest Representation in Administrative Procedures. Representative Democracy vs. Participatory Democracy in the EU and the US: A Comment', in R Caranta (ed), *Interest Representation in Administrative Proceedings* (Jovene, 2008) 143.

[48] See, however, the decision of the US Supreme Court in *Perez v Mortgage Bankers Association* (April 2015) (federal agencies are exempt from notice-and-comment requirements when amending or repealing interpretative rules).

[49] House of Lords, *Bushell v Secretary of State for the Environment* [1980] 2 All ER 608.

3. A Transnational Minimum Standard

At the beginning of this book it was suggested that the traditional assumption that the State, each State, is master of its own procedures is simply not consistent with the evolving legal realities of our epoch. That this is not the case can be seen from two points of view: there is not only an increasing specification of the requirements of due process by international and supranational bodies, but also an increasing use of such requirements by national and international courts, as well as by arbitral tribunals.

Hearing requirements imposed on national authorities

Even a quick look at international documents shows an increase, in the number and in the typology, of due process requirements. The technical distinction between recommendations and norms can be helpful in this respect, together with the degree of specificity of such requirements.

Consider again the Resolution passed by the Council of Europe's Committee of Ministers aiming at protecting individuals in relation to the acts of administrative authorities.[50] Interestingly, the Resolution was based on the assumption that a broad consensus existed 'concerning the fundamental principles which should guide the administrative procedures and particularly the necessity to ensure fairness in the relations between the individual and administrative authorities'. It recognized several rights, including the rights to be heard ('the person concerned may put forward facts and arguments and, in appropriate cases, call evidence'),[51] to have access to both essential facts and legal advice, and to be assisted or represented within the administrative procedure. The Resolution imposed other duties on public authorities, notably the requirement to take into account evidence brought by the person concerned, and the duty to give reasons and to indicate available remedies. Three years later, the Committee of Ministers adopted a recommendation on the exercise of discretionary powers by administrative authorities, establishing, inter alia, the principles of impartiality, proportionality, and reasonable time limits.

Unlike these standards, those laid down by the EU are fully binding, due to the principle of direct effect and primacy of EU law over national law. One of the most interesting examples is that of electronic communications. This body of law has been considered for many years simply as a body of law relating to market forces. However, to the extent to which it increasingly defines the powers and duties of national regulatory authorities (NRAs), it imposes on them both broad standards of objectivity and transparency and more specific procedural requirements. When an NRA intends to impose certain duties on the providers of networks of electronic

[50] Committee of Ministers, Resolution (77) 31 of 28 September 1977 on 'the protection of the individual in relation to the acts of administrative authorities'.

[51] Committee of Ministers, Resolution (77) 31, Article I.

communications, particularly the sharing of essential facilities, it can do so only after an adequate period of time devoted to public consultation, in the context of which all affected parties are provided with an opportunity to express their views.[52] The significant point about this legal framework is that, whatever the nationality of providers, procedural requirements are increasingly harmonized. There is, however, no general duty to consult the public that is imposed either by positive norms (the Treaties and EU legislation) or judge-made law. It is, however, a general principle of law shared by the legal systems of the Member States, and thus constituting a general principle of EU law, that public authorities must provide individuals with an opportunity to be heard before decisions adversely affecting them are taken.[53]

While EU rules apply to its Member States and the few other countries included in the European legal space, the Aarhus Convention (1998) applies not only to European countries but also to some neighbouring States, such as Kazakhstan. In the Convention there are two broad mechanisms that are relevant for our purposes: access and participation. Access is designed to ensure that information is available, a precondition for participation. In this respect, the Convention provides that each contracting party shall ensure that, in response to a request for environmental information, public authorities make such information available 'without an interest having to be stated'.[54] Participation takes the form of notice and comment. Public authorities must inform not only individuals of the proposed activity, but also the 'public concerned', a very broad notion which includes environmental associations and committees. They must also ensure that the envisaged procedure provides opportunities for the public to take part in it.[55] Considered as a whole, access and participation allow the public to intervene in the decision-making process and the focus will be upon the merit of the decision as well its technical aspects. Judicial supervision by way of contrast is *ex post facto* and the same applies to the enforcement mechanism provided by the Convention.[56]

The fact that administrative procedures matter and will increasingly matter can be seen also from a worldwide viewpoint. We have already mentioned the procedural constraints imposed on public authorities in the context of the Government Procurement Agreement (GPA). Unlike the GPA, the Agreement on Trade-Related Aspects of Intellectual Property Rights (the TRIPS Agreement), an annex to the Marrakech Agreement establishing the WTO (1994), is compulsory for all contracting parties. These parties may neither retain nor introduce

[52] Article 12(2), Directive n 2009/140 of the European Parliament and Council of Ministers of 25 November 2009.

[53] John A Usher, *General Principles of EC Law* (Longman, 1998) 95.

[54] Aarhus Convention, Article 4(1)(a).

[55] Aarhus Convention, Article 6(2). See also the ruling of the CJEU in Case C-240/09, *Lesoochranárske zoskupenie VLK v Ministerstvo životného prostredia Slovenskej republiky* (holding that, though the Convention has no direct effect in domestic law, national courts must interpret rules concerning administrative and judicial proceedings in accordance with the Convention's objectives, as set out by Article 9).

[56] Marco Macchia, 'Global Administrative Review Mechanism: The Case of the Aarhus Convention', in G della Cananea and A Sandulli (eds), *Global Standards for Public Authorities* (Editoriale Scientifica, 2012) 109.

any discrimination on grounds of nationality in the field of intellectual property. This substantive rule is complemented by some procedural rules, both general and particular. The general rule is that procedures concerning the enforcement of intellectual property rights must be 'fair and equitable'.[57] The particular rules which are established for judicial proceedings but are applicable also to administrative procedures[58] provide intellectual rights holders with process rights: notice, comment, and legal counsel.[59] Such process rights are qualitatively strengthened by the requirement that notice is timely and contains sufficient detail and that all parties are 'duly entitled to substantiate their claims' and to present all evidence that is relevant to the case.

Another domain in which standards of procedural fairness are increasingly emerging is that of bilateral investment treaties (BITs). Following the US BIT Model,[60] the Central America Free Trade Agreement (CAFTA)[61] combines the 'fair and equitable treatment' (FET) standard with 'the obligation not to deny justice in criminal, civil, or administrative adjudicatory proceedings in accordance with the principle of due process embodied in the principal legal systems of the world'. This provision has influenced various BITs agreed by Latin American countries, between themselves and with the US. An interesting example is the US–Uruguay BIT: not only does it replicate the connection between the FET standard and the 'the principle of due process embodied in the principal legal systems of the world', but it also lays down the principle of transparency with regard to public decision-making processes, in particular administrative procedures.[62] Similarly, Article 6(2)(a) of the Association of Southeast Asian Nations–Australia–New Zealand BIT provides, literally, that the FET standard 'requires each party not to deny justice in any legal or administrative proceeding'.

Two preliminary conclusions may be drawn from this. First, procedural due process rights are recognized for individuals and businesses in order to prevent any discrimination on grounds of nationality. An instrumental rationale thus prevails, in contrast with the non-instrumental one that characterizes national legal systems. Second, international regulatory regimes increasingly require public authorities to provide a hearing before an order or a measure is taken if it may adversely affect someone. This gives claimants an important opportunity in national judicial proceedings.[63]

[57] TRIPS Agreement, Article 41(2). [58] TRIPS Agreement, Article 49.

[59] TRIPS Agreement, Article 42. On GATS, see Panagiotis Delimatsis, 'Due Process and "Good" Regulation Embedded in the GATS—Disciplining Regulatory Behaviour in Services Through Article VI of the GATS' (2006) 13 J Int'l Econ L 10, 19.

[60] See Article 6(1)(d) of the 2004 US Model BIT.

[61] CAFTA has been signed by the US with five Central American countries (Costa Rica, El Salvador, Guatemala, Honduras, and Nicaragua) and the Dominican Republic, and has now entered into force in all of them.

[62] See Articles 5(2) a) and 10(4), respectively, of the US–Uruguay BIT. See also the Argentina–US BIT, where Article IV refers to 'due process of law and the general principles of treatment provided for in Article II (2)', thus distinguishing due process.

[63] See Sabino Cassese, *Global Standards for National Administrative Procedure* (2005) 68 Law & Contemp Probs 109, 109–10.

The strategic use of international requirements by national courts

National courts have, of course, an essential importance for ensuring the implementation of transnational requirements of due process. They are the guardians of legality and must, thus, ensure that the law, including the law coming from external sources, is respected. National remedies must also be exhausted before other remedies can be used by claimants, as far as the European and American courts of human rights are concerned, for example. This is sometimes seen as a kind of tribute that must be paid to national sovereignties or to the reluctance by the State's professional judges to cede their powers to other authorities.

However, this is not necessarily the case. Indeed, individuals and groups such as environmental associations or civil rights movements can, and often do, seek to use an international treaty or a precedent as an *escamotage* in order to promote a new interpretation of an existing piece of legislation or to convince lawmakers to change it. National courts may, and sometimes do, use transnational standards in order to overcome certain obstacles to the exercise of process rights and, thus, to affirm their role as guarantors of such rights. This point is well illustrated by the Yellowstone case, in which American environmental groups opposed the issuing of a concession for exploiting a mine close to the Yellowstone national park, relying on its inclusion within UNESCO's list of the sites that are part of the collective patrimony of humanity.[64]

A more recent case arose in Italy at the end of the twentieth century in the metropolitan area of Naples. Local administrators' incapacity to implement correctly the norms laid down by the European Waste Directive,[65] particularly by ensuring waste is disposed of without endangering human health or harming the environment, gave rise to a serious crisis. While the Commission initiated an infringement procedure,[66] the Italian government decided to entrust an ad hoc body with special powers to resolve the crisis. The exercising of such powers was exempted from following the ordinary processes of the law, including access to documents held by the administration and citizens' involvement in administrative procedures. A group of citizens then contested these derogations and the regional administrative court endorsed their claim. It did not put into doubt the existence of a government's power to introduce exceptions to the general rules of administrative procedure. Rather, it observed that after those exceptions had been introduced, the Italian Parliament ratified and executed an international document, the Charter of Aalborg.[67] This Charter provided, among other things, public access and participation.[68]

[64] UNESCO, World Heritage Committee, Proceedings of the Twenty-first session, 1–6 December 1997, available at http://whc.unesco.org.

[65] Directive n 2006/12 of the European Parliament and of the Council of 5 April 2006 [2006] OJ L/190, 1.

[66] The Court declared that Italy had failed to fulfil its obligations under EU law: Case C-297/08, *Commission v Italy* [2010] ECR I, 1749.

[67] *Aalborg Charter of European Cities & Towns Towards Sustainability* (1994), available at http://www.sustainablecities.eu/aalborg-process/charter.

[68] The contracting parties (European cities and towns) urged governments to 'ensure that all citizens and interested groups have access to information and are able to participate in local decision-making processes' (Section 1.14).

Legally, the problem with the Aalborg Charter was that, unlike the Aarhus Convention, it was neither negotiated by national governments, nor was meant to produce any binding effect. However, the administrative judge observed, once the Charter had been ratified, that the ordinary legal criteria applied, including that of *lex posterior*.[69]

This case is then a strong illustration of the way in which national courts can use transnational requirements of due process as a remedy for the problems caused by recalcitrant legislators and governments unwilling to respect the ordinary processes of the law. From this point of view, it is a case of 'strategic' use of transnational standards by the courts.[70] This case also confirms the importance of transnational public law litigation brought by non-governmental organizations (NGOs), the decisions of which provoke judicial action.[71] In this respect, NGOs are not just observers of transnational legal processes but are involved in them, thus contributing to shaping the normative dimension of procedures. Both these features—individual activation of remedies against government and the development of procedural requirements—also characterize other instruments as enforcing transnational standards.

International tribunals enforcing due process: Foreign investment and world trade

What procedural requirements concretely imply and whether they can be granted in the absence of specific provisions are the questions that will now be addressed in two fields: foreign investment and world trade.

One of ICSID's early arbitral awards was *Amco*.[72] The dispute concerned the construction and operation of a hotel in Indonesia. Once the hotel construction was substantially completed, the national government's agency, claiming that the investor had not fulfilled certain financial commitments, seized the hotel and replaced its management, aided by police and military forces. In its award, the *Amco* tribunal strongly criticized Indonesia, among other things, for granting the company only a one-hour hearing, which it characterized as a violation of a fundamental principle of due process.[73] Since Indonesian law provided that sanctions against foreign investors, including the revocation of a licence, could be adopted only after prior notice had been given, which had not been adequately provided in this case, the State had not followed its own rules.[74] Moreover, according to the tribunal, the conduct of the State had infringed the general principles of law, more specifically that of due process.

[69] Regional Administrative Court for the Regione Campania, decision of 12 June 2007, n 6075, available at http://www.giustizia-amministrativa.it.

[70] This expression is drawn from Harold H Koh, *Transnational Public Law Litigation*, 2371 and Eyal Benvenisti, 'Reclaiming Democracy: The Strategic Uses of Foreign and International Law by National Courts' (2008) *Tel Aviv Law School Faculty Papers* n 59.

[71] See Harold H. Koh, *Transnational Legal Processes*, 182.

[72] *Amco Asia Corporation and others v Republic of Indonesia* (ICSID Case No ARB/81/1), Award of 20 November 1984.

[73] *Amco*, paragraph 202.

[74] *Amco*, paragraph 202.

Some decades later, arbitrators are clearly predisposed to inquire into the procedural law in place in States whose treatment of investors is under review. Since *Amco*, tribunals have elaborated and enforced a test. Consider one of the most cited and controversial arbitral awards, *Metalclad*.[75] After attracting a US waste disposal company to invest in Mexico, a local authority refused to permit the firm to operate a hazardous waste facility in order to protect the environment and health. The arbitral tribunal put problems of procedural propriety quite neatly under the FET standard heading. As it noted, '[t]he permit was denied at a meeting of the Municipal Town Council of which *Metalclad* received no notice, to which it received no invitation, and at which it was given no opportunity to appear'.[76] Arbitrators thus elaborated a simple test that an arbitral tribunal can carry out on procedural grounds when reviewing the exercise of power by a national authority, one that is based on the duty to give notice of the commencement of an administrative procedure that is likely to affect adversely the foreign investor and to provide some kind of hearing.

Other arbitral tribunals used such a test in *Genin*[77] and *ADC*,[78] in the latter case with a significant innovation. The *ADC* tribunal specified that the hearing must be 'fair' and added a third element to the test, that is to say, the need for 'an unbiased and impartial adjudicator'. In so doing, it referred to a traditional principle of international law[79] and established a connection between the two elements that have historically been thought essential to ensure that the fundamental obligations of natural justice are respected, namely the maxims *audi alteram partem* and *nemo judex in causa propria* respectively.[80]

A connection between legal requirements more or less shared by modern legal systems emerged also in the field of world trade. The most important WTO ruling on due process requirements borne by States under international trade law is that issued in *Shrimp*. A dispute arose in the 1990s with regard to the legitimacy of a US ban on the import of shrimps and shrimp-related products, a ban imposed under the US Endangered Species Act (1973) for the purposes of safeguarding sea turtles. Since shrimp harvesting endangered sea turtles, obliging shrimp trawl vessels to use turtle-excluder devices appeared an appropriate solution. This solution was imposed on national fleets, but the problem of significant sea turtle mortality abroad remained unresolved. For this reason, the rules adopted by the US

[75] *Metalclad Corporation v United Mexican States* (*Metalclad*), ICSID Case No ARB(AF)/97/1, Award of 30 August 2000.

[76] *Metalclad*, paragraph 91.

[77] *Alex Genin and others v Republic of Estonia* (*Genin*), ICSID Case No ARB/99/2, Award of 25 June 2001.

[78] *ADC Affiliate Limited and ADC & ADMC Management Limited v Republic of Hungary* (*ADC*), ICSID Case No ARB/03/16, Award of 2 October 2006.

[79] See E de Vattel, *Le droit des gens*, I, paragraph 164 (holding that it is not suitable for the sovereign to be a judge in his own case) and B Cheng, *General Principles of Law as Applied by International Courts and Tribunals* (Cambridge University Press, 2006) 257.

[80] Martin Loughlin and Gus Van Harten, *Investment Treaty Arbitration as a Species of Global Administrative Law* (2006) 17 Eur J Int'l L 121 (holding that 'the regime of international investment arbitration ... provides ... a singularly important and under-appreciated manifestation of an evolving system of global administrative law').

administration from 1991 onwards prohibited the importation of shrimps, unless turtle-excluder devices had been used. Import licences were only granted to exporters that had a specific form of certification. In order to obtain such certification, the nation of would-be exporters had to provide documentary evidence of a regulatory programme designed to comply with US requirements. Moreover, the impact of the ban on shrimp exporters worldwide was diverse. The US administration had negotiated a more favourable agreement with Caribbean shrimp exporters whilst, by contrast, Asian exporters had received non-negotiable terms requiring compliance with the new fishing rules which were, moreover, more burdensome. For this reason, India, Pakistan, Malaysia, and Thailand brought an action before the WTO. The Panel rejected the US argument that environmental protection could offer a sound basis for prohibiting certain imports.[81]

The Appellate Body (AB) took a different view in two respects. First, after hearing the parties, it received (to the dismay of the Asian countries) the *amicus curiae* briefs presented by environmental associations. Second, it rejected the panel's conclusion that Article XX of the General Agreement on Tariffs and Trade (GATT) was not applicable. It interpreted Article XX of GATT in the sense that the protection of the environment could justify national measures having discriminatory effects.[82] Such measures must satisfy two requirements, however: they must not be arbitrary or unjustifiable in character and they must not create discrimination between countries where the same conditions prevail. Since the AB reached the conclusion that such requirements had not been met, it rejected the US appeal.

A more detailed analysis of the reasoning followed by the AB will be carried out in Chapter 7. Meanwhile, two aspects ought to be highlighted. The AB found the process through which the US had taken the measure was arbitrary and unjustifiable. Not only had the US government not consulted with certain countries whose industries would be affected prior to the rule's entry into force, but it had also adopted the rule without observing basic notice and comment requirements. Nor had it provided reasons for the rejection of applications for certification. The informality of these processes therefore failed to protect the rights of the shrimp exporting nations and their individual exporters to 'basic fairness and due process'.[83]

4. A Minimum Standard for Non-State Authorities

After observing that the requirements of administrative due process of law—in particular, the right to be heard—that are shared by most modern legal systems are also referred to by transnational standards, it is now time to consider whether the same requirements are imposed on international and supranational authorities. In

[81] *United States – Import Prohibition of Certain Shrimps and Shrimps Products*, Panel Report, WT/DS58R, 15 May 1998 (hereinafter *Shrimp I*).

[82] The AB adopted two reports: *United States – Import Prohibition of Certain Shrimps and Shrimps Products*, WT/DS58/AB/R, 12 October 1998 and WT/DS587AB7RW, 22 October 2001. They are referred to as *Shrimp II* and *Shrimp III*. *Shrimp II*, paragraph 127 acknowledged the admissibility of limits upon imports.

[83] *Shrimp II*, paragraph 181.

discussing the operation of due process requirements, separate treatment will be helpful in connection with their effects on two distinct kinds of subjects: the civil servants of international bodies and other individuals or businesses.

Due process in disciplinary procedures for international civil servants

When considering staff disputes, international courts have not hesitated to affirm that disciplinary procedures must allow civil servants to be heard before an adverse measure is taken.

In the European Community (EC), the Court of Justice has ruled in this way since its earliest case, *Alvis*.[84] The applicant, who had a contract with the Secretariat of the Council of Ministers, claimed that administratively his case had not been handled fairly and objectively. The reason was that the administration had terminated his contract with a measure that was clearly of a disciplinary nature without hearing him. Advocate General Lagrange stated at the outset that staff rules did not expressly lay down a duty to provide a hearing in the case of contractual relations, while they did so for Community officers. This might have suggested adherence to the traditional doctrine according to which the availability of due process requirements depended upon the nature of the employment relationship.[85] Lagrange argued, instead, that even though there is no specific duty to provide a hearing, without it the deprivation of office was unlawful. His starting point was that, whatever the mutual obligations contractually established by the parties, their relationship was governed by public law because what the individual retained was an office connected with public functions. Accordingly, particularly when exercising disciplinary powers, public authorities were subject to 'strict requirements'. Such requirements, he argued, included the 'the opportunity to give a complete explanation' and, to this end, the servant had to be fully informed of the allegations against him. The purpose of this requirement was to avoid arbitrariness. The Court of Justice agreed with its Advocate General. It refused to bring the distinction between the two kinds of servants, based either on appointment or on contract, to the consequence that only the former would be granted the right to be heard. It enriched this line of reasoning, affirming that if due process required a hearing prior to termination of public employment it was also because the requirement inhered to a 'generally accepted principle of administrative law' in the legal systems of the Member States.

The legal doctrine according to which general principles of law are included in the rules with which international courts must ensure compliance is not a peculiarity of the EU, but is used also by other courts. An illuminating example is that of the Administrative Tribunal of the International Labour Organization (ILO), which hears the complaints brought by civil servants against the institutions and

[84] Case 33/62, *Maurice Alvis v Council of the EEC* [1962] ECR 109.
[85] Paul Craig, *Administrative Law*, 446.

bodies of the United Nations (UN).[86] For example, in *Ferrecchia*, a case very similar to *Alvis* (a staff member was dismissed after an inspection confirmed his negligence, but was given no opportunity to take part in the examination of the evidence), the Tribunal held that, before adopting any disciplinary measure, the administration must provide the affected staff member with the right to be heard. It added that, since this right derives from a general principle of law, 'it must be respected even where contrary provisions exist or in the absence of any explicit text'. It concluded that the contested decision was invalid on procedural grounds.[87] When international servants bring claims regarding the requirements of procedural due process of law, therefore, neither the strict adherence to the legal text nor a scant attention to issues of form characterize judicial review.

That said, the techniques developed by the Administrative Tribunal for introducing into the contractual employment relationship the advantages associated with due process—such as order and prevention of arbitrariness—do not exclude the employer's power to dismiss the employee. Consider a 'hard' case, *Bustani v Organisation for the Prohibition of Chemical Weapons* (OPCW), concerning the premature dismissal of the Organisation's Director General.[88] At the root of this dispute there were the concerns expressed by an influential Member State, the US, about Bustani's conduct. The majority of the conference of national representatives shared those concerns. It took the decision to terminate the appointment prematurely and with immediate effect. While the Tribunal refrained from discussing the 'real motivation' for Bustani's dismissal, it observed that he had been afforded no procedural guarantee 'in contrast with the principle of due process'.[89] Moreover, the tribunal held, to concede that the authority entrusted with the power of appointment and dismissal is free to terminate the mandate of a top official would 'constitute an unacceptable violation of the principles of the international civil service'. For these reasons, the contested decision was set aside, though it would have been politically unfeasible to reinstate Bustani. Being aware of this, he himself clarified that he was not seeking reinstatement and this facilitated the work of the Tribunal, which accorded him compensation for the injury caused by his unlawful dismissal.

This case confirms the existence of a tension between the interests of an organization and those of its members.[90] It represents a move away from the idea that

[86] See Karel Wellens, *Remedies Against International Organizations* (2nd edn, Cambridge University Press, 2004).

[87] ILO Administrative Tribunal, Judgment No 203 of 14 May 1973, *Ferrecchia v International Centre for Advanced Technical and Vocational Training*. This ruling and the others that are cited here are available at http://www.ilo.org/tribunal/lang--en/index.htm.

[88] ILO Administrative Tribunal, judgment n 2232 of 16 July 2003, *Bustani v Organisation for the Prohibition of Chemical Weapons*.

[89] ILO Administrative Tribunal, judgment n 2232 of 17 July 2003, *Bustani v OPCW*, § 16. For further analysis, see the comment by Ana Stanic (2004) 98 Am J Int'l L 811. See also Chittharanjan F Amerasinghe, 'The Future of International Administrative Law' (1996) 45 Int'l & Comp L Q 773, 788, for whom the 'law has been refined by a general elaboration of the broad concept of due process'.

[90] Jan Klabbers, *An Introduction to International Institutional Law* (Cambridge University Press, 2002) 39; Chris de Cooker (ed), *Accountability, Investigation and Due Process in International Organizations* (Martinus Nijhoff, 2005).

the appointing authority enjoys an unfettered discretion. A relationship of confidence and trust between employer and employee is still legally relevant. A premature dismissal in case of grave misconduct must be contemplated, especially if the officer's conduct can be detrimental to the public interest, in this case because lack of confidence in the Director General put in jeopardy 'the preservation and effective functioning of the Organisation'.[91] But there is no possibility of exercising such a significant power without following fair procedures. Following this line of reasoning, the Tribunal held that a measure of this kind, 'being punitive in nature', can only be taken 'in full compliance with the principle of due process', following an adequate procedure.[92]

An important implication of this, to which we will return in Chapter 9, is that precisely because due process is a variable standard, it applies with different intensity, in the sense that the need to respect it is more intense when exceptional powers are exercised (in this case there was no provision expressly providing for the removal of the Director General during his or her term). Whether the courts will protect process rights unless, for instance, global security is at stake is the question that will now be addressed.

The right to be heard in EU administrative procedures

EU administrative law provides another important demonstration of the gradual transplant of due process requirements from the national to the supranational level.

The leading case is *Transocean Marine Paint Association v Commission*,[93] where the Court expanded on the reasoning in *Alvis*. The claimant, a Dutch corporation, sued the Commission for refusing to renew certain exemptions to the Treaty of Rome's antitrust rules. It held that it should have been provided with an opportunity to be heard before the decision was taken. The Commission argued that the special rules governing that type of procedure did not provide a requirement to hear affected parties. But Advocate General Warner, on the basis of a comparative analysis of the legal systems of the Member States, observed that they shared the same general principle of law, expressed by the maxim *audi alteram partem*, and that such principle could thus be invoked by private parties in the EC.[94] The Court followed this opinion and annulled the contested decision. In the following decades, EU courts have referred to this fundamental principle of due process in hundreds of cases, in areas such as agriculture and competition, structural funds, and tax cooperation. The right to be heard, along with other general principles generated by the Court under the rubric of 'good and fair administration', is now codified as Article 41 of the Charter.[95]

[91] For further remarks, see Jan Klabbers, 'The Bustani Case before the ILOAT: Constitutionalism in Disguise?' (2004) 63 Int'l & Comp L Quart 455.

[92] ILO Administrative Tribunal, judgment n 2232, *Bustani v OPCW*, paragraph 16.

[93] Case 17/74, *Transocean Marine Paint Association v Commission* [1974] ECR 1063. For further remarks, see John A Usher, *General Principles of EC Law*, 77.

[94] Opinion of Advocate General Werner [1974] ECR 1088.

[95] See Treaty on European Union, Article 6(3) (stating that the Charter has the 'same legal value' as EU Treaties).

However, the institutions of the EU were involved, together with national governments, in the management of the anti-terrorism measures provided by UN resolutions. When affected individuals and groups, such as *Kadi*[96] and *OMPI*[97] contested such measures, one of the arguments brought by the defendants, supported by the UK government, was that the requirements of due process could be derogated in exceptional circumstances. In the *Kadi* case this argument was vigorously criticized by Advocate General Maduro, who, among other things, referred to the opinion enounced by Justice Murphy in the US Supreme Court ruling in *Korematsu*, to exclude any limitation based on the doctrine of political questions.[98] The ECJ followed its Advocate General[99] and held that, despite the fact that targeted sanctions were based on UN resolutions, in the field of EU law such measures could not infringe fundamental principles such as the right to be heard. Both the Court's concern not to interfere with the measures taken by UN authorities and its emphasis on procedural due process clearly emerge from the following part of the ruling:

> Because the Council neither communicated to the appellants the evidence used against them to justify the restrictive measures imposed on them nor afforded them the right to be informed of that evidence within a reasonable period after those measures were enacted, the appellants were not in a position to make their point of view in that respect known to advantage. Therefore, the appellants' ... *right to be heard* [was] not respected.[100]

Whether the problem with those measures was that they infringed the right to be heard or, more precisely, its essential content,[101] is another question and a very important one in the light of interest balancing, to which we will return in Chapter 6. Meanwhile, it is important to devote some thoughts to the relationship between EU and UN standards.

Adjusting UN procedures for suspect terrorists

Referring to the *Kadi* ruling is helpful in understanding the gradual adjustment of the requirements of due process provided by UN resolutions. In other words, if we want to understand the development of due process of law, it is necessary to place *Kadi* in context not only from the viewpoint of EU law, but also from the gradual adjustment of UN administrative procedures.

96 CFI, Case T-315/01 *Kadi v Council and Commission* [2005] ECR II-3649; Case T-306/01 *Yusuf and Al Barakaat International Foundation v Council and Commission* [2005] ECR II-3533.

97 CFI, Case T-228/02, *OMPI v Council*, paragraph 127.

98 Opinion of AG Maduro, Joined Cases C-402/05 and 415/05, *Kadi v Council and Al Barakaat v Council and Commission* [2008] ECR 1, 18, §§ 30–34.

99 ECJ, Joined Cases C-402/05 and 415/05, *Kadi v Council and Al Barakaat v Council and Commission*.

100 ECJ, Joined Cases C-402/05 and 415/05, *Kadi v Council and Al Barakaat v Council and Commission*, paragraph 348 (emphasis added).

101 Pasquale De Sena and Maria Chiara Vitucci, *The European Courts and the Security Council: Between Dédoublement Fonctionnel and Balancing of Values* (2009) 20 Eur J Int'l L 193, 208.

Initially, due process requirements were simply ignored by the Security Council. Individuals and groups suspected of being involved in terrorist activities were targeted by the Sanctions Committee on the basis of information gathered by national agencies and were included in a 'black list' without receiving any prior notice. Nor were they provided with an opportunity to be heard in any form before being listed. If we add to this that targeted individuals and groups did not have access to files and had no judicial protection in the legal order of the UN, the CJEU's reluctance to give away all the guarantees provided by EU law can be understood. But my intent here is not to justify its judicial policy. It is, rather, to look at the progress of UN law that was acknowledged by the Court.

After paying tribute to the role of the Security Council in the maintenance of peace and security at the global level, the Court considered UN procedures not only as they were before the decision to include *Kadi* in the list had been taken, but also on the basis of the *Guidelines of the Sanctions Committee*, as amended in February 2007. It used a two-tier test for determining whether the UN guidelines were consistent with EU principles. The first part of the test was the consideration of whether the Sanctions Committee Guidelines were open to affected interests. An evident change had taken place in that respect, and the Court was ready to take notice of it, affirming that while initially UN officials would not provide targeted individuals with any notice, the UN procedure had been opened to any person or entity to approach the Sanctions Committee directly, submitting a request to be removed from the summary list at what is called the 'focal point'.

Ascertaining whether some kind of openness had been introduced, however, was not enough for the Court, which also applied the second part of the test, which was whether this openness was adequate, that is to say, whether the procedure was coherent with its own settled standards of procedural fairness. This second part of the test had a negative outcome, for the Court found several weaknesses in the procedure, which was 'still in essence diplomatic and intergovernmental'.[102] The affected person or legal entity might in no way 'assert his rights himself during the procedure before the Sanctions Committee or be represented for that purpose'.[103]

It can be argued that the two-tier test used by the ECJ shows that, though the Court found that the progress made by the UN guidelines was not sufficient, at least some elements of parallelism between UN procedures and the standards that must be respected within the EU did exist. In other words, not only did the 2007 UN guidelines put an end to the incommensurability of procedural requirements, but the progress made by UN institutions was also moving in the direction envisaged by the EU.[104] Other rules governing the conduct of

[102] ECJ, Joined Cases C-402/05 and 415/05, *Kadi v Council and Al Barakaat v Council and Commission*, § 323.

[103] ECJ, Joined Cases C-402/05 and 415/05, *Kadi v Council and Al Barakaat v Council and Commission*, § 322.

[104] See Ian Johnstone, *Legislation and Adjudication in the UN Security Council: Bringing Down the Deliberative Deficit* (2008) 102 Am J Int'l L 275, 297 (pointing out the connection between procedural fairness and the 'deliberative deficit' of UN bodies).

international bodies confirm this trend. For example, Article 34 of the Patent Cooperation Treaty (PCT) recognizes the right of applicants to communicate both in writing and orally with the authority that carried out the preliminary examination. Higher standards are also imposed in some fields. For example, the Bylaws governing the assignment of domain names on the internet provide that the Internet Corporation for Assigned Names and Numbers (ICANN) shall 'provide public notice' and 'a reasonable opportunity for parties to comment on the adoption of the proposed policies, to see the comments of others and to reply to those comments'.[105]

5. Conclusions

In this chapter I have sought to look at a traditional legal maxim, *audi alteram partem*, from the same angle used earlier with regard to the requirement to carry out a procedure, that is to say, a comparative analysis of national legal systems, followed by an analysis of the transnational requirements imposed both on the States and the institutions they have set up regionally and globally. This has set the framework for our consideration in Part II of the rationales of such requirements, including the giving reasons requirement that will be examined in the next chapter.

In view of these further steps, it is helpful to highlight three main points. First, not only in order to avoid a denial of justice but also give concrete meaning to the norms protecting interests, State and non-State courts, as well as arbitral tribunals, increasingly interpret constitutions, statutes, and treaties as imposing some basic requirements of due process. If a public authority is in the process of issuing a decision that may adversely affect some interests, the affected persons must receive a notice of it and must be afforded with a reasonable opportunity to be heard, which implies adequate time to prepare and access to the documents and evidence gathered by the decision-maker. In so doing, courts and other bodies go beyond an interpretation that is strictly textual. The requirements of due process are thus conceived beyond written provisions. The second point is that, especially when faced with due process problems that have no compelling historical analogies, both courts and arbitral bodies tend to look at other legal systems and due process, seen as a general principle of law, is particularly helpful in this respect. Last but not least, the shift from national to transnational legal disputes is not without consequences. Indeed, sometimes process rights are not directly claimed by an individual, but by one public authority against another. This justifies a caveat against the expectation that national doctrines of due process may simply be reproduced in a transnational context. More thought, therefore, will be given in Part II to understanding the nature of the balancing process.

105 ICANN Bylaws (as amended and effective since 2006) Article III, Section 6.

4

The Giving Reasons Requirement

The giving reasons requirement might appear to be a rather simple and common sense requirement, the mildest of all. However, its practical importance must not be underestimated. Its gradual shift from judicial to non-judicial decisions and from national to international and supranational decisions confirms that the giving reasons requirement is 'replete with potential development'.[1] It is, moreover, an 'under-theorized topic'[2] as far as administrative decisions and rules as concerned. It is useful first of all to attempt to gain a measure of it from a historical perspective. As a second step, we will confront the giving reasons requirements laid down by national legal systems in order to see if a common denominator emerges and, if so, whether it is to such common denominator that transnational rules refer when imposing similar duties on national, international, and supranational authorities. Next, we will consider the interactions between this requirement and those considered in previous chapters.

1. Origins and Variety of Giving Reasons Requirements

The giving reasons requirement for judicial decisions

The current acceptance of the giving reasons requirement for the executive branch of government may be viewed as an important development. Yet it should not be forgotten that this requirement was initially established for another branch, that is to say, the judiciary.

The origins of the judges' giving reasons requirement are, compared with the other two branches of government, quite ancient. Historic and comparative analysis shows very clearly that a different choice has been made in different countries and epochs. If such a variety of choices could ideally be placed in a sort of *continuum*, we could find at one extreme the prohibition on stating the grounds for the decisions taken by judicial bodies, which was taken by the *Parlement de Paris* in the early fourteenth century.[3] At the other extreme, there would be the duty to provide the

[1] See Martin Shapiro, 'The Giving Reasons Requirement' (1992) 7 Un Chi Legal Forum 179.

[2] Jerry Mashaw, 'Reasoned Administration: The European Union, the United States, and the Project of Democratic Governance' (2007) 77 George Wash L Rev 101.

[3] See John P Dawson, *The Oracles of the Law* (University of Michigan Law School, 1968) 287; Georg Bergholtz, 'Ratio et Auctoritas: A Comparative Study of the Significance of Reasoned Decisions with

reasons for any judgment and order, in conjunction with the principle that justice is rendered in the name of the people.[4]

However, this would be a rather abstract and naïf way to consider a serious legal issue. First, the reluctance to disclose the secrets of the courts' decisions was not at all a distinctive feature of the French judiciary, but it was shared by their colleagues elsewhere, particularly on the other side of the Channel.[5] Indeed, the earliest doctrines of judicial review were based on the assumption that the reasons for judgments must be collected from the records. Secondly, a more accurate account shows a trend towards the codification of the duty to give reasons, from the Swedish codification of 1734 to the constitutions of the twentieth century. In addition to obliging judges to provide reasons, modern legal orders distinguish between lack of reasons and inadequate or contradictory reasons and provide a variety of remedies for them. Sometimes, the judgments contain only a short statement, which is even shorter when a higher court concurs with the reasoning of the lower court.[6] Thirdly, different explanations have been suggested for the requirement to provide reasons for judicial decisions, including the need to allow review by higher courts and to justify and legitimate the exercise of power.

The ancient origins of this requirement combined with the proliferation of forms in the various States make it hard to say more than that it is a general principle of law common to the laws of Western countries. In the West, according to a widespread belief, giving reasons is a necessary feature of the 'impartial judge' that predated modern democracy. Some countries in East Asia, such as Japan and Korea, more recently recognized the giving reasons requirement. The significance of these findings, however, is ambiguous. It may suggest that the requirement to provide reasons for judicial decisions is common to liberal democracies, but it is not a universal principle. Or, it may suggest that, if an independent judiciary exists, some reasons must be provided for its decisions. Only in this limited sense could it be regarded as a 'natural' requirement of justice.

Advantages of establishing a giving reasons requirement

Moving from the judiciary to the other branches of government, particularly to the executive, several advantages can be obtained by laying down a giving reasons

Special Reference to Civil Cases', in Volker Gessner et al (eds), *European Legal Cultures* (Dartmouth, 1997) 122.

4 See, for example, Article 121 of the Dutch Constitution (providing that 'except in cases laid down by Act of Parliament, trials shall be held in public and judgements shall specify the grounds on which they are based'); Article 93(IX) of the Brazilian Constitution (providing that 'all judgements of the bodies of the Judicial Power shall be public, and all decisions shall be justified, under penalty of nullity'); Article 139(5) of the Peruvian Constitution (requiring that all court orders have a 'written explanation').

5 Whether a constitutional duty to state reasons for judicial decisions exists in the UK is, at the least, questionable: See *R v Knightsbridge Crown Court, ex p. International Sporting Club* [1982] 2 QB 304.

6 See Jerry Mashaw, *Creating the American Constitution* (Yale University Press, 2012) 113 (for Chief Justice Marshall's view that legality contained a requirement to give reasons).

requirement.[7] Such a requirement can be seen, first, as a function of judicial review of administrative actions. Second, it can be an instrument for protecting rights and, thus, preventing inequality in their exercise. The same requirement can also be seen as a function of democratic government.

The idea that the giving reasons requirement is a function of judicial review is deeply rooted in the jurisprudence of both French and Italian administrative courts. It was shared also by German courts, which considered the duty to give reasons as a corollary of the fundamental principle of *Rechtsstaat*.[8] The same idea was not foreign to English courts in their supervisory function. There is a practical reason why this duty is acceptable in cultural environments that differ in many respects, culturally and institutionally.[9] The giving reasons requirement does not constitute an intolerable burden on the executive if the courts do not go so far as to replace the reasons provided by administrators with their own. Seen in this light, the giving reasons requirement is acceptable to political systems that are not based on the American conception of separation of powers, such as British cabinet government and the continental systems of parliamentary government that adhered to a 'thin' version of the Rule of Law.[10] It can probably be acceptable also within political systems that are reluctant to recognize individual rights, such as modern China.[11] The argument may perhaps be brought even further, by affirming that accuracy and respect of political guidelines may be acceptable to a despotic government: a tyrant may be interested to know if and how public officers respect his prescriptions.

From the perspective of the parties affected by the decision taken by a public authority, the giving reasons requirement has a remarkable and instrumental importance. It is a fundamental instrument to allow the parties to know why and how a certain measure has been adopted.[12] In this sense, the giving reasons requirement is a shield against any attempt to encroach on rights. Things are quite different, however, if the giving reasons requirement is associated with public sector values such as openness, accountability, and democratic governance. This dimension of the giving reasons requirement, therefore, is not a simple variant of the

[7] Paul Craig, *EU Administrative Law* (Oxford University Press, 2006) 382.

[8] Otto Bachof, 'German Administrative Law' (1953) 2 Int'l & Comp LQ 373; Christian Autexier, *Introduction au droit public allemand* (PUF, 1997) 290; Giovanni Miele, 'Italian Administrative Law' (1954) 3 Int'l & Comp LQ 421, 446.

[9] Martin Shapiro, 'The Giving Reasons Requirement', 182 noted that British conservatives had sought to 'constrain the growing administrative state by pushing reasons requirements'. For further remarks, see Carol Harlow and Richard Rawlings, *Law and Administration* (2nd edn, Butterworths, 1998) 110.

[10] For similar remarks, see Martin Shapiro, 'The Giving Reasons Requirement', 181 and John S Bell, 'Comparative Administrative Law', in Matthias Reinmann and Rheinard Zimmermann (eds), *The Oxford Handbook of Comparative Law* (Oxford University Press, 2006) 1277.

[11] For this remark, see Kanishka Jayasuriya, 'Riding the Accountability Wave', in Tom Ginsburg and Albert HY Chen (eds), *Administrative Law and Governance in Asia* (Routledge, 2008) 62. For another example, see Martin Shapiro, 'Islam and Appeal' (1980), in Csaba Varga (ed), *Comparing Legal Cultures* (Dartmouth, 1997) 299 (pointing out that appeal is often chosen by authoritative and even totalitarian regimes in order to facilitate tighter control of judicial decisions).

[12] See Paul Craig, *EU Administrative Law*, 382.

first, which emphasizes the importance of accountability through the courts. It can be seen, rather, as a function of democratic governance. However, democracy is not 'the' *raison d'être* of the giving reasons requirement, but one of its rationales, together with sound management and control.[13]

Procedural and substantive versions of the giving reasons requirement

Another preliminary point should be borne in mind: there are two conceptions of the giving reasons requirement that are related, but distinct. While the first is procedural, the other is substantive.

A procedural conception of this requirement emerges when public authorities must simply keep a record of their activities and make them public. Sometimes they are required either by legislators or by the courts to provide reasons in terms of both fact and law. This is already a limit to arbitrariness because administrators must produce and keep a record of their activities. However, it is not a limit to discretion, properly intended. Not only may public administrators make choices between equivalent solutions, but they are the only ones who can fully appreciate complex situations of fact. Consider, for example, a situation in which the historic or environmental value of a site must be appreciated or a situation in which, in view of floods or other natural emergencies, a certain number of cars or houses must be requisitioned in order to bring support to affected individuals. Consider also a situation in which a local or regional government must decide whether it is wise to use force against citizens who have occupied a piece of land where a waste recycling plant is going to be built. In all these situations, administrators really know what should be done. Their easy access to facts and superior expertise lie at the base of their autonomy. However, if factual reasons must be provided for justifying a decision adversely affecting the interests of individuals and groups, there are at least two important elements in favour of the latter: no decision can be simply unreasoned and there is room for ascertaining whether the reasons adduced by the public authority are prima facie reasonable.

If a court, or another reviewing body, takes this second step, the giving reasons requirement changes from a duty to give reasons, whatever their extent and content, to a duty to give reasons that are not manifestly irrational or 'adequate' or even 'good'. Consider, for example, the ECJ's ruling in *Sytraval*, according to which it is 'settled case law that the statement of reasons ... must disclose in a clear and unequivocal fashion the reasoning followed by the institution'.[14] Alternatively, the court or other agency may request administrators to explain why they did not accept the evidence and arguments provided by private parties, as happened in the US.[15] If either circumstance occurs, the outcome is not simply that a more

[13] Réné Chapus, *Droit administratif general* (10th edn, Montchrestien, 2001) I, 1141; John A Usher, *General Principles of EC Law* (2nd edn, Longman, 1998) 114.

[14] See ECJ, Case C-367/95, *Commission v Sytraval* [1998] ECR-I, 1719.

[15] See Martin Shapiro, 'The Giving Reasons Requirement', 181.

demanding standard has been adopted. It is, rather, that the giving reasons requirement, which is normally considered a procedural constraint on power, turns into a substantive constraint. This shift is important not only when the court or other reviewing body is entrusted with the power to quash the contested decision, but also if its power consists in deciding whether, if the decision was unlawful, damages must be accorded to the claimant. A blatantly unreasonable decision may therefore determine the court's assessment of damages.

2. A Minimum Standard for State Authorities: Justifying Disadvantageous Distinctions

The remarks just made can help us in better understanding the common and distinctive elements between the giving reasons requirements laid down by national legal systems. Our focus will be initially on differences and then on what might be regarded as a sort of common denominator standard, that is to say, requesting reasons at least for all decisions that adversely affect an individual or a group. We shall also develop in this respect the distinction made in the previous chapter between adjudication and rulemaking and analyse the countervailing considerations that lead to imposing reasons with regard to the former, but not to the latter.

Variety of giving reasons requirements

As noted earlier, the duty to give reasons for administrative decisions is a relatively recent development. In Continental Europe, it was introduced only in the last quarter of the nineteenth century, due to the influence of the French *Conseil d'État*. When it was entrusted with the power to render justice after 1872, it begun to develop safeguards for citizens.[16] It argued that the judge must have an adequate knowledge of the ways in which the public authority has balanced relevant interests in order to prevent misuses of powers. At the root of this way of looking at the giving reasons requirement there was thus a concern for the protection of individual rights. By contrast, for German administrative courts the rationale for giving reasons was the need to prevent an infringement of the law, considered objectively.[17] In practical terms, however, the effects of these judicial doctrines were very similar and they are now even more similar since the laws on procedures have codified the duty to give reasons.[18]

Nor do striking differences, in practical terms, arise from the giving reasons requirement being directly laid down by a constitutional provision[19] or being

[16] Eduard Laferrière, *Traité de la juridiction administrative et des recours contentieux* (2nd edn, Berger-Lavrault, 1896) 435.

[17] Ernst Forsthoff, *Lehrbuch des Verwaltungsrechts* (1950), *Traité de droit administratif allemand* (Michel Fromont (tr), Brussels, Bruylant, 1969) 367; Hermann Maurer, *Droit administratif allemand* (Michel Fromont (tr), 2nd edn, LGDJ, 1992) 276.

[18] Céline Wiener, 'La motivation des décisions administratives en droit comparé' (1969) 21 Rev Int Dr Comparé 788.

[19] See Article 268(3) of the Portuguese Constitution.

derived from broader principles, such as the principle of objectivity in Spain and the due process clause in the US. Three other differences are more relevant for present purposes: generally the giving reasons requirement only applies to certain individual decisions; seldom does it apply to administrative rulemaking; and sometimes the courts require the administration to give not simply reasons, but adequate reasons.

Although there are a number of advantages that can be secured by requesting reasons for the decisions of public authorities, there is no general duty to give reasons in two important European liberal democracies, France and the UK. The French administrative court expressly excluded the fact that the various norms imposing on public authorities the duty to give reasons are manifestations of a general duty.[20] It pointed out that the only general norms are those that impose on public administrations the duty to provide reasons for decisions adversely affecting individuals and those that derogate from existing rules against the principle of equality. Eventually, this judicial doctrine was codified by legislation in 1979.[21] Similarly, English courts have been reluctant to develop a general rule requiring administrative bodies to provide adequate reasons for their decisions. Absent such a general rule, the courts have held that the lack of reasons is a symptom of either an error on grounds of law or unreasonableness. In other cases unreasoned decisions have been quashed in order to ensure transparency.[22] Although this judicial policy is questionable in the opinion of many commentators, because the possibility to know the reasons underlying the authority's decision could be justified by the ordinary man's sense of justice,[23] this quick look at the two sides of the Channel shows that their developments are not so different. Only a portion of individual decisions must be reasoned. Reasons are required when the decision of a public authority produces unfavourable effects for some individual or collective interests. Reasons are due, too, when the authority deviates from existing rules or precedents.

In other parts of Europe, as well as in the Americas, legislation has been modified following the recommendation to require the giving of reasons. This duty has been enacted, for example, in Germany and Italy.[24] Their legislative provisions follow the same form. As a first step, they lay down the general rule according to which reasons must be given. They also specify that both grounds of fact and law must be provided. Moreover, they request public authorities to specify the points of view that they considered when exercising their discretionary powers. However, the rule is not without exceptions. German law dispenses with the administration's duty to give reasons when there is no decision adversely affecting anyone, when the adverse

[20] *Conseil d'Etat*, 10 April 1992, *M. Aykan*.

[21] French law n 79–587 of 11 July 1979, as later amended in 2011.

[22] *R v Secretary of State ex parte Doody* [1994] 1 AC 531; Carol Harlow and Richard Rawlings, *Law and Administration*, 523.

[23] See Paul Craig, 'The Common Law, Reasons and Administrative Justice' (1994) 53 Cambridge LJ 282; Paul R Verkuil, 'Crosscurrents in Anglo-American Administrative Law' (1986) 27 Wm & Mary L Rev 685, 701 (noting that Americans find a conception of due process without a requirement that decision-makers give reasons 'inexplicable').

[24] See Article 39 of the German APA and Article 3 of the Italian APA.

effect derives directly from legislation, or when a general order is taken. Similarly, Italian law does not require that grounds be given when an act containing rules is adopted.[25]

A general duty to give reasons has also been laid down by Spain, as well as by the Latin American countries that have been influenced by its legislation. The Spanish Act of 1992, later amended, requires public administrations to give a written statement of the reasons for a decision and the Constitutional Court has clarified that this is a general requirement, as distinct from the more stringent requisite that applies to measures such as sanctions and the expulsion of foreigners.[26] Argentinian and Venezuelan legislation, too, includes reasons among the requisites of an administrative act and specifies that both elements of fact and grounds of law must be provided.[27] The legislative framework of Peru contains a more synthetic but no less significant requirement. It affirms that the governed have a right to receive a decision that is reasoned and includes this right among its due process requirements.[28] Interestingly, the Peruvian Constitutional Court has held that the right to a reasoned decision has a special relevance because there must be a reasonable connection between the facts that underlie a certain decision and the rules of law that it applies or must respect. It has also held that the reasons must be 'sufficient', affirming that this is a safeguard against arbitrariness. The lack of an adequately reasonable basis, therefore, is incompatible with due process.[29]

The scope of the giving reasons requirement differs in another important respect because sometimes reasons are not required only for individual decisions, but also for rules. This is not provided for by legislation, for example, in France and Italy. Nor is giving reasons a requirement that applies to rules in South Africa: the reason is, as observed by its Constitutional Court, that the right to be given reasons fits in 'closely with adjudicative justice for individuals'.[30] By contrast, in the US the APA imposes on all agencies the duty to provide a full explanation of the reasons behind their decisions. Even when adopting informal rules, they must provide a 'concise general statement of their basis and purpose'. This assures that the grounds of a decision will not come as a surprise and will be linked to findings of fact and

[25] The Italian APA, Article 3(1) provides: 'The statement of reasons must set out the factual premises and the points of law that determined the authority's decision, as these emerge from the preliminary fact-finding activities.'

[26] Spanish Constitutional Court, judgments n 82/2009 of 23 March 2009 and n 186/2013 of 4 November 2013, paragraphs 3–4 (*motivación reforzada* in the original), available at http://www.tribunalconstitucional.es.

[27] See the APAs of Argentina (1972), Article 7(e) and Venezuela (1981), Article 8.

[28] Peruvian Law n 27444 (2001), Article IV(2); Diego Zegarra Valdivia, 'La motivación del acto administrativo en la Ley 27444, nueva ley de procedimento administrativo general del Peru' (2003) 10 Revista iberoamericana de administración publica 119.

[29] Constitutional Court of Peru, judgment of 26 May 2011 (application no 02638/2010), paragraph 5, available at http://www.tc.gob.pe/tc.

[30] Constitutional Court of South Africa, *Minister of Health v New Clicks South Africa (Pty) Ltd*, 2006 (2) SA 311 (CC), paragraph 596 (per Justice Sachs), available at http://www.constitutionalcourt.org.za/. For further remarks, see Michael Asimow, 'Administrative Law under South Africa's Interim Constitution' (1996) 44 Am J Comp L 389, 396 (noting that, in this respect, there was no right under prior law).

elements of law. Once reasons must be provided not only for individual measures, but also for secondary and tertiary rules, the formal distinction between legislative and administrative rules simply loses its importance and the courts are encouraged to review even the reasons adduced by the legislator.

The other distinctive feature of national duties to give reasons concerns its nature, which is either procedural or substantive. There is not, however, a clear-cut divide. There is, rather, as we saw in earlier chapters, a sort of continuum. In some cases, public authorities must simply keep a record of their activities and make it public, either *ex officio* or if requested by the affected individual. In these cases, the giving reasons requirement is regarded as being a fundamental requisite of procedural protection. In other cases, for example, in Belgium and the Netherlands, there is a more stringent duty because the reasons given must be intelligible and adequate.[31] Their adequacy is not only assessed internally, from the point of view of their coherence, but also externally, that is to say, that such reasons must deal with all the substantial points that were raised in the course of the administrative procedure. Also, the French and Italian administrative courts have affirmed that a decision inadequately reasoned is invalid.[32] Similarly, some English statutes that impose a duty to give reasons in specific situations are regarded by the courts as requiring that such reasons be clear and adequate in order to assess whether the administration is exercising power coherently with the will of Parliament, as well as to enable the individual to assess their potential weaknesses. However, the courts have clarified that such alleged weaknesses justify the quashing of the contested decision only if the applicant has suffered from a substantial prejudice.[33]

A minimum standard

When considering these examples, and others that can easily be adduced on a comparative basis, a caveat is necessary. A general theory of the giving reasons requirement may not be grounded on them. If making reasons available to the courts or to the citizenry were the only *raison d'être* of the giving reasons requirement, then it should apply to all decisions, not only to those having adverse effects or derogating to general rules of law. Those examples suggest, rather, first, that there are growing analogies between modern legal orders; secondly, that it is in the field of administrative law that such analogies become most visible, and, thirdly, that a common element or denominator is the prohibition of disadvantageous distinctions that are not based on a valid justification. 'Valid' means here not only grounded on interests protected by the legal order, but also adequate or reasonable.[34]

[31] See, for example, the Dutch GALA, Section 4(16) (providing that 'a decision shall be based on proper reasons'). See also the Belgian Law of 29 July 1991, Article 3, which provides that reasons must be 'adequate', and the judgment of the Belgian Constitutional Court n 2014/74 of 8 May 2014, § B.9.3, according to which legislation creates an individual right.

[32] George Vedel and Pierre Delvolvé, *Le système français de protection des administrés contre l'administration* (Sirey, 1991) 142.

[33] Paul Craig, *Administrative Law* (5th edn, Sweet & Maxwell, 2003) 437.

[34] Jerry Mashaw, 'Reasoned Administration', 101.

A US case dramatically illustrates the potentials of the duty to give reasons—the ruling of the Supreme Court in *Palmer v Thompson* in 1971, a few years after the Civil Rights Act. The case concerned racial desegregation in public swimming pools. What was at issue was whether the decision taken by the city council of Jackson, Mississippi to desegregate its public recreational facilities, with the exception of swimming pools, was an undue reaction to desegregation, though it was justified on other grounds. The city council held that the pools could not be operated safely and economically on an integrated basis. It added that the decision did not infringe the principle of equality, since it had closed the public pools to black and white alike. Since the majority of the Court thought that it would have been extremely difficult to ascertain the real reasons underlying the closing of public swimming pools, it confirmed the lower court's ruling. However, three justices dissented on the grounds that it was clear that the city's action in closing the pools, after the prohibition of segregation, was an exercise of the state police power at war with the principle of equality.[35] A factual element such as the local authority's decision to close the pools because of opposition to the District Court judgment may shed some light on the real reasons for a choice that, while damaging all citizens, is in conflict with the goal of racial integration.

From this point of view, not only is a rule denying certain individuals or groups access to a public service unconstitutional, in contrast with the equal subjection of all classes to one law,[36] but also a rule that terminates such a service is contrary to the principle of equality. The difference between these situations is that, while the former is characterized by discrimination on ethnic grounds and is therefore intrinsically unacceptable; the latter is unacceptable to the extent that it is unjustified. The clearest formulation of this principle can be found in the Constitution of South Africa, which provides: 'Everyone whose rights have been adversely affected by administrative action has the right to be given written reasons.'[37]

These remarks can help us understand better the minimum standard concerning reasons. What is prohibited by most, if not all, modern legal systems is not that an administrative measure confirms or creates a disadvantageous distinction between citizens or other individuals, as well as businesses, but, rather, an unjustified disadvantageous distinction.[38] The reasonableness of any distinction is, in other words, the fundamental legal aspect. The disadvantageous distinction, either confirmed or created by the decision taken by the authority, must be justified by giving reasons on grounds of fact and law, though such grounds may be provided by another

[35] Justice White, writing for the minority—*Palmer v Thompson* (403 US 217).

[36] This is one of the central tenets of the Rule of Law, according to Albert V Dicey, *Introduction to the Study of the Law of the Constitution* (10th edn, MacMillan, 1956) 193.

[37] Constitution of South Africa, Article 33(2). The constitutional requirement of 'just administrative action' was implemented by the *Promotion of Administrative Justice Act* (2000), Section 5 of which sets out requirements about giving reasons.

[38] See John H Ely, 'Legislative and Administrative Motivation in Constitutional Law' (1970) 79 Yale LJ 1205; *On Constitutional Ground* (Princeton University Press, 1996) 362. See also Ronald Dworkin, *Taking Rights Seriously* (Harvard University Press, 1977) 229 (distinguishing between the right to equal treatment and the right to be treated as an equal).

document to which such decision refers.[39] It is in this sense and within these limits that a public authority is obliged to make the reasons underlying its decision known because its effects are potentially in contrast with equality before the law.[40]

3. A Transnational Minimum Standard

Having sketched some of the ways in which national legal systems deal with the giving reasons requirement and what can be regarded as being the minimum standard, let us turn now to how non-State entities deal with such requirement and, in particular, to how courts and other bodies carry out checks in this respect. Such a minimum standard, that is to say, giving reasons for disadvantageous distinctions, will be of relevance for the argument to be presented in the remaining portions of this chapter. The argument is that, with respect to the conduct of national authorities, international and supranational requirements coincide with the minimum standard, although higher standards can be imposed in specific situations. To the extent to which the materials referred to include some decisions taken by courts and arbitral bodies in the exercise of their supervisory function, it is not surprising that they focus particularly on certain rationales of the giving reasons requirement, notably facilitating such supervision and preventing unjustified discrimination. This is not, however, detrimental to the construction of the giving reasons requirement as a function of democratic government, in the sense that reasons make government more accountable to the public.

Particular reasons requirements established by international norms

As a first step, it ought to be clarified that there is no general basis for imposing a giving reasons requirement on States' institutions and agencies. There are, rather, specific requirements imposed either by bilateral or multilateral treaties or by the norms enacted by the common institutions created by such treaties.[41]

Consider, first, a multilateral treaty that was already referred to in the previous chapter, the Aarhus Convention. It requests its contracting parties to provide information to all those who seek it. It also lays down a time limit for doing so of one month. Although this term may be extended to two months in particular cases, the Convention obliges any decision of this kind to state the reasons.[42] Once again, no

[39] See, for example, the Dutch GALA, Section 4(19). Italian and Spanish administrative law follow the same solution, that is to say, to give reasons *per relationem.*

[40] The principle of equality, in this sense, is affirmed by most, if not all, constitutions of the world: see, for example, the constitutions of Argentina (Article 16), Peru (Article 2), South Africa (Articles 1, 7, and 9), South Korea (Article 11), and Turkey (where Article X specifically urges administrative authorities to 'act in compliance with the principle of equality before the law').

[41] See Benedict Kingsbury, 'The Concept of "Law" in Global Administrative Law' (2009) 20 Eur J Int'l L 23 (pointing out the growing use of publicness criteria in practices of judicial review, including the requirement of reason-giving).

[42] Aarhus Convention, Article 4(2).

giving reasons requirement is established in general terms; rather, a specific requirement is laid down in order to prevent abuses.

Consider also the World Trade Organization (WTO)'s Agreement on Subsidies and Countervailing Measures, one of the agreements that are binding for all contracting parties. It deals with subsidies, that is to say, with financial contributions delivered in whatsoever form by a government or any public body to businesses,[43] and with the measures that a government can be authorized to take in order to combat unfair trade practices. Under this Agreement, if the authorities of the importing State refuse the offers made by the exporter State's undertakings for a variety of reasons, including 'reasons of general policy', they 'shall provide the reasons' which have led them to adopt a certain measure.[44] Similarly, if national authorities exercise their powers to impose provisional measures, they are requested to 'refer to the matters of fact and law' which have led them to impose measures of this kind.[45]

While these provisions clearly impose duties to give reasons whenever specific undertakings are adversely affected by State measures, it remains to be seen whether such duties are of either a procedural or substantive character. As we saw earlier, failure to provide reasons is one of the grounds on which the AB dismissed the claim made by the US administration with regard to the ban imposed on the import of shrimps and shrimp-related products.[46] The AB clarified that it was not willing to accept just any set of reasons in support of the ban, in view of its established doctrine according to which national limits to trade must not produce unjustified discrimination between the producers of different countries.

There are some analogies, but also some differences between this dispute and another concerning US subsidies to the steel industry, *US Steel*.[47] Both the panel and the AB placed the burden on the US to provide a 'reasoned and adequate explanation' of how the facts supported its findings of importation in increased quantities. The panel and the AB disagreed, instead, on another aspect. The former found that the US had produced irreconcilable elements of fact and held, therefore, that the reasons provided were incoherent, while the latter held that the panel should have reviewed each of those findings autonomously. The administrative decision could, accordingly, be based alternatively on each of them. In this way, the AB ensured a higher degree of deference with regard to the reasons of fact rendered by the administration. This solution has two different sides. It may make the exercise of authority less vulnerable to external review. However, the obligation imposed on national authorities is not simply to provide some reasons of fact, but also to give a 'reasoned and adequate explanation' of the contested measures. Such an explanation must allow the retracing of the administrators' decision-making

[43] Agreement on Subsidies and Countervailing Measures, Section 2.1.

[44] Agreement on Subsidies and Countervailing Measures, Section 18.3.

[45] Agreement on Subsidies and Countervailing Measures, Section 22.4.

[46] The panel's report has been followed by two reports of the Appellate Body: *Panel Report*, WT/DS58R (1998); *Report of the Appellate Body*, WT/DS58/AB/R (1998); *Report of the Appellate Body*, WT/DS58/AB (2001), available at: http://www.wto.org/.

[47] WTO Appellate Body report: *United States—Definitive Safeguard Measures on Imports of Certain Steel Products*, WT7DS248–254 and 258, 259/AB/R, adopted 10 December 2003, paragraph 368.

process. The political choice to introduce safeguard measures, therefore, is lawful only if it is supported by facts and well reasoned in terms of law. In sum, unlike in *Shrimp*, in *US Steel* the AB neither imposed a new duty on national authorities nor refused to exclude the fact that national measures were lawful if at least some of the reasons provided would suffice to justify them. The procedural conception of the giving reasons requirement looks therefore coherent with a principal–agent model of relationships between national politicians and international tribunals.

The giving reasons requirement in the investment field

A more procedural version of the giving reasons requirement seems to emerge in the jurisprudence of the ICSID arbitral tribunals. An early case is *Middle East*, adjudicated in 1992. Like in *Amco*, the foreign investor had stipulated a contract for the construction and operation of a hotel. But in this case the national administration decided to discontinue the contract on the grounds that the corporation lacked the requisite expertise and experience to properly implement the project. The Tribunal rejected this claim and added that there was no evidence of the irregular conduct of the claimant. To put it more simply, it observed that there was no evidence for this in the records.[48]

A more recent, and controversial, case is *Metalclad*. As we saw in the previous chapter, *Metalclad*, a US waste disposal company, created a subsidiary in Mexico, with a view to carrying out the same activity abroad. Although the Mexican central government encouraged this project, the local authority eventually refused to permit the subsidiary to open and operate a hazardous waste facility. The denial of the permit to build was based on concerns for its impact on the environment. When the investor instituted arbitration proceedings against Mexico under the ICSID rules, it alleged breaches of several North American Free Trade Agreement (NAFTA) articles and sought damages. It relied, in particular, on Article 1105, according to which 'each party shall accord to investments or investors of another party *treatment in accordance with international law*, including *fair and equitable treatment and full protection and security*'. The arbitral tribunal upheld this line of reasoning. It found that the Municipality's denial of the permit did not make any reference to any aspect of the facility that the investor aimed at building. The decision producing adverse effects, therefore, lacked proper reasons.

Two aspects of this ruling are particularly relevant for our analysis. First, the arbitral tribunal included the giving reasons requirements among the manifestations of the 'fair and equitable treatment' standard, similar to what we found earlier with regard to the right to be heard. This standard thus provides a basis for procedural due process requirements. Second, once factual reasons have been provided for justifying a decision adversely affecting the interests of investors, their reasonableness can be assessed.

[48] *Middle East Cement Shipping and Handling Co. S.A. v Arab Republic of Egypt* (*Middle East*), ICSID Case No ARB/99/6, Award of 12 April 2002, paragraphs 126–32.

From particular to general giving reasons requirements

Another body of law in which specific giving reasons requirements have been imposed on national authorities is that of European Union (EU) law. Such requirements have developed so as to provide protection for the citizens of the EU against measures affecting their freedom to move and live in another Member State,[49] as well as for professionals, such as lawyers, whose right to carry out their profession is denied by national authorities.[50] These developments do not represent a move away from the traditional reluctance of the EU legislator, whose competence is sector-specific, to impose general duties on the institutions and agencies of the Member States. Thus, the cases where the giving reasons requirement is granted are specific, though not exceptional.

However, the Court of Justice has generalized this requirement in *Heylens*. The dispute regarded the free movement of workers, and the Court's concern was how to make effective both this 'fundamental principle' and the broader prohibition of any discrimination on grounds of nationality. Both principles allow workers to seek employment within the single market once they have obtained the recognition of equivalence of their diplomas with those issued by the host Member State. Neither the Treaty nor the specific directives gave individuals any right to obtain such recognition, which could be refused for various reasons. However, the Court held that national authorities were obliged to provide those reasons in order to avoid discrimination.

The Court thus had to explain what the reasons were for demanding reasons and it did so in two ways. First, it emphasized the relationship between reasons giving and judicial review. Only if the national authority gives the reasons for its decision will the affected individuals have the possibility of deciding, with full knowledge of the relevant facts, whether there is any point in bringing an action before the national judge. Second, only if those reasons are known can the judge review the legality of the contested measure and assess whether it results in unjustified discrimination. Interestingly, the Court specified that the duty to give reasons was limited to the adverse decision and did not extend to other stages of the administrative action.[51] Only a decision that produces a situation disadvantageous with respect to a citizen, therefore, must be reasoned; that is to say, that any distinction of this kind is unlawful unless it is based on adequate reasons.

Another general requirement to provide reasons is laid down, according to the other European Court, that of human rights, by Article 6 of the European Convention on Human Rights (ECHR). Since this provision affirms the right to a fair trial, there is no doubt that its scope of application includes all national

49 Council Directive 2009/50 of 25 May 2009 on the conditions of entry and stay of third country citizens who intend to carry out particularly qualified work, Article 11(3) [2009] OJ L/155, 5.

50 EC Directive 98/5 of 16 February 1998, Article 9 [1998] OJ L/77, 36.

51 ECJ, Case 222/86, *Unectef v Heylens and Others* [1987] ECR I-1987, 4097. For further remarks, see Louis Dubouis, 'A propos de deux principes généraux de droit communautaire' (1988) Revue française de droit administratif, 691.

courts and its content includes typical process rights, such as the right to be heard and to counsel, as well as the duty to give reasons. The question that arises is, however, whether Article 6 also applies to administrative procedures. The Court has responded in the affirmative, for example, with regard to disciplinary procedures. But it has been confronted with different problems in more recent cases.

For instance, in *Lombardi Vallauri*,[52] the Catholic University of Milan terminated its contract with a professor of jurisprudence. The contract had been renewed for several years, but after Lombardi Vallauri publicly expressed views that were regarded as being 'in clear opposition to Catholic doctrine', the Faculty Board decided not to take his application into account on the grounds that an essential requisite was lacking, the approval of the Congregation for Catholic Education. The applicant then brought a claim before the Italian administrative courts, arguing, among other things, that his right to be heard and to obtain reasons had been infringed by the University. Both the lower and the higher administrative courts dismissed his claim, however. They observed that no part of the agreement between Italy and the Holy See, a foreign State, imposed a giving reasons requirement on the latter. Nor could the courts examine the lawfulness of its decisions. This argument, incidentally, was similar to that of the CFI in *Kadi*, where it affirmed that EU courts could not judge on the validity of the measures taken by United Nations (UN) bodies. Relying on the same provision of the ECHR, Article 6(1),[53] the applicant brought his case before the European Court of Human Rights (ECtHR). The Court agreed with the national courts that it was not for them to review the substance of any decision taken by the ecclesiastical authority. However, it endorsed the applicant's argument that the University had failed to provide adequate reasons for refusing to consider his application.

The interest of this case is not limited to the interpretation of Article 6, a provision to which we will return later, in Part II. *Lombardi Vallauri* also sheds some light on the significance of procedural due process for the protection of basic human rights, such as freedom of expression. The ECHR protects this and other rights, but its protection does not prevent considerations of public policy from being taken into account. In fact, the ECtHR acknowledges that public authorities have a margin of discretion. This does not imply an unlimited discretionary power, however. Indeed, the problem in *Lombardi Vallauri* was that the essential content of the right

[52] Eur Ct HR, *Lombardi Vallauri v Italy* (application no 39128/05) 20 October 2009.

[53] Article 6 of the ECHR establishes the right to a fair trial. It guarantees a public hearing within a reasonable time, and formally states the presumption of innocence. Paragraph 1 provides: 'In the determination of his civil rights and obligations or of any criminal charge against him, everyone is entitled to a fair and public hearing within a reasonable time by an independent and impartial tribunal established by law. Judgment shall be pronounced publicly but the press and public may be excluded from all or part of the trial in the interests of morals, public order or national security in a democratic society, where the interests of juveniles or the protection of the private life of the parties so require, or to the extent strictly necessary in the opinion of the court in special circumstances where publicity would prejudice the interests of justice.' The ECtHR has enforced this provision in a number of cases, mainly in criminal proceedings, but recently also in administrative procedures.

to be heard had been limited well beyond what can be deemed as 'necessary in a democratic society'.

4. A Minimum Standard for Non-State Authorities

Having clarified in which sense and within which limits it can be affirmed that there is a common standard for States, we should seek to test its applicability beyond their borders. The question that will be examined is, therefore, whether the same, or a similar, giving reasons requirement applies to the UN and the EU when they exercise powers internally and externally.

The giving reasons requirement in staff cases: The EU and the UN

We may begin our analysis with a case of 'ordinary' injustice. More than thirty years ago, there was a reluctance by national courts to allow international civil servants to take legal action against their employers and even to pursue allegations of discrimination. A situation of this kind arose from US judgments when applying the International Organizations Immunities Act. US courts denied the right to a hearing of an Argentinian national, Susana Mendaro, against her employer, the World Bank, on an alleged case of unjustified discrimination.[54] In the following twenty-five years the ILO Administrative Court gradually improved this situation. It did not call into question the traditional assumption that political bodies have a broad margin of discretion. Nevertheless, it ordered them to provide their grounds, using arguments similar to those developed at the beginning of the nineteenth century by the French *Conseil d'État.*

In 1993 a dispute arose between the Universal postal union and one of its administrators. The latter applied for a vacant post and was included in the shortlist. When the first candidate withdrew, the applicant thought that he was entitled to get the post. However, the post was again put up for internal competition. The applicant argued that the appointing authority had failed to substantiate the contested decision because the reasons given were sketchy and thus contrary to the general principles of law. The tribunal disagreed on the grounds that 'there is no rule or principle of law that requires the Director General to state in so many words just why he has turned someone down for promotion or appointment. What matters is that, if the official asks, the reasons must be revealed'.[55] Records and findings must, therefore, support every decision. To use the words of the Tribunal, without reasons 'the Tribunal may not exercise its power of review and determine whether

[54] *Mendaro v World Bank*, 717 F2d 610 (DC Cir 1983).

[55] See judgment n 1355 of 14 July 1994, *Subrapto v UPU*, paragraph 6. For an account of principles protecting international civil servants, see Robert A Gorman, 'The Development of International Employment Law: My Experience on International Administrative Tribunals at the World Bank and the Asian Development Bank' (2005) 25 Comparative Labour Law and Policy Journal 423.

the reasons are lawful'. It exercised self-restraint, however, to the extent to which it refrained from investigating the reasons stated by the administration.

In a more recent judgment concerning the Atomic Energy Agency, the Tribunal adopted a more intrusive approach. It had to deal with a refusal to renew a contract. The starting point was, again, the wide discretionary powers of the appointing authority. Its policy was not to be put into question. In this case, however, the Tribunal observed that the 'Agency failed to give any timely reasons in support of the decision not to extend the complainant's appointment'. Moreover, no rational explanation was provided as to why some requests were accepted, while others were refused. The Tribunal thus came to the conclusion that the decision was made for some 'undisclosed or purely arbitrary reason'.[56]

This judicial policy cannot be regarded as being complacent with respect to employers. The Court rejected the stronger version of the obligation to provide justification, namely that the authority was required to provide a detailed justification for each choice. Instead, it upheld an apparently milder version, that is to say, that all reasoning should be disclosed if requested by the parties. This implies that keeping records and findings of a specific procedure are not sufficient. Since the outcomes of several procedures must be considered and confronted, the authority has a heavier burden. It must provide reasons which are not simply coherent with a certain policy, but which demonstrate that that policy is coherently carried out. Moreover, the Court has extended the obligation to give reasons, even to the point of configuring it as a kind of duty to respond to petitions and objections raised by private parties. Consequently, the administration is not simply required to provide all the grounds on which its decisions are based; it has to answer *all* questions on matters of fact and law, as well as the choice between the various options available, such as the sanctions to be applied. The aim is to ensure the observance of a general principle that regulates the relationship between employer and employee.

A similar development has emerged also in the case law of the Court of Justice. Commentators on its jurisprudence have not failed to emphasize how the Court had initially stated that there was no need to justify a decision to promote one candidate over the others. Using a rhetorical device, it even argued that to justify a decision not to choose the other candidates might harm them.[57] More recently, this position has been rectified, especially in legal proceedings having an effect on business. The Court attached importance not only to the existence of grounds, but also to their adequacy. While shrinking from drawing all the necessary conclusions in terms of the investigation to be carried out on the legality of the contested measures, it found in favour of requests for compensation for undue damage caused by the inadequacy of the grounds. It endorsed the view that a judgment on annulment and one on claims for compensation are distinct and may result in different outcomes.

[56] See judgment n 2513 of 1st February 2006, *J.F. . IAEA*, paragraph 11.
[57] John A Usher, *General Principles of EC Law*, 115.

Reasoned administration in the EU

The giving reasons requirement, as noted earlier, is an established principle of EU law. It has a specific textual basis. The Charter of Fundamental Rights of the EU also confirms its importance by affirming that the right to a good administration includes, among other things, 'the obligation of the administration to give reasons for its decisions'.[58] That said, it must be added that the giving reasons requirement does not apply to all the activities of public institutions. It applies only to the 'acts' adopted by the institutions of the EU and to the extent to which such acts have binding effects. Opinions and recommendations are, therefore, excluded. Moreover, as the ECJ has constantly argued, the duty to give reasons must be adapted to the specific context. It is less demanding for general rules, such as those laid down by regulations and directives, while it is more demanding for individual decisions, particularly if they adversely affect certain individuals or groups.[59] The giving reasons requirement, thus intended, has an important impact on the exercise of discretionary powers. Its impact is even greater because EU judges check the adequacy of the reasons provided, which means that administrators cannot simply adopt boilerplate statements. A further step would be to oblige them to give reasons on all the issues considered by the discontents of those choices. If this happens,[60] the procedural requirement is converted into a substantive one.

If considered in general terms, this approach is clear enough. However, the problems it raises are neither few nor irrelevant. Some of these problems emerged in a recent dispute concerning the fight against terrorism. At the heart of this dispute, that preceded the *Kadi* ruling discussed earlier, there was the inclusion of a political movement, the *Organisation des Modhahedins du Peuple de l'Iran* (OMPI), in the list of individuals and other legal entities suspected of supporting terrorism. As a consequence, it was subject to measures such as the freezing of funds. OMPI brought an action against such measures, contending that its rights had been adversely affected without reasons being provided. The EU lower court agreed that, as a matter of principle, the giving reasons requirement applied to all measures having binding effects and adversely affecting individuals and groups, including the contested measures. However, it affirmed that a detailed disclosure of the reasons and sources upon which the freezing of funds was based could jeopardize the collective interests that it was aimed at protecting, that is to say, national security. This justified an 'exceptional' limit to the duty to give reasons. However, the Court continued, when such a fundamental procedural safeguard is limited, judicial review is 'all the more imperative'.[61]

58 EU Charter of Fundamental Rights (as revised in 2007), Article 41(2).

59 ECJ, Joined Cases 43, 45, and 48/59, *von Lachmuller et al. v Commission* [1960] ECR 453, paragraphs 6–7. For further analysis, see Jerry Mashaw, 'Reasoned Administration', 78.

60 Martin Shapiro, 'The Giving Reasons Requirement', 179. For the thesis that the ECJ has developed a dialogue requirement similar to that imposed by US courts, see Hans-Paul Nehl, *Principles of Administrative Procedure in EC Law* (Hart, 2003) 119.

61 CFI, Case T-228/02, *Organisation de Modjahedins du Peuple de l'Iran v Council* [2006] ECR-II, 4674, paragraph 127. For further analysis, see Giacinto della Cananea, 'Return to the Due Process of Law: The European Union and the Fight Against Terrorism' (2007) 32 Eur L Rev 895.

What emerges from this case, consequently, is a twofold lesson. First, any exercise of power by a public authority must be duly justified; otherwise, the courts will annul the measure that such authority has taken unless compelling public interests exist. That being the case, exercises of power are subject to a more stringent judicial review, a harder look, to borrow an American expression. This brings us to the second lesson: instead of considering each requirement of due process as if it were isolated, we must take their connections into account.

5. The Global Diffusion of Due Process Requirements: Two Caveats

My argument in this chapter has been that, although there is a variety of giving reasons requirements (procedural and substantive, limited to decisions or including administrative rules), a minimum standard has emerged. I have identified such minimum standard in the duty to provide reasons in order to justify disadvantageous distinctions affecting individuals, companies, or other legal entities. In order to fully understand the importance of this requirement, we must reflect on the sense in which it can be regarded as a 'minimum' standard. We will thus be in a position to reflect on the current diffusion of procedural due process requirements.

'Minimum' requirements of due process

This giving reasons requirement for disadvantageous distinctions is not a 'minimum' standard in the sense that it is a useless constraint on exercises of power. Indeed, a giving reasons requirement generates a record about the facts that preceded and justified the decision that adversely affected the interests of individuals or legal persons. It is true that this requirement does not challenge the discretionary powers of decision-makers. However, as observed by Shapiro, if factual reasons must be provided for justifying a decision adversely affecting the interests of individuals or businesses, there are at least two important elements in favour of the latter. First, no decision can be simply unreasoned. Administrators are at least obliged to provide evidence for their choices and this may improve the quality of their decisions.[62] Second, there is a room for ascertaining whether the reasons adduced by the State are prima facie reasonable.[63] This impinges on the quality and significance of supervisory mechanisms, as observed before with regard to the reasons that underlie the giving reasons requirement. It accentuates an important distinctive trait—decisions must be justified—of both law and politics, as opposed to markets.[64]

[62] See Frederick Schauer, 'Giving Reasons' (1995) 47 Stanford L Rev 633, at 656 (pointing out that the 'time required to give reasons may reduce excess haste and thus produce better decisions').

[63] Martin Shapiro, 'The Giving Reasons Requirement', 187.

[64] Giandomenico Majone, *Evidence, Argument & Persuasion in the Policy Process* (Yale University Press, 1989).

The giving reasons requirement for disadvantageous distinctions is, thus, a 'minimum' standard in another sense: precisely because it is mild, it is shared by most legal systems of the world and is established by several regulatory regimes set up by the States. But each national legal system responds in its own specific way to the requirement that public decision-making be subjected to this type of constraint. Accordingly, nothing prevents a State or a union of States from imposing such a requirement on a broader class of administrative decisions, by establishing that reasons must be given for all administrative acts that affect rights or interests, without any specification of their 'adverse' effects.[65] Similarly, a State or a union of States may wish to establish a more demanding standard by requiring that public authorities provide not simply reasons, but adequate or good reasons.

There are some similarities to and connections with the other procedural requirements examined in the previous chapters. The spread of codification, in the form of either an all-embracing procedural code or of a sector-specific code, does not necessarily imply that there is such thing as a 'model' on which every administrative procedure is based. It implies, rather, that there is a general requirement that a certain degree of order is necessary when broadly conceived administrative action is taken. This allows differentiation in relation to the interests at stake, as well as to the degree of autonomy which public authorities enjoy. Similarly, there is a variety of hearing requirements. But the legislative or judicial assertion of a right to be heard implies that no measure can be taken by a public authority if it is likely to adversely affect the interests of individuals and groups without providing them with a meaningful opportunity to be heard. The advantage of such a requirement is that it provides a standard for assessing whether administrative action is lawful and sound. In short, the right to be heard only implies that public authorities are obliged to carry out 'some kind of hearing'.[66] However, the huge variety of fields subject to administrative adjudication and regulation often means that the minimum requirement, a sort of *lex generalis*, will be supplemented by sector-specific legislation (*lex specialis*). There may in addition be judicial discretion as to the right to be heard depending on interest balancing exercises.

Caveats (I): Similar, not uniform, procedural requirements

Although the three requirements of procedural due process of law (ensuring that a certain order is respected through a procedure; providing a hearing; stating reasons) are no longer an exclusive patrimony of the legal systems where they were initially set out, those of the States, a twofold caveat is necessary regarding their significance. First and foremost, there is no harmonization. Second, a progress is hardly discernible.

The three requirements of administrative procedure are no longer an exclusive patrimony of the States in two respects, concerning their legal sources and scope of application. The first innovation is that procedural requirements are increasingly

[65] Portuguese Constitution, Article 268(3).
[66] Henry J Friendly, 'Some Kind of Hearing' (1975) 123 Un Pa L Rev 1267.

set out by 'regional' and global regulatory regimes and are viewed as standards for national authorities. The second innovation relates to the authorities to which such procedural requirements apply. They do not only belong to the class of subjects that have traditionally been considered by academic work in this field, the States. Similar requirements are imposed on national and supranational authorities. There is clearly, therefore, not simply an increasing importance of due process requirements, but also an evident similarity between the requirements.

However, I am not suggesting that all legal institutions can be neatly fitted into a certain pre-defined model, as that would imply a degree of coherence between various legal developments, while it is part of my thesis to suggest that this does not exist. Such coherence does not exist, in particular, because regional and global regulatory regimes do not simply adopt the requirements of due process of law that are common to their Member States, or to most of them.[67] While in national legal systems detailed legal provisions often define those procedural requirements, this is seldom the case beyond the States, where courts and arbitral tribunals enforce broad standards of justice. Whether this difference is simply due to the fact that regional and global regulatory regimes are more recent or it is a consequence of a preference for looser regulation,[68] is another question, to which we will return in Chapter 9.

The lack of uniformity may also be perceived by focusing on the distinction between the structure of the requirements imposed on public authorities (ie the manner in which they are to be performed) and their function. While the structure of the duty to provide a hearing or to give reasons is largely the same as that of the corresponding duty existing in domestic jurisdictions, its function is different. The law of world trade provides illuminating examples, with the giving reasons requirement being imposed on all contracting parties in the interest of the others. Similarly, when the AB imposes a consultation requirement concerning a national administrative procedure, the contracting parties are not only subject to duties, but they may also exercise a previously unknown right. These examples raise an important question; that is, whether the new requirements of procedural due process are based on the same rationales as those to which we are accustomed in a national context. In the field of world trade law a procedural requirement such as the hearing within an administrative procedure is justified neither by the traditional concern of protecting individuals nor by the will to involve civil society. It is justified, instead, by the need to ensure cooperation between States, as will be observed in Chapter 7.

To conclude, although the metaphor of the 'legal transplant' is controversial,[69] it can be helpful for present purposes as it suggests that transporting a legal institution

[67] For the statement that even within a closer union such as the EU important differences persist, see Michel Fromont, *Droits administratifs des Etats européens* (PUF, 2006) 219.

[68] See Sabino Cassese, *The Global Polity: Global Dimensions of Democracy and the Rule of Law* (Global Law Press, 2012) (asserting that at global level 'participatory rights are rudimentary' and that 'the rule of law is not fully developed in the global legal system').

[69] See Alan Watson, *Legal Transplants: An Approach to Comparative Law* (2nd edn, University of Georgia Press, 1993).

into a different legal environment may cause not only a reaction, but also adaptation and change. In other words, although a sort of 'spill-over' effect is clearly discernible,[70] it implies neither the homogenization of laws nor their harmonization in the strict sense. Rather, it leaves room for regulatory *arbitrages* and promotes a new kind of legal pluralism.[71]

Caveats (II): A development, not an achievement

Another caveat is warranted. We should not take for granted that there is such a thing as a continuous extension of legal safeguards.[72] Three reasons support this view. Firstly, and generally, the history of legal and political institutions shows that a clear and linear progression, not to say progress, is barely discernible.[73] Every attempt to read the complex events of human history (and particularly the history of legal institutions) from an evolutionary perspective is inevitably doomed.

Secondly, a comparative analysis of administrative procedure shows that there has not just been progress. For example, English judges, who had elaborated the principles of natural justice, attenuated them during the first part of the twentieth century[74] and the same happened in the US after 1941. Procedural safeguards against public authorities were even more drastically attenuated in Austria, Germany, and Italy during the same period. Similarly, legislation may set out requirements for fair procedures, but these may remain ineffective if an independent judiciary is lacking, as happened in Hungary. Still today, the constraints that a group of countries have accepted—for example, arbitration in the investment field—can be, and are, contested by some of them, thus leading to self-restraint by arbitrators.

Thirdly, we need to be adequately aware that, while we are witnessing legal developments that are faster than those that occurred in several national systems, they are meeting with several obstacles. One obstacle is, of course, the aversion that all administrators, worldwide, feel for formalities. Another is the absence of an architect's design.[75] Transnational standards do not just evolve by virtue of a sovereign's orders, but also as a result of a variety of factors, among which an important role is played by judicial decisions, which themselves are influenced by the actions brought by private parties and their lawyers. These parties—plaintiffs and defendants, lawyers and judges—do not usually pursue 'great' change-oriented objectives. They have more limited goals that are sometimes quite prosaic.

70 See Paul Craig, *Administrative Law*, 209.

71 Francis G Snyder, *The EU, the WTO and China. Legal Pluralism and International Trade Regulation* (Hart, 2008).

72 Gordon Silverstein, 'Globalization and the rule of law: "A machine that runs of itself?"' (2003) 1 Int J Const L 427 (criticizing the belief in a spontaneous adjustment).

73 For a similar remark, from the viewpoint of legal history, see Antonio Manoel Hespanha, *Panorama historico da cultura jurìdica europea* (2nd edn, PEA, 1999).

74 Patrick Birkinshaw, *European Public Law* (Butterworths, 2003) 331.

75 Although Eyal Benvenisti and George W Downs, 'Political Economy and the Fragmentation of International Law' (2007) 60 Stanford L Rev 597 acknowledge that there is no such thing as a 'plan', they identify individual States' strategies that aim at creating a more favourable legal framework.

PART II

RATIONALES FOR DUE PROCESS REQUIREMENTS

5

Variety of Rationales for Due Process Requirements

As indicated before, it is part of the thesis of this book that a growing concern for the requirements of due process characterizes two different classes of subjects: States and the regulatory regimes set up at regional or global level. The deepest significance of the operation of similar—or even the same—legal institutions is that it undermines the theory that there is a profound separation, a divide, between the two provinces of public law, within and beyond the borders of the States. Before reconsidering critically such theory in the last chapter, more thought has to be given to the rationales underlying the requirements of due process of law. Later chapters will explore them in more detail. My main purpose here is, first, to clarify the meaning of 'rationales' and, second, to observe that in a transnational context such rationales are partly different from those that are usually observed in a national context.

1. The Concept of 'Rationales'

I begin with two basic points that will review some matters discussed in Part I and introduce the concepts we are about to examine: the distinction between principles and values and its implications for understanding the 'rationales' for the requirements of administrative due process of law.

The ambiguity of 'values'

In Chapter 1, when discussing traditional philosophical approaches to due process of law, I observed that they are confronted with two problems. The first is that, since the starting point of such theories is a given premise such as a certain idea of justice, they are inevitably abstract. This rationalistic approach tends to neglect the importance of experience and this is especially a problem for jurisprudence because it is practical and theoretical at the same time. The other problem with an approach of this type is that it is unsuitable for making sense not only of the various interests that emerge in modern societies, but also of the different visions for good that are formulated therein. If the premise is not shared, the conclusions that follow from it are less likely to be accepted. This problem is, of course, particularly relevant in a transnational context, where there is no such thing as a community that can be conceived organically.

However, this method also has some advantages. Methodologically, by choosing a certain value, such as justice, it is easier to present a theory of due process as a coherent whole and thus to attempt to systematize the particularities that emerge from the practice of law and government. Moreover, and more importantly for present purposes, since this method emphasizes the importance of values, it is easier to give meaning to the facts that emerge from reality and to give legal acknowledgement to the interests that the legal system aims to protect and promote. Accordingly, values have a teleological and deontological dimension.[1]

Consider, for example, deprivation of offices, as occurred in *Bagg*'s case and in many other cases in a variety of legal systems across time. Even in a legal system that is primarily concerned with the issue of authority, there is room for requiring the head of an office to proceed accurately and objectively. *A fortiori*, in a legal system that is concerned with liberty and is constructed on the prevention of any arbitrary and capricious exercise of power, the decision-maker must be unbiased (*nemo judex in causa sua*) and must hear the other side (*audi alteram partem*) before taking an unfavourable decision. Principles, as distinct from rules, are particularly helpful for this due to their indeterminacy, while rules regulate specific conduct and 'weight' or importance, in the sense that they express values that are socially relevant.[2]

It is precisely because principles, especially general principles of law, have such 'weight' that there is some overlapping with 'values'. European Union (EU) law furnishes a practical example of the ambiguous distinction between 'principles' and 'values'. While initially Article F TEU conceptualized the Rule of Law and the protection of fundamental rights as principles of law, when the treaties were modified in an attempt to strengthen the (contested) legitimacy of the EU, they were included in a list of 'values upon which the Union is founded' (Article 4). But in two different parts of the TEU's preamble the Rule of Law and fundamental rights are qualified as ('universal') values and as principles, respectively.

A certain ambiguity also characterizes scholarly writings on administrative procedure, for example, when they note that the underlying 'values grow out of the traditions of due process and the related notions of fair procedure'.[3] Although these terms are not inherently tautological, a sort of circularity emerges when the value of the administrative process is identified in the notion of a fair procedure. Such circularity would not disappear by affirming that due process expresses the ideals of the Rule of Law.[4] In fact, the Rule of Law has meant many things to many

[1] Dawn Oliver, *Common Values and the Public-Private Divide* (Cambridge University Press, 1999) 57.

[2] Ronald Dworkin, *Taking Rights Seriously* (Harvard University Press, 1999) 26.

[3] See Paul R Verkuil, 'The Emerging Concept of Administrative Procedure' (1978) 78 Colum LR 258, 279.

[4] See Carol Harlow and Richard Rawlings, *Process and Procedure in EU Administration* (Hart, 2014) 2–3; José Araujo Juarez, *Principios generales del derecho administrativo formal* (Vadell, 1989) 69.

people within different institutional frameworks, from the ideal of the exclusion of officials' discretion[5] to the opinion that officials must exercise discretion though within certain parameters.[6] Moreover, the Rule of Law ideal of protecting liberty from government interference may collide with the achievement of the goals set by the people's representatives.[7] Last but not least, while some commentators think that with the Rule of Law there is at least the potential for empowerment for all,[8] and point out its importance from a global perspective,[9] others assert that the Rule of Law is often an instrument of mystification of force and hegemony, if not of plunder.[10]

Despite this diversity of opinion, there is an important dimension which recent studies about public law values share in common with an apparently diverging theory of Carl Schmitt; namely, the dimension of conflict. Both theories argue that secularized societies express a variety of interests and values, which require complex balancing exercises. It is precisely because our conceptions of good differ, and are thus profoundly divisive, that, in order to make conflicts between such values manageable, we need acceptable procedures for conflict resolution.[11] Schmitt went further, warning legal scholarship about the use of values.[12] First, he observed, the concept of value is not neutral. It is often associated with the idea that in a bourgeois society all—not only things, but also persons—are converted into something that has an economic value.[13] Money thus becomes the measure of all, objects and subjects. Secondly, values are less easily discernible than legal principles. Thirdly, unlike legal principles, values are intrinsically divisive. As a consequence, it is inevitably the case that values come into conflict with countervailing values, with the further consequence that it is very hard for legal scholarship to keep itself distinct from politics. Even the attempt to identify and propose 'objective' values is doomed to stifle conflict, Schmitt held, because any theory that proposes a system of values will regard any other as false.[14]

While there is no need for us to take a side in this debate, a twofold aspect is instructive for our analysis. We must explore the possibility of using a concept that captures the meaning of 'values', viewed as the normative foundations of procedural

[5] Albert V Dicey, *The Law of the Constitution*, 188; Guido Zanobini, *L'attività amministrativa e la legge* (1922), in *Scritti di diritto pubblico* (Giuffrè, 1956) 25.

[6] Kenneth C Davis, *Discretionary Justice. A Preliminary Inquiry* (Greenwood Press, 1969) 5.

[7] See Jeffrey Jowell, *The Rule of Law Today*, in Jeffrey Jowell and Dawn Oliver (eds), *The Changing Constitution* (2nd edn, Oxford University Press, 1996) 57.

[8] Lord Bingham, 'The Rule of Law' (2007) 66 Cambridge LJ 67.

[9] Gordon Anthony et al (eds), *Values in Global Administrative Law* (Hart, 2011).

[10] Ugo Mattei and Laura Nader, *Plunder: Why the Rule of Law is Illegal* (Wiley, 2008).

[11] Isaiah Berlin, *Two Concepts of Liberty* (Clarendon Press, 1958) 15; Stuart Hampshire, *Justice is Conflict* (Princeton University Press, 2000) 5.

[12] Carl Schmitt, *The Tyranny of Values* (1967, Simona Draghici (tr), Plutarch Press, 1996).

[13] For a recent reassertion of the dangers deriving from an economic approach detached from morals, see Michael J Sandel, *What Money Can't Buy. The Moral Limits of Markets* (Farrar, Straus and Giraux, 2012) 7.

[14] From a different angle, Susan Rose-Ackerman, 'Regulation and Public Law in Comparative Perspective' (2010) 60 Un Toronto LJ 519, 528 notes that neither competence nor method eliminates disagreement over values.

due process requirements, but avoids its ambiguity. If so, the further question that arises is how such a concept may also reflect the fact that such normative foundations may come into conflict with one another.

From values to 'rationales'

Fortunately or not, there is no agreed list of foundations for the requirements of administrative procedure. However, some scholarly works that discuss them provide us with some insights for both the issues just mentioned by using the concept of 'rationales' and distinguishing them on the basis of the interests or values that they 'serve'.[15] Using this concept, instead of that of values, is not simply coherent with the tradition of legal studies in this field. It also provides a key for understanding the foundations of due process requirements in two respects. First, a 'rationale' is not simply an explanation for something, as the definitions provided by some vocabularies suggest. It designates something more important and more closely related to the genesis and development of a legal institution or a set of legal institutions, that is to say, the fundamental reason why it exists and has been shaped in the way it exists, in brief its *raison d'être*.[16] From this point of view, the concept of 'rationale' has a teleological sense.

Second, this concept has a deontological sense, which is that it designates the normative foundations of procedural due process requirements. From this angle, rationales are not themselves principles of law, although such principles reflect one or several rationales, which operate at a higher level of abstraction. Rationales are legally relevant, therefore, notwithstanding the fact that a certain rationale has or has not a special place in positive law. Similarly, rationales are not themselves rights but, rather, provide the foundations for process rights.[17]

Focusing on rationales, as distinct from rights, has a further advantage, which can be appreciated through a slight historical digression. Western constitutionalism has always been concerned with constraints on the power of the executive,[18] which ultimately rest on moral grounds.[19] This concern for injury has not waned in the twentieth century. It emerges, for example, in the US Supreme Court use of the expression 'Star Chamber proceedings' to refer to the activities of New Deal agencies.[20] However, avoiding arbitrariness is not the only rationale for procedural

[15] See Paul Craig, 'Procedures and Administrative Decisionmaking: A Common Law Perspective' (1993) 3 Eur Rev Public L 56; Dawn Oliver, *Common Values*, 98; Michael Asimow, 'Administrative Law under South Africa's Interim Constitution' (1996) 44 Am J Comp L 389, 398 (distinguishing utilitarian and dignitarian justifications).

[16] Guy Isaac, *La procédure administrative non contentieuse* (LGDJ, 1968) 147.

[17] Servulo Correia, 'Administrative Due or Fair Process: Different Paths in the Evolutionary Formation of a Global Principle and of a Global Right', in Gordon Anthony et al (eds), *Values in Global Administrative Law*, 313–61.

[18] See Geoffrey Marshall, 'Due Process in England', in J Roland Pennock and James W Chapman (eds), *Due Process: Nomos XVIII* (New York University Press, 1977) 69.

[19] See Thomas M Scanlon, 'Due Process', in J Roland Pennock and James W Chapman (eds), *Due Process*, 93 (for the thesis that 'claims in due process are grounded in moral principles of political right').

[20] Paul R Verkuil, 'The Emerging Concept of Administrative Procedure', 268.

due process requirements. Another one is sound governance, which is important not only for the richer countries of the world which administer our lives from the cradle to the grave but also in other countries where traditional essential functions (internal and external defence, the administration of justice, and the building of material and non-material infrastructures)[21] are carried out. There is still another rationale for procedural requirements, namely the achievement of political control over administrative action.

Instrumental and non-instrumental rationales

If there is not a single and unitary *raison d'être* for due process requirements, the further questions that arise are, conceptually, how it is possible to distinguish them and, practically, how they interact. Whether the rationales of due process work in the same direction or are in conflict, and whether there are significant differences in a national and in a transnational context, is what will be discussed in the remaining portions of this chapter. Meanwhile, the conceptual distinction between instrumental and non-instrumental rationales will be considered.

Historically, as observed before, non-instrumental rationales have been central to the construction of process rights. Despite the different institutional premises of theories of the Rule of Law and *Rechtsstaat*, these theories nevertheless share certain affinities with respect to the limitation of exercises of power by public authorities.[22] The underlying assumption is that the law, whilst conferring powers on government, provides a set of principles to keep it within legal bounds. Consider the rule against bias, expressed by the maxim *nemo judex in re propria*: it requires public administrators to avoid conflicts of interest, as well as to act impartially when deciding whether a sanction must be imposed on a group of undertakings, thus ensuring that justice is done from a procedural point of view. Similarly, the maxim *audi alteram partem* requires that a reasonable opportunity to be heard be provided to a civil servant in all procedures that may lead to a deprivation of office. The emphasis here is on process rights, with a view to providing procedural protections for individuals against government.[23]

At the root of this argument there is the theory, contractarian in nature, that has been elaborated by Immanuel Kant. The central tenets of this theory are that a philosophically sound foundation of rights must be based on reason, not on experience, from which empirical principles are derived; that human action must, therefore, be coherent with a maxim that can be regarded as being universal, not

[21] Adam Smith, *An Inquiry into the Nature and Causes of the Wealth of Nations* (1776) (Penguin, 1987) V.I.3–4.

[22] Christian Starck, *Droits fondamentaux, État de droit et Principe démocratique en tant que fondements de la procédure administrative non contentieuse* (1993) 3 Eur Rev Public L 35.

[23] Alfred C Aman, *The Democracy Deficit. Taming Globalization through Law Reform* (New York University Press, 2004) 13 (observing that administrative law also allows 'for input by citizens regarding policy').

simply general; and that it is imperative that every person be treated as a goal, not as a means.[24] In the same tradition of thought, it has been suggested that citizens must be described according to a constitutional imperative that does not simply emphasize certain goals of a political association, but ensures that all citizens are treated as 'free and equal'.[25]

For all the attractiveness of this model, it should be observed that it raises the question whether not only citizens but also other individuals should be treated as 'free and equal' in administrative procedure, unless an overriding reason of public interest precludes it. Moreover, a procedural requirement such as the duty to give reasons can equally rest on an instrumental rationale, which emphasizes the connection between procedural due process and the substantive goals of government's policies, especially when they are defined by legislation. A typical manifestation of this manner of looking at due process is to affirm that hearing a private party before taking a decision that may adversely affect it, for example, by issuing a concession for exploiting a gold mine to someone instead of someone else, can help ensure that such decision is coherent with government goals, and that the relevant elements of fact have been correctly gathered and weighed before deciding. Especially from the latter viewpoint, the focus is not so much on process rights, but on procedural requirements, following the logic according to which a proper procedure plays an important role in helping to attain an accurate decision. This logic becomes even more evident when considering administrative rulemaking. Citizens and businesses potentially affected by an agency's decision to formulate or amend a rule are in a position to provide that agency with information and experience that its officers may not have. In this sense, although public authorities alone begin rulemaking procedures, consultation can positively affect the quality of rules.[26] While the non-instrumental rationale can be associated with the Kantian ideal, the intellectual origins of instrumental rationales are to be found in the work of utilitarians such as Jeremy Bentham.[27]

In conclusion, both instrumental and non-instrumental rationales pervade the procedural requirements that law imposes on public authorities. It is by respecting them that a governmental authority ensures its legitimacy, differently from the mere possession of superior powers by the State. However, instrumental and non-instrumental rationales have different intellectual origins, serve different purposes, and must thus be kept distinct. Whether, practically, they are also in conflict remains to be seen.

[24] Immanuel Kant, *Grundlegung zur Metaphysik der Sitten* (1785) IV.429. See also Jeffrey Jowell, *The Rule of Law Today*, 19 (viewing the Rule of Law as a 'principle of institutional morality').

[25] John Rawls, *Justice as Fairness* (Harvard University Press, 2003) 81.

[26] OECD, *Recommendations of the Council on Regulatory Policy and Governance*, paragraph 3.

[27] Jeremy Bentham, *An Introduction to the Principles of Morals and Legislation* (first published 1781; Blackwell, 1948) 125 (holding that 'the business of government is to promote the happiness of the society').

2. Rationales of Due Process Within the State

There are various interactions between instrumental and non-instrumental rationales. Such interactions will be considered, first of all, in the context in which the requirements of due process have been set out initially, that of the State. This will permit a comparison with the requirements that emerge in a transnational context.

Concurring and conflicting rationales

Instrumental and non-instrumental rationales may work in the same direction, as is the case in the examples just mentioned, where both the administration and the affected parties have an interest in the accuracy of the procedure. Suppose that a public authority, acting as employer, is informed that an employee frequently fails to fulfil the obligations stemming from contract and begins a disciplinary procedure. The employee's right to be heard before any sanction is imposed is not in contrast with the employer's interest to gather all relevant elements of fact, following the logic of accuracy, impartiality, and objectivity. Suppose also that a government agency begins a procurement procedure to buy the goods and services it needs. Although the particular interest of each participant in the tendering procedure is obviously to be selected, such interest is not necessarily in contrast with procedural propriety and fairness, which serve the general interests related to workable competition and to value for money. In the light of these and other examples that may easily be added, it can be argued that instrumental and non-instrumental rationales may act as 'twin rationales' for the existence of process rights and the related duties imposed on public authorities.[28]

However, as Paul Craig has argued, instrumental and non-instrumental rationales can have 'ambivalent' relationships and can even be in conflict.[29] This is the case, in particular, when the level of accuracy that a public authority deems proper for its decision-making process, in the light of constraints concerning money and time, is in contrast with the process rights of individuals and especially of social groups. Consider, for example, the ruling of the US Supreme Court in *Overton Park*.[30] Federal funds were used to finance construction of an interstate highway through a public park in Memphis. A group of citizens claimed that the project ran against the rule that this was not legitimate if a 'feasible and prudent' alternative route existed. A conflict thus emerged, because enabling citizens to take part in the decision-making process had a negative impact on costs and time and thus on efficiency and effectiveness. The Court ultimately found that the District Court had to check whether the exercise of administrative discretion was justifiable. Interestingly,

[28] See Paul Craig, *Administrative Law* (5th edn, Sweet & Maxwell, 2003) 408–9; John A Usher, *General Principles of EC Law* (Longman, 1998) 2.

[29] Peter L Strauss, 'The Rulemaking Continuum' (1992) 31 Duke LJ 1463.

[30] US Supreme Court, *Citizens to Preserve Overton Park v Volpe*, 401 US 402 (1971).

in their separate concurring opinions, justices Black and Brennan affirmed that 'whatever the hearing requirements might be, the Department of Transportation failed to meet them'.

The ruling of the Court in *Mathews v Eldridge* expressed the potential contrast between the interests at stake in clearer terms and sought to find a remedy by devising a test:

> The identification of the specific dictates of due process generally requires consideration of three distinct factors. First, the private interest that will be affected by the official action; second, the risk of erroneous deprivation of such interest through the procedures used, and the probable value, if any, of additional or substantive procedural safeguards; and, finally, the Government interest, including the function involved and the fiscal and administrative burdens that the additional or substitute procedural requirements would entail.[31]

A few years later, the Supreme Court reiterated in another ruling, regarding authorization for the building and management of a nuclear plant, its concern for the formalized procedures then in force that could cause parties to engage in expensive and time-consuming litigation over agency rules.[32] The interest of these cases, considered as a whole, goes beyond the particular legal environment in which they have arisen. First, they confirm the caveat enounced at the end of Chapter 4: the protection given by the courts to individual and collective interests through the requirements of due process of law is not always incremental, but may, and sometimes does, decrease. Second, these cases show that due processes of law can be approached from several viewpoints, some of which may be systematically structured as 'models'.

Competing 'models' of due process

In order to understand the foundations and implications of the competing 'models' of due process, insight will be sought through an examination of the analysis carried out by Jerry Mashaw with regard to due process in US public law. His approach has been chosen because it seems to be one of the most insightful of the theories on the legal institutions that are examined in this book, as it devotes considerable attention to the history of legal institutions, but presents them in a systematic, as distinct from chronological, manner.[33] This choice may raise a problem, that is whether his approach is representative in respect of other thoughts about due process in the US and, *a fortiori*, in other institutional settings. But my intent is to focus on his

[31] US Supreme Court, *Mathews v Eldridge*, 424 US 319, 334–5 (1976). For further remarks, see Jerry Mashaw, 'The Supreme Court's Due Process Calculus for Administrative Adjudication in Mathews v. Eldridge: Three Factors in Search of a Theory' (1976) 44 U Chi L Rev 28.

[32] US Supreme Court, *Vermont Yankee Nuclear Power Corp v Natural Resources Defense Council Inc.*, 435 US 519 (1978). See, in favour and against the Court's ruling, Antonin Scalia, 'Vermont Yankee: The APA, the D.C. Circuit, and The Supreme Court' [1978] Supreme Court Rev 345 and Steven Breyer, 'Vermont Yankee and the Court's role in the Nuclear Energy Controversy, (1978) 91 Harv L Rev 1833.

[33] For an approach of this kind, instead, see Alfred C Aman, *The Democracy Deficit*, 14.

approach in order to show that, whatever their intrinsic plausibility, the ideas and thoughts about due process of law elaborated in the context of a liberal democracy are less susceptible to making sense of legal realities in a transnational context.[34]

Although initially already presented in a series of essays, Jerry Mashaw's work has been systematically exposed in his book *Due Process in the Administrative State*. This book is particularly interesting for it provides a comprehensive account of administrative due process. Mashaw elaborated 'three related, but somewhat different models', which he qualified as the models of appropriateness, competence, and dignitary values.[35] He thus emphasized how in addition to the traditional concerns regarding the appropriateness of the decision and the competence of the decision-maker, in a vision functionally oriented and inspired by the scientific method (as in the test elaborated by the Supreme Court in *Mathews v Eldridge*), there is a growing awareness of the importance of human dignity, seen in connection with assertions of fundamental fairness.

In order to understand the originality of Mashaw's theory of due process we must appreciate its epistemological roots and normative nature. In view of a variety of legal realities (the US Supreme Court's doctrines about due process in taxation and personal freedom, as well as regarding welfare entitlements), he constructs three 'somewhat different models'. He is not, however, in a position of indifference in respect of such models. Quite the opposite, Mashaw argues about the 'normative superiority of one',[36] which emphasizes human dignity by reinterpreting the natural rights approach and integrating procedural and substantive concerns.[37]

This is, of course, objectionable, as the debate about due process in that particular legal context shows.[38] However, three other aspects are more relevant for present purposes. First, the rejection of a philosophical approach to due process of law, particularly in the form of a deduction from abstract concepts such as justice in favour of an approach based on experience, presents us with a problem. It is the problem of how we can make sense of the practice of law and government that, as worldwide practice, lacks coherence.[39] It is precisely because he is aware of this problem that Mashaw does not try to present his theory of due process as a coherent whole, but constructs three models.

Secondly, although such models are analytically distinct and emphasize different values, either on the side of authority or on the side of an individual's autonomy, they do not coincide with the rationales of due process. These models are abstractions that allow the author to give an account of several legal realities from partial and defective points of view. Incidentally, this explains why an argument about the normative superiority of one is possible, though objectionable. Quite the contrary,

[34] For a different viewpoint, Richard B Stewart, 'US Administrative Law: A Model for Global Administrative Law' (2005) 68 Law & Cont Probl 63 (holding that in some respects US administrative law can be viewed as a model for global law).

[35] Jerry Mashaw, *Due Process in the Administrative State* (Yale University Press, 1985) 48.

[36] Jerry Mashaw, *Due Process*, 43.

[37] Jerry Mashaw, *Due Process*, 49.

[38] See Ronald A Cass, *Review of Jerry Mashaw, Due Process in the Administrative State* (1986) 3 Constitutional Commentary 525, 529.

[39] Martin Loughlin, *Public Law and Political Theory* (Clarendon Press, 1992) 67.

instrumental and non-instrumental rationales indicate the goals that are served by the requirements of procedural due process of law.[40] The conjecture that will be explored in the remaining portions of this chapter is that, especially in a transnational context, such rationales cannot be ordered in a hierarchy.

Last but not least, Mashaw has not sought to identify the ideal character of due process in any human association, but in a particular one, though clearly an important one from a comparative viewpoint, and this is the reason why his approach constitutes a valuable starting point in terms of method. A widespread approach, common especially in economic and social theories that are based on rational choice, is instead based on the assumption that there is a sort of 'optimal' model of legal institutions which ought to be used everywhere, regardless of the current state of a certain political system, of its cultural roots, and of its institutional particularities. This approach emerges in the reports of global institutions that propose a somewhat stereotyped view of sound governance.[41] The least that can be said is that the intellectual soundness and practical adequacy of this approach are questionable. Critics convincingly argue that law cannot be simply regarded as a method of solving problems in the manner of an engineer, whose exclusive problem consists in finding and using the appropriate technique.[42] Legal institutions are not shaped only by rational intent, but also by history and culture, and thus are influenced by values.

3. Rationales of Due Process Beyond the State

After explaining the doubts that, on grounds of method, concern any search for an 'optimal' law, in our case a procedural law, it is now time to survey what would seem to be the main features of modern regulatory regimes. This analysis will be developed normatively and empirically. Normatively, it is helpful to highlight the limits of the theories of justice centred on the State. Empirically, it is important to understand whether in the transnational arena the rationales for due process are more or less the same that emerge in the national arena.

The limits of theories of procedural justice centred on the State

In Chapter 1 it was suggested that one should not assume in advance that certain requirements of procedural due process of law that are regarded as being just or

[40] For example, Christian Starck, *Droits fondamentaux, État de droit et Principe démocratique*, 25 focuses on the Rule of Law, democracy, and fundamental rights.

[41] See the OECD's request for 'regulatory coherence' between the various levels of government: OECD, *Recommendations of the Council on Regulatory Policy and Governance*, paragraph 10. See also Daniel C Esty, 'Good Governance at the Supranational Scale: Globalizing Administrative Law' (2006) 115 Yale LJ 1491.

[42] See Martti Koskenniemi, *The Politics of International Law* (Hart, 2001) 73 (for a critique of 'managerialism').

reasonable in a particular institutional framework are also just or reasonable everywhere. This suggestion can now be developed in two respects, which are distinct but related.

A first limit that is common not only to the 'models' of due process just sketched, particularly in view of the asserted superiority of the model that focuses on dignity, but also to several theories about justice—for example, Rawls' theory of justice—is that they have been elaborated in the context of a particular type of polity, that is, a liberal democracy,[43] and it cannot be assumed that other types of polities share the same values. It is perhaps possible to individuate some principles of justice that public authorities must abide by in liberal societies as well as in a larger group, corresponding to what Rawls calls 'well-ordered societies', which include non-liberal societies that are characterized by the respect for at least some elements of political rights and justice.[44] However, the problem with this is not so much that such 'well-ordered societies' are distinct from others that exist in the world we live in;[45] the problem is, rather, that the similarities and dissimilarities that can be observed with regard to those elements of political rights and justice do not necessarily imply the existence of similar and distinctive traits in the regulation of administrative procedure. In fact, the analysis carried out has showed that some requirements—for example, the right to a hearing before a hearing officer, as distinct from an exchange of documents, and the giving reasons requirement for all administrative decisions, as well as for rules—are common to some liberal democracies, but not to all. Hence, a set of procedural due process requirements that suits one group of countries, even though it can be regarded as including the most advanced legal systems of the world, does not necessarily suit another, at least not under the same conditions.[46] On the other hand, some of those requirements—for instance, the respect for a pre-established procedure—are common to liberal and non-liberal democracies, and possibly to polities that have only the appearance of a democracy. In short, analogies and differences concerning administrative procedure are traceable on lines that are much more complex than those of a single type of polity, even assuming that it includes the major legal systems of the world.

Another way to establish a connection between the values upon which liberal democracies are founded and the transnational arena might be to argue that public power must be ordered with reference to such values because they are at the heart of the global community in which we live. The central premise of an important strand in legal literature, known as 'global administrative law',[47] is that most of the issues that concern exercises of power by regional and global authorities are

[43] John Rawls, *Justice as Fairness* (Harvard University Press, 2003) 6–7.

[44] John Rawls, *The Law of Peoples* (Harvard University Press, 1999) 2.

[45] John Rawls, *The Law of Peoples*, 3–4 (distinguishing 'well-ordered societies' from outlaw states, societies burdened by unfavourable conditions, and societies that have a sort of benevolent absolutism).

[46] Thomas Nagel, 'The Problem of Global Justice' (2005) 33 Phil & Public Affairs 113.

[47] Benedict Kingsbury, Nico Krisch, and Richard B Stewart, 'The Emergence of Global Administrative Law' (2005) 68 Law & Cont Probl 15; Nico Krisch and Benedict Kingsbury, 'Introduction: Global Governance and Global Administrative Law in the International Legal Order' (2006) 17 Eur J Int L 1, 3.

administrative in nature and can thus be analysed with reference to values that include the Rule of Law, accountability, and participation.[48] There are, however, two problems with this line of argumentation. First, this framework must be confronted with the traditional strand in international law according to which domestic public law and international public law are separated. This is not to say that I agree with this traditional strand. Quite the contrary, it will be critically examined in Chapter 10. But the question it poses, namely the distinctiveness of international law matters, cannot be ignored or underestimated. The other problem with the 'global administrative law' framework has been its 'disengagement with wider debates about constitutionalism'.[49] Affirming, as it is sometimes done, that the emphasis on accountability and openness provides a means for legitimating global decision-making processes leaves unresolved the question of which ideas and values underlie procedural requirements. In the pages that follow, it will be argued that the legal situations that emerge transnationally often call for distinct consideration on their merits, though 'distinct' does not mean wholly separated.

Rationales for due process requirements: Common traits

Even a quick look at some recent cases, analysed by scholarly writings and even selected in a casebook,[50] shows that there are some common features of due process requirements within and outside the State.

Let us consider, first, a traditional transnational situation, that is to say, the confiscation of a foreign vessel. The *Juno Trader* case furnishes a clear illustration of this. *Juno Trader*, a cargo vessel, under the flag of Saint Vincent and the Grenadines, was confiscated by maritime officers of Guinea-Bissau on grounds that it was illegally fishing inside the exclusive economic zone of that country. The home country brought an action before the International Tribunal for the Law of the Sea (ITLOS), claiming that the provisions of the United Nations Convention on the Law of the Sea (UNCLOS) of 1994 had been breached. The Tribunal endorsed this claim. It found that the host State had infringed both Article 73(2) of the Convention, which provides that arrested vessels and their crews shall be promptly released upon the posting of a reasonable bond or other security. It thus ordered the vessel and crew be promptly released.[51]

The importance of this ruling goes far beyond the correctness of the procedure by which a country's government may exercise its *imperium* against the vessel

[48] Benedict Kingsbury, 'The Concept of "Law" in Global Administrative Law' (2009) 20 Eur J Int'l L 23, 34–41.

[49] Gordon Anthony, 'EU Law's Fundamental Rights Regime and Post-national Constitutionalism: Kadi's Global Setting', in Patrick Birkinshaw and Mike Varney (eds), *The European Union Legal Order after Lisbon* (Kluwer, 2010) 179, 183. His critique is explicitly recognized by Sabino Cassese, 'Administrative Law Without the State? The Challenge of Global Regulation' (2005) 37 NYU J Int'l L & Pol 663 (pointing out that global administrative law lacks 'constitutional foundation').

[50] Sabino Cassese et al, *Global Administrative Law: The Casebook* (3rd edn, IRPA, 2012).

[51] ITLOS, *Juno Trader* (*Saint Vincent and the Grenadines v Guinea Bissau*), Prompt Release, Judgment (2004) ITLOS Reports, 17.

of another country.[52] The Tribunal held that the requirement that the bond or other financial security must be reasonable 'indicates that concern for fairness is' enshrined in it; additionally, it pointed out that the obligation of prompt release includes 'elementary considerations of humanity and due process'.[53] There is discussion, in international law scholarship, as to whether 'elementary considerations of humanity' may already have attained the status of customary international law[54] and probably this is not the way in which the Tribunal intended them. Similarly, it interpreted the provisions agreed by the contracting parties in the light of due process, viewed as a general principle of law. Also, the Tribunal being aware that the contents of due process differ throughout the world, what it imposed was just an 'elementary' standard.

While this way of looking at due process from the traditional perspective of natural justice reflects the traditional adversarial conception of process rights,[55] the standards of conduct imposed on public authorities can be fashioned in other ways, which may be better suited to the particular needs of the interests of groups. That the interest of a group of citizens, as distinct from their individual interests, implies different needs is what was noted before with regard to *Overton Park*. In that case, the Supreme Court deemed that a hearing was necessary, and one that permitted public participation. Interestingly, in this and in other cases interest groups do not merely seek to influence government decision-making, but are involved in it, in order to protect certain collective goals.[56]

A similar need emerged two decades later in a transnational case concerning the exploitation of a gold mine, the Marlin Mine, close to the villages of the Sipakapa population, an ethnic minority of Guatemala. Feasibility studies were carried out and the excavation concession was issued by the national government, which also obtained funds from the International Finance Corporation (IFC). But a non-governmental organization (NGO) aiming at protecting the rights of indigenous peoples brought a complaint to the Compliance Advisor Ombudsman (CAO), an independent agency operating within the framework of World Bank guidelines. It upheld the complaint, referring to the ILO Convention that protects the rights of Indigenous Groups.[57] The Convention covers both issues of substance, such as the safeguarding of both natural resources and cultural traditions, and process, specifying that their protection must be 'effective'.[58] While the CAO dismissed the claims on grounds of substance, it pointed out the need to develop a 'consultation process

[52] Under Article 73, such powers include boarding, inspection, and arrest.

[53] ITLOS, *Juno Trader*, paragraph 77. For further analysis, see Michael White, 'Prompt Release in ITLOS', in Tafsir Malick Ndiaye and Rüdiger Wolfrum (eds), *Law of the Sea, Environmental Law and Settlement of Disputes: Liber Amicorum Judge Thomas A. Mensah* (Martinus Nijhoff, 2009) 1051.

[54] Theodor Meron, *Human Rights and Humanitarian Norms as Customary Law* (Clarendon Press, 1989) 35.

[55] Michael D Bayles, *Procedural Justice. Allocating to Individuals* (Kluwer, 1990) 15.

[56] Martin Shapiro, 'Administrative Law Unbounded: Reflections on Government and Governance' (2001) 8 Indiana J Global Legal St 369, 373.

[57] Convention concerning Indigenous and Tribal Peoples in Independent Countries, n 169 (adopted on 1989 and entered into force in 1991).

[58] Convention concerning Indigenous and Tribal Peoples in Independent Countries, Article 14(2).

that gives affected communities real participation in decisions that will affect them'.[59] Eventually, when the national government organized a public consultation, a clear majority voted against the mining activities and the Constitutional Court dismissed an action aimed at invalidating the vote.[60] Despite several institutional differences with *Overton Park*, concerning the combination of international rules with the guidelines of the World Bank and the role of its ombudsman, two analogies should be noted. One is the non-instrumental justification for procedural due process requirements, the other is the shift from the adversarial conception to consultation processes.[61]

Rationales for due process requirements: Distinctive traits

While the cases just examined are characterized by evident analogies with the cases that arise within a purely national context, a quick look at other cases will bring out some distinctive features. One important difference is the weight that is given to technical expertise and, most of all, to cooperation between national governments. Another is regarding the role played by *raison d'état.*

Consider, first, a case that regards fishing rules for a particular species, the Southern Blue Tuna, in the Pacific Ocean.[62] A few years after the establishment of a particular international regime, the studies it promoted showed and blamed excessive fishing for the impoverishment of the stock of this species of tuna fish. They warned of the risk of reaching the point of no return. After long negotiations, national governments reached an agreement on limits to fishing in order to minimize the risk. But one government—Japan—changed its mind, producing more optimistic studies and deciding to act unilaterally. A complex dispute ensued before a number of courts, including ITLOS, which concluded in a call for more decisive negotiation. Hence the importance of procedures which will allow negotiations to take place under suitable conditions. Interestingly, the rationale served by procedural requirements is not some sort of legal right, even though some theorists discuss whether the collective interest in the preservation of exhaustible natural resources can be considered as a right. It is, rather, cooperation between public authorities, more specifically national governments. The use of this kind of procedure may perhaps not obtain the consent of the supporters of traditional diplomatic methods, but it might be the only way to stop the radicalization of conflicting interests becoming endemic.[63]

[59] CAO, *Follow up Report on Marling Mining Project*, May 2006, 9. Another case concerned the building of a dam in the Himalayas: see Complaint Advisory Ombudsman, *Complaint Regarding the Allain Duhangeon Hydropower Project in Himachal Pradesh—Progress Report*, 2006.

[60] While this case gave rise to litigation before the national constitutional court, others have been brought to the Inter-American Court of Human Rights: see the case of *Saramaka People v Suriname*, Judgment of 28 November 2007, available at http://www.corteidh.or.cr.

[61] See Alfred C Aman, *The Democracy Deficit*, 8 (holding that what is needed is 'more than providing negative rights and remedies').

[62] This dispute is examined more in depth in Chapter 7, paragraph 2, p. 125.

[63] Cesare Romano, 'The Southern Bluefin Tuna Dispute. Hints of a World to Come ... Like it or Not' (2001) 32 Ocean Development & Int'l L 314.

Both interest balancing and cooperation lie at the heart of a dispute that is particularly important for present purposes, the *Shrimp* case. As observed in Chapter 3, before introducing new rules about fishing for shrimps with turtle-excluder devices, the US administration consulted its regulated industry and received evidence and arguments brought by environmental associations. It also negotiated a gradual adjustment of fishing regulation with some neighbour States. From the first point of view, the question that arose was whether the national regulator was pursuing the general public interest or, rather, the interests of a specific firm or group of firms,[64] which was partially coincidental with the view of NGOs. From the second point of view, there was a clear prima facie case that the US administration had treated its partners differently, discriminating against some of them.

The decisions taken by panel and, in particular, by the AB have already been discussed in Chapters 3 and 4. For our purposes here it suffices to observe that the AB did not substitute its own view on what the decision-maker—the US government—should have decided to do, but on how it should have done so. What should be considered now is why it did so. It devoted attention to both the internal and external dimension of decision-making processes. Externally, it held, the US government failed to respect the principle according to which all World Trade Organization (WTO) contracting parties must be given 'similar opportunities to negotiate'.[65] It pointed out the failure of the US to engage in serious negotiations with the aim of concluding fair agreements with Asian countries, while some Caribbean countries were provided with a period of time for adjusting their own standards. Internally, when the ban on imports coming from countries that did not use turtle-excluder devices was introduced, the administration failed to respect basic notice and comment requirements; nor did it provide reasons for the rejection of applications for certification.

One way to look at this decision is to observe that there is a logic in the line of reasoning followed by the AB, although the first flaw can be understood in terms of lack of fairness or good faith in negotiation, while the other concerns more specifically procedural due process of law. It might be argued, by way of response, that this way of looking at procedural aspects misses a very important dimension of due process; that is, the AB erred because procedural protections against any arbitrary and capricious conduct rest on the necessity to cope with the asymmetry between holders of public powers and individuals, while this was a dispute between national governments. This argument, however, must be sustained, not merely stated. It is by no means self-evidently true. The contention that there is an improper use of procedural protections will be considered in Chapter 6. Leaving this aside for the present, it ought to be mentioned that, while issues of process can be distinguished from issues of substance, the dissatisfaction with the way in which the AB has dealt with the protection of the environment[66] is not unrelated to its procedural path.

[64] See Gregory S Shaffer, *Defending Interests: Public–private Partnerships in WTO Litigation* (The Brookings Institution, 2003).

[65] *Shrimp III*, paragraphs 115 and 122.

[66] Martin Rietvelt, 'Multilateral Failure: A Comprehensive Analysis of the Shrimp/Turtle Decision' (2004–5) 15 Indiana Int'l & Comp L Rev 473.

Similarly, what is at stake in the disputes concerning individuals and groups targeted by the antiterrorism measures taken by the institutions of the EU and the United Nations (UN) is not simply an old issue of public law, the impact of *raison d'état* ('reasons of State') on legal rights. It would be wrong to conceive *raison d'état* simply as a justification for arbitrariness or as a general derogation from the rule of law. It should be seen, rather, as an attempt to bring the fundamental interest of a community to be preserved as such into the legal dimension.[67] Even in this guise, however, *raison d'état* has had a huge impact on legal rights, as observed by Charles McIlwain.[68] However, what is at stake in such disputes is the interest of collective security that lies at the heart of the resolutions adopted by the UN Security Council. When such disputes reach the EU, its courts acknowledge the existence of such an interest, but they follow different approaches. The lower court asserts that such an interest cannot be balanced with the procedural and substantive rights of individuals and groups targeted by the freezing of the funds, unless such rights are included within the peremptory norms of international law (*jus cogens*).[69] By contrast, the ECJ follows the consolidated approach of interest balancing, thus weighing collective security and individual process rights, and reaches the conclusion that the contested regulation must be annulled. There are few doubts that the lower court erred in affirming that only *jus cogens* might limit exercises of power by UN authorities. There are many more differing views as to whether maximizing process rights, following the logic of preserving and enhancing the autonomy of the legal order of the EU, undermines the primacy of international law and thus frustrates recent attempts to achieve cooperation against global threats, such as transnational terrorism.[70]

While the main concern of academics and politicians is with the relations between regional and global legal systems, I have a distinct concern. I will argue that the failure to identify, if not all, the main values protected by due process in the transnational arena would lead to an inadequate conception not only of the rationales for due process requirements, but also of their functioning. In particular, I will propose an approach that stresses the importance of a plurality of rationales.

[67] See Christian Autexier, *Introduction au droit public allemand* (Presses universitaires de France, 1997) 279 (noting that in Germany the right to be heard can be limited if an overriding public interest so requires, but this derogation has been strictly interpreted).

[68] Charles H McIlwain, *Constitutionalism—Ancient and Modern* (first published 1948; The Law Book Exchange, 2006) 147 ('all the rights of personality we hold dearest … have always been endangered when "reasons of state" have been thought to require it').

[69] This view has been adumbrated by Christian Tomuschat, 'Comment to Case T-315/01', 549.

[70] Andrea Gattini, 'Comment—Joined Cases C-402/05 & 415/05, *Kadi v. Council and Al Barakaat v. Council and Commission*' (2009) 46 Common Mkt L Rev 213; Gráinne de Búrca, *The European Court of Justice and the International Legal Order After Kadi* (2010) 51 Harvard Int'l LJ 1, 36. See also Eric Barbier de la Serre, 'Procedural Justice in the European Community Case-law concerning the Right of the Defence: Essentialist and Instrumental Trends' (2006) 12 Eur P L 225 (for the thesis that the ECJ has traditionally oscillated between an approach focused on procedural fairness and another focused on the specific interests protected by procedural constraints).

4. A First Cut at the Argument

In earlier chapters I observed that the requirements of procedural due process of law that are set out by national legal systems and those that are set out by regional and global regulatory regimes have both common and distinctive traits. Sometimes such requirements are largely similar, if not the same. For example, regardless of the national or international nature of the employer, when disciplinary procedures are brought against civil servants, the procedure previously defined must be respected, 'some kind of hearing' must be provided, and reasons, even adequate reasons, must be given. Sometimes, procedural requirements are instead shaped in a different manner. Precisely because their use is invoked by a more differentiated typology of subjects, including public authorities such as States, the same procedural device becomes an instrument to achieve a different goal, for example, a State's involvement in the administrative procedure of another, as it emerged in the WTO's *Shrimp* case. There is not simply a difference of standards, therefore, but a different function performed by procedural requirements.

It would be wrong, moreover, to overestimate the importance of the adversarial type of logic that inspires some legal institutions.[71] This dialectical kind of logic is not the only important one in law. There are others. Giving an authority the possibility to use the contribution of individuals expresses a logic that is not necessarily *adversarial.* Many procedural safeguards are not directed at bringing to a halt the course of a public action or blocking its effects. They ensure that a certain activity (hearings, consulting) is carried out first. Otherwise, they enable individuals and groups to invest the authority with the power to enact a rule or a decision with high costs, and not only economic ones, which make a particular course of action inadvisable. Or they require the final decision to be expressed in a specific way.

In order to make sense of both the particularities and complexities of transnational legal situations, two sets of rationales, instrumental and non-instrumental, will be outlined. The first goes beyond the traditional viewpoint of the right of defence, emphasizes the importance of dignity, and considers distinctively collaboration and participation. The other two rationales are, instead, centred on good administration, with its various interpretations, and cooperation between public authorities. In the discussion over the next two chapters of this Part attempts will be made to clarify the various aspects of such rationales, as they emerge from legal texts, such as bilateral treaties and multilateral conventions, as well as from arbitral and judicial decisions.

[71] Robert Kagan, *Adversarial Legalism. The American Way of Law* (Harvard University Press, 2001).

6

Dignity and Participation

This chapter focuses on non-instrumental rationales for due process requirements. First, it examines legal interactions between private parties—including citizens and other individuals, social groups, such as environmental associations, and businesses—and public authorities in a transnational context, in an attempt to shed light on the various ways in which the requirements of procedural due process of law are influenced by the ideal of dignity. Second, in contrast with the widespread tendency to define all such legal interactions, generically, as 'participation', a distinction will be made between the right of defence, consultation, and participation. The next chapter will consider instrumental rationales.

1. The Right of Defence

A helpful starting point for our analysis is Adam Smith's assertion that 'the end of justice is to secure from injury and that is the foundation of civil government'.[1] Smith used this characterization of justice as the basis for his argument according to which the sovereign's duty is not simply to administer justice, but to do so fairly and that this is a precondition for promoting trade and cooperation between nations.

This line of reasoning is not ahistorical or merely theoretical. It lies at the roots of general and particular rules of international law, such as the prohibition to deny justice to aliens and the obligation to release vessels with the flag of another State respectively. Under the Law of the Sea Convention, State officers have several and relevant discretionary powers, including boarding, inspection, and confiscation of vessels. Arrest of the crew is also allowed. However, State officers are required to act in accordance with the rules of law that reflect the engagements they have reciprocally exchanged. A good example is Article 73(2) of United Nations Convention on the Law of the Sea (UNCLOS), which provides that arrested vessels and their crews shall be promptly released upon the posting of a reasonable bond or other security. The scope for arbitrary action that in former times frequently occasioned conflict, political and sometimes military, between States is reduced. It is reduced, *a fortiori*, when courts interpret this requirement in the light of general principles

[1] Adam Smith, *Lectures on Justice, Police, Revenue and Arms* (1763, first published by Clarendon Press, 1896) 4.

Due Process of Law Beyond the State. First Edition. Giacinto della Cananea. © Giacinto della Cananea 2016.
Published 2016 by Oxford University Press.

of law, as the International Tribunal for the Law of the Sea (ITLOS) did in the *Juno Trader* case.

The Tribunal referred to 'elementary considerations of humanity and *due process*'.[2] Both 'humanity' and 'due process' clearly rest on moral considerations. However, it would be wrong to think that ITLOS used these concepts merely rhetorically. Such concepts, in particular due process of law, reflect the idea that individuals enjoy rights in relation to the State, not only that of which they are nationals. Individuals must therefore be treated, relatively at least, with respect. More importantly, their freedom cannot be arbitrarily limited. Accordingly, absent any overriding and duly justified reason of public interest, they must be promptly released, that is, be left free to leave. This transnational legal situation is not, of course, immune from practical problems. However, it shows the importance of a trend towards recognition of the importance of individuals and their interests.

For some decades this trend has also affected supranational authorities. Consider, for example, the ruling of the ECJ in *Hoechst*, a 'classic' competition case. Under regulation n 17/1962, the Commission found that there were grounds to suspect the existence of agreements or concerted practices for the fixing of prices. It then asked the German competition authority to carry out an inspection and a search warrant was obtained from the *Amstgericht Frankfurt am Main*. The inspection confirmed the suspicions of the Commission, which issued a fine. *Hoechst* contested it on the grounds that the inspection infringed its fundamental right to the inviolability of the home and that its process rights had been violated. The Court dismissed the first argument, devoting considerable attention to the second. It attributed its respect for the inviolability of home, seen as a general principle of public law common to the legal systems of the Member States. However, it held, such right was affirmed in regard to the private dwellings of natural persons, but not to business premises.[3] Nor did the Court find any limit to the intervention of public authorities in this respect in Article 8 of the European Convention on Human Rights (ECHR).[4] The reason given was that 'the protective scope of that article is concerned with the development of man's personal freedom and may not therefore be extended to business premises'.[5]

In the other respect, the Court summarized its established case law about the right of defence. It began by affirming that protection against arbitrary or disproportionate intervention was a general principle of Community law. It then specified

[2] ITLOS, *Juno Trader* (*Saint Vincent and the Grenadines v Guinea Bissau*), Prompt Release, Judgment [2004] ITLOS Reports, 17, paragraph 77 (emphasis added).

[3] ECJ, Joined Cases 46/87 and 227/88, *Hoechst AG v Commission* [1988] ECR 2859, paragraph 17.

[4] Article 8(2) ECHR provides: 'There shall be no interference by a public authority with the exercise of this right except such as is in accordance with the law and is necessary in a democratic society in the interests of national security, public safety or the economic well-being of the country, for the prevention of disorder or crime, for the protection of health or morals, or for the protection of the rights and freedoms of others.'

[5] ECJ, Joined Cases 46/87 and 227/88, *Hoechst AG v Commission*, paragraph 18. In another ruling, the lower court stressed that the Commission cannot rely on documents undisclosed to the undertaking: CFI, Case T-148/99, *Tréfilunion v Commission* [1995] ECR II-1063.

that Commission officials were entitled to carry out searches only in respect of certain essential procedural guarantees. An opportunity to be heard had to be provided and this implied that the undertaking should be 'entitled to an opportunity to know and meet, with the weapons of rebuttal evidence, ... unfavorable evidence'.[6] Moreover, the Commission had to state the essential reasons upon which its decision ordering an inspection was based. This was, the Court said, 'a fundamental guarantee of the rights of the defence of the undertakings concerned'.[7]

This approach was quite similar to that of the French administrative court. This is hardly surprising, since the influence of French administrative law, especially on the European Community (EC) system of judicial review, is well known. It was natural, therefore, to look first at French law, as Advocate General Warner did in *Transocean Marine Paint Association*.[8] But the French doctrine of *droit de la défense* that had been developed in the 1940s was based on the idea that, although general principles of administrative law could be identified without a textual basis, such principles could not prevail over statutory legislation.[9] Moreover, the French doctrine of *droit de la défense* only applied where an administrative measure adversely affected an individual interest.[10] Though encapsulating the Treaty's concern for the respect of 'essential procedural requirements', this conception failed to fully appreciate the constitutional dimension of due process, though it emerged from the bill of rights that the Court of Justice had referred to since the early 1970s, the ECHR. In particular, according to the European Court of Human Rights (ECtHR), the protection accorded to a residence may, under certain circumstances, extend to business premises.[11] It is, however, another aspect of the constitutional dimension of due process emerging from the ECHR that is particularly relevant for present purposes, namely its importance for the protection of human dignity.

2. From the Right of Defence to the Protection of Dignity

It is commonplace that, especially after 1945, considerations of human dignity have assumed an ever increasing importance in modern legal systems. Both modern constitutions and treaties refer to dignity,[12] regarded as being 'inherent' to human persons. Provisions of this type carry with them implications that are important for procedural due process of law.

[6] Kenneth C Davis, *Administrative Law: Cases, Texts, Problems* (6th edn, West Publishing, 1972) 160.

[7] ECJ, Joined Cases 46/87 and 227/88, *Hoechst AG v Commission*, paragraph 14.

[8] ECJ, Case 17/74, *Transocean Marine Paint Association v Commission* [1974] ECR 1063.

[9] The 'classic' analysis is that of Benoît Jeanneau, *Les principes généraux du droit dans la jurisprudence administrative* (Sirey, 1954) (considering the different roles of general principles).

[10] John A Usher, *The General Principles of EC Law* (Longman, 1998) 73.

[11] Eur Ct HR, judgment of 16 December 1992, case *Niemietz v Germany* (application no 13710/88) Series A, No 251-B, 33.

[12] See W Michael Reisman, *The Quest for World Order and Human Dignity in the Twenty-first Century* (The Hague Academy of International Law, 2012) 263 (examining external ways to change national arrangements concerning human rights).

The dignitarian value of process rights

The concept of human dignity characterizes the constitutions of peoples belonging to the various portions of the globe, though it has been convincingly held that their norms are often designed to achieve different purposes. It also characterizes international documents, including the Rousseauvian incipit of the Universal Declaration of Human Rights ('all human beings are born free and equal in dignity and rights'), the similar incipit of the ECHR (opening with a 'full recognition of the inherent dignity of all human beings'), and the more sober provision of the American Convention on Human Rights (whose Article 11 provides that 'everyone has the right to have his honor respected and his dignity recognized'). Under these provisions, and others having more or less similar contents, dignity is regarded substantively as a value in itself. There is also a potential value-generating impact of dignity that may allow a reinterpretation of process rights such as the right to be heard and the right to know the reasons that justify the disadvantageous decision taken by a public authority. In short, respect for the dignity of any individual is also a rationale for due process values.[13]

A recent dispute shows well the potential value of dignity in terms of procedural due process of law—the judgment of the ECtHR in *Tysiac*.[14] Tysiac, a Polish citizen mother of two children and expecting a third one, was diagnosed as seriously risking her sight if she went ahead with the pregnancy. She contacted the health service and presented them with this diagnosis, applying for an exemption from the prohibition of termination of pregnancy. But the doctors of the public health service failed to take into consideration the documents exhibited. They listened to her very briefly and in a desultory manner. Ultimately, they rejected her request for an abortion. The pregnancy thus went ahead, but unfortunately its consequences on the woman's sight were even worse than expected. When Polish courts dismissed her application for compensation, she appealed to the Strasbourg Court.

More than one option was available for the Court. It could have endorsed the applicant's attempt to found her claim on the right to the integrity of family life, which is affirmed by Article 8 ECHR.[15] It could have used it as a basis to discount any interference by the State in a choice pertaining to the couple or to the woman alone. An alternative reasoning could be based on Article 6, which guarantees the right to a fair trial. There was no shortage of earlier and well-known, albeit controversial, precedents, particularly that followed by the US Supreme Court since 1977.[16] This would, of course, have been a questionable choice, and much more political than is usual in the Court's judgments.

[13] Sanford H Kadish, 'Methodology and Criteria in Due Process Adjudication' (1974) 66 Yale L Rev 319, 346; Robert S Summers, 'Evaluating and Improving Legal Processes—A Plea for Process Values' (1974) 60 Cornell L Rev 1, 4.

[14] Eur Ct HR, judgment of 20 March 2007, case *Tysiac v Poland* (application no 5410/03) [2007] ECHR 219, I, § 4.

[15] For further analysis of the Court's precedents, see Frederick Sudre (ed), *Le droit au respect de la vie privée au sens de la Convention européenne des droits de l'homme* (Bruylant, 2005).

[16] US Supreme Court, *Roe v Wade*, 410 US, 113, 164 (1973).

A strong obstacle opposed a solution of the first kind. Polish legislation on abortion may appear particularly restrictive in comparison to others, and also with legislation previously in force in Poland. However, it reflects the widespread feeling of the majority of Poles, and they are not isolated in Europe. Suffice it to mention the tenacity with which the majority of Irish people included the prohibition of abortion in the Constitution, and insisted on it again when it came to ratifying the TEU.[17] But even if the majority decision in Poland were completely isolated, it would not be any less valid. The ECHR recognizes that it is a prerogative of political institutions to decide how best to balance the various interests expressed by society. The basic assumption is that the majority can decide what is considered to be the public interest.[18] On the basis of this assumption, the Court has often (even too often, according to some critics)[19] applied the 'margin of appreciation'. This doctrine is not unknown, though differently formulated, to other supranational judges such as the CJEU. It implies a degree of deference to the limitations to the fundamental rights that States deem it necessary to impose. This makes it possible to balance legal and political necessities, an exercise which is common to several higher courts.

In *Tysiac*, the Court initially followed this line of reasoning, but later changed its approach. It pointed out in its premises the various choices that States have made in regulating the termination of pregnancy and in establishing the procedures that must be followed by individuals. But after doing so, the Court made an observation that may seem obvious and almost axiomatic: a State may autonomously create its own rules, but once they have been produced, it must abide by them. This stylized remark implies that the choice to establish a procedure takes on a certain significance. Whatever a State's substantive choices about abortion, it must apply its own procedures properly and accurately. The problem with the conduct of the Polish government was that, despite the fact that a 'relatively simple procedure for obtaining a lawful abortion' existed, the procedure did not deal with the disagreement between the woman and the doctors.[20] Nor, in *Tysiac*'s case had any particular procedural technique been used to deal with such disagreement and to take into account the woman's volition. The Court thus came—with a striking 6 to 1 majority—to the conclusion that the Polish government had failed to fulfil the obligations stemming from the ECHR.

There are various possible rationales for this reading of the Convention. The first refers, following the logic of good faith, to a standard affirmed by most legal systems, by virtue of which no body can act incoherently with its previous conduct

[17] See Protocol n 35 added to the TEU, providing that 'nothing in the Treaties ... shall affect the application in Ireland of Article 40.3.3 of the Constitution of Ireland'.

[18] John H Ely, *Democracy and Distrust. A Theory of Judicial Review* (Harvard University Press, 1980) 7.

[19] See Jeffrey A Brauch, 'The Margin of Appreciation and the Jurisprudence of the European Court of Human Rights: Threats to the Rule of Law' (2005) 11 Columbia J Eur L 113.

[20] Eur Ct HR, judgment of 20 March 2007, case *Tysiac v Poland*, paragraph 121. See also the Court's former President's extrajudicial assertion that its policy is to protect weaker subjects: Jean-Paul Costa, *La Cour européenne des droits de l'homme. Des juges pour la liberté* (Dalloz, 2013) 113.

(*venire contra factum proprium*), if this behaviour damages other interests that have obtained legal acknowledgement and protection. Another rationale may be found in the Rule of Law values of legal certainty and protection of legitimate expectations. The ECHR provides still another and more specific rationale because Article 6 recognizes and protects the right to a fair trial. From this point of view, Article 6 goes far beyond the necessary coherence between the conduct of a public authority and the standards of conduct previously set out. It emphasizes the importance that those standards have for human beings. Hence the emphasis placed by the Court on the lack of any procedural guarantee for the patient and the resulting situation of uncertainty.

This does not, however, mean that Article 6, a typically procedural clause, has been converted into a substantive provision, whereby the Court can substitute its own view for that of national elected officials. In my reading, Article 6 retains its own wholly procedural significance. But, precisely for this reason, it implies that an administrative procedure must be applied properly, particularly because public officers act on behalf of society seen as a whole. As a consequence of this, they can neither deny a human being a meaningful opportunity to be heard before a decision potentially affecting his or her life and health is taken, nor comply with this procedural requirement only formalistically and hastily, as they did in *Tysiac*. A procedure is, therefore, not simply an instrument for ensuring the respect of a certain interest that has been acknowledged by the legal system. It is, rather, an instrument for protecting human dignity, by ensuring that each person is enabled to take part in the decision-making process that may adversely affect his or her rights and is told why he or she is being treated unfavourably.[21] In a case such as that of *Tysiac*, the applicant's dignity was affected by the fact that the decision was taken without her participation, as if nothing she could say on the matter of her health could be useful or relevant. Moreover, the consequences of such decision deprived her of the right to live her life the way she wanted.

The dignitarian rationale and its implications

When considering *Tysiac* and other cases where basic process rights are at stake, the distinction sketched before between the models of appropriateness and competence and the model that maximizes dignity reveals all its importance in both its explanatory and its normative potentials. What is particularly problematic in a case such as *Tysiac* is not the deviation from procedural rules, which is susceptible of generating uncertainty,[22] or the risk of inaccuracy, that is particularly evident when the views

[21] See Denis J Galligan, *Due Process and Fair Procedures. A Study of Administrative Procedures* (Clarendon Press, 1996) 140–41 (holding that 'if the person has a special claim because his interests are at stake … he ought to be able to defend or promote his interest in the process') and Christian Autexier, *Introduction au droit public allemand* (Presses universitaires de France, 1997) 278 (noting that in Germany the right to be heard has been based not only on traditional theories of *Rechtsstaat*, but also on the dignity of every human being, as affirmed by Article 1 of the *Grundgesetz*).

[22] Joseph Raz, *The Authority of Law* (Clarendon Press, 1979) 22.

of the affected person are ignored. The model that emphasizes dignity explains all the necessary consequences of the choice to establish a procedure that provides some form of interaction among individuals, though each with a different role (the applicant, the health officers, the decision-maker). At the same time, this model also suggests that a public authority is constrained in its conduct by requirements previously set out by the rules of law.

Clearly, the approach to due process of law in this case is modelled on ideas of fairness and justice, if not of equity. It is not surprising that this model seems more congenial to lawyers who are concerned with government interference with fundamental rights.[23] The model suggests that when two or several interests are legally relevant for the decision a public authority is going to take, they must all be taken into account. Individuals do not simply have an expectation that public officials act benevolently when taking a decision that can adversely affect their lives, but have a right to be heard before such decision is taken, as well as a right to be adequately informed of all implications deriving from the decision potentially affecting them. This understanding of procedures, which appears to be more consistent with the choice to give value to a series of rights because they are considered essential for a decent existence, is based on an assumption and has further implications that are worth mentioning. The underlying assumption is that procedural requirements must be viewed as providing individuals with rights that are part of what it means to be a human person. If an authority either takes a decision that potentially has an adverse effect on the life of an individual without even giving him or her an opportunity to be heard or does not give any kind of explanation for such decision, then such conduct is susceptible of affecting negatively the individual's sense of autonomy and personhood.[24] As observed in the previous chapter, at the root of this argument there is the theory that it is imperative that every person be treated as a goal, not as a means. This line of reasoning comes close to Lon Fuller's argument that every deviation from the principles that assure the law's inner morality 'is an affront to man's dignity'.[25]

This may suggest that individual rights as such or at least some of them are inherently 'absolute' and do not allow, therefore, any interference by public authorities. However, whatever the attractiveness of the idea that 'absolute' rights exist as a matter of legal theory,[26] procedural requirements have both advantages and costs, which must be carefully weighed. For instance, while the individual's sense of autonomy and personhood would be irremediably and intolerably infringed by the lack of any kind of hearing whatsoever, compelling reasons of public interest may justify the public authority's choice to grant a hearing after a provisional decision has already been taken. In this sense, it has been held that informing the person

[23] Jerry Mashaw, *Due Process in the Administrative State* (Yale University Press, 1985) 151.

[24] Paul Craig, 'Procedures and Administrative Decisionmaking: A Common Law Perspective' (1993) 3 Eur Rev Public L 56, 58.

[25] Lon Fuller, *The Morality of Law* (2nd edn, Yale University Press, 1967) 162.

[26] For a contrary opinion, see George Christie, 'The Adjudication of Human Rights', in *Philosophia Practica Universalis. Festschrift fur Hruschka* (Duncker & Humblot, 2005) 427.

targeted as a suspected terrorist that his funds are going to be frozen risks jeopardizing the effectiveness of this measure and, thus, the collective security interest that it serves.[27] In short, there is a need for a balance.[28] A balancing exercise may also imply that administrative procedures can vary depending on the context.[29] Moreover, procedures may vary because of their consequences in terms of costs or *lourdeur*. Several legal systems, for example, provide different types of notice, depending on the number of persons that must receive it. Whether involving a large number of persons in that procedure raises not simply more complex issues, but a different type of issue is the question that will now be addressed.

3. From the Right of Defence to Collaboration and Participation

At the beginning of this chapter I suggested that a central theme of this book is that the classic doctrine of the right of defence offers only one part of a theory of procedural due process of law, as there is a variety of forms of interactions between individuals and groups, on the one hand, and public authorities, on the other. In the remaining portions of the chapter an attempt will be made to present a more differentiated picture, based on a distinction between three kinds of relationships: the defence of the individual, cooperation between private parties and public authorities, and participation in a narrower sense.[30] The crucial normative question is whether not only individuals but also groups should be involved in administrative procedures, while the crucial empirical question is whether they are involved and, if so, how.

The case for and against involving the public in administrative procedures

In this respect, the distinction traced before between consultation and participation is both theoretically and practically justified. Theoretically, consultation and participation rest on instrumental and non-instrumental rationales respectively. Consultation performs an instrumental role in the sense that it may help the administration attain an accurate decision, for example, by providing regulators with better knowledge of the available technical standards for electronic communications.

[27] CFI, Case T-284/08, *OMPI v Council* [2008] ECR II-334.

[28] Bruce Ackerman, *Before the Next Attack. Preserving Civil Liberties in an Age of Terrorism* (Yale University Press, 2006) 29.

[29] Eur Ct HR, judgment of 10 May 2001, application 23452/94, *Osman v United Kingdom* [1998] ECHR 101.

[30] For this approach, see Sabino Cassese, *Il privato e il procedimento amministrativo. Una analisi della legislazione e della giurisprudenza* (Mucchi, 1971). See also Alfred C Aman, *The Democracy Deficit. Taming Globalization through Law Reform* (New York University Press, 2004) 10 (distinguishing participation from 'negative rights and remedies').

It is in this sense, for example, that if an agency is considering where a waste storage facility should be built, providing access opportunities to environmental associations is said to be susceptible of improving the quality of decision-making, as well as the implementation of decisions[31] which might otherwise be regarded as lacking the necessary legitimacy. By contrast, participation is based on a non-instrumental rationale, in the sense that it ensures that human dignity is adequately respected by public administrators when taking decisions that potentially affect the lives of individuals and groups. Following another line of reasoning, participation performs a democratic role, in the sense of allowing citizens to express their views within decision-making processes.[32] The distinction between consultation and participation is also relevant from a practical point of view, given the clear preference of administrators for the former. The explanation is simple: since consultation can minimize disagreements, and thus transaction costs, for administrators it is desirable to have appropriate procedures for consulting affected parties without the obstacles that may derive from participation.

Normatively, two main arguments are used against the involvement of groups such as associations of citizens or organizations of entrepreneurs: the first excludes any involvement in these procedures because of their administrative nature; the second criticizes its impact on administrative action.

The argument that criticizes any involvement of the public in administrative procedures is related to traditional theories of government and can be better understood by distinguishing between two variants. The first variant, that Richard Stewart has called the 'transmission belt' model of administration, holds that, whatever the reasons in favour of the maxim *audi alteram partem* as far as individuals are concerned, there is no need for the public to be involved in administrative procedures. The reason is that, within a democratic institutional framework, administrators implement policies decided by the people's representatives, particularly through legislation. The legitimacy of their decisions, therefore, is based on their coherence with legislative prescriptions.[33] Another variant holds that there is a reciprocal exclusion between democracy and administration, the former being about the pursuit of the interests of society seen as a whole, while the latter is about individual interests. As a consequence of this, with the possible exception of local government, in administrative action there is no representation.[34]

The problem with this argument is that it is based on the traditional assumption—a certain view of separation of powers—according to which the administration exercises discretionary powers in individual cases, while rules concerning an

[31] These positive outcomes are associated with consultation by the guidelines issued for the implementation of the Convention of Aarhus: see UN ECE *Almaty* Decision II/4 (2005), available at http://www.unece.org/.

[32] For a discussion of these arguments, see Paul Craig, *Public Law and Democracy in the United Kingdom and the United States of America* (Oxford University Press, 1991).

[33] Richard B Stewart, 'The Reformation of American Administrative Law' (1974–75) 88 Harvard L Rev 1675.

[34] Carl Schmitt, *Verfassungslehre* (Duncker & Humblot, 1928) paragraph 20.IV. See also Hans Kelsen, *Von Wesen und Wert der Demokratie* (Mohr, 1929), especially Chapter 7.

undetermined class of subjects or even all of them are reserved to Parliament. But this view fails to provide an account of much of today's activities of public administrations in two respects. First, there are individual decisions potentially affecting a large part of the population, such as the authorization to build and manage a nuclear plant. In these cases, open procedures are susceptible of improving the quality of decisions and, to the extent to that they admit conflict (between ideas and interests) within the public sphere, they can play a legitimizing role, as observed by Luhmann.[35] Second, modern societies are not regulated only by legislation, but also by innumerable rules, often having a technical nature, issued by public administrations, for example, with regard to the marketing of pharmaceutical products and to the delivery of electronic communications. Awareness of these weaknesses lies at the base of the idea that administrative procedures should ensure an adequate involvement of affected interests in the process of administrative policy formation.[36]

That the exercise of administrative power should be influenced by openness and participation in order to be acceptable is, however, criticized on another ground. The troubling element is that opening procedures to the holders of collective interests entails a serious risk. It is the risk of making things worse. At the root of this critique there is an assumption that ought to be made explicit. The assumption is that, since public administrators are often captured by the economically stronger, such as multinational corporations, opening administrative procedures is either futile or perverse:[37] futile because other voices are unlikely to be heard, or even perverse, in the sense that it can strengthen those who can spend more money on presenting documents and evidence and on hiring skilled consultants and lawyers.[38] This scepticism is particularly strong among some discontents of globalization. They use a variant of this argument, holding that, whatever the desirability and feasibility of consultation and participation in national decision-making processes, they are not suitable to a transnational context because they negatively affect national styles of policymaking.

On normative grounds, a first response to the argument of futility or perversity is that, because organized or wealthier social groups have many ways to influence the work of administrators, openness and participation can provide all citizens with fair and equal opportunities to engage in a public debate. Underlying this way of looking at public decision-making is the idea that open competition between affected interests is desirable and healthy, as suggested by some theories of democracy. Another response emphasizes the central importance of dignity in modern

[35] See Niklas Luhmann, *Legitimation durch Verfahren*, Chapter 4 and, in secondary literature, Stefan Machura, 'The Individual in the Shadow of Powerful Institutions: Niklas Luhmann's Legitimation by Procedure as Seen by Critics', in Klaus F Rohl and Stefan Machura (eds), *Procedural Justice* (Ashgate, 1997) 183.

[36] Jerry Mashaw, *Due Process in the Administrative State*, 23.

[37] This terminology is borrowed from Alfred O Hirschmann, *The Rhetoric of Reaction: Perversity, Futility, Jeopardy* (Harvard University Press, 1991).

[38] Matthew McCubbins, Roger Noll, and Barry Weingast, 'Administrative Procedures as Instruments of Political Control' (1987) 33 J Law & Org 257, 266 highlight the problem of 'subsidized representation'.

legal systems. The idea is that in many instances people are not affected by the consequences of administrative action as individuals, but as members of a social group. It is only if administrative procedures are open to such groups, therefore, that they can obtain information about issues of public significance,[39] acquire or improve socially relevant skills, and, thus, fully develop their sense of dignity and worthiness. Following this line of reasoning, the objection based on futility and perversity is met by affirming that an equal opportunity to be involved in the process of administrative policy formation is a condition for ensuring that human dignity is fully respected.

Consulting requirements

If, as the analysis just exposed suggests, the normative objections to opening administrative procedures can be met on different grounds, it remains to be seen whether, empirically, procedures are open to stakeholders in a transnational context and, if so, how.

There are a variety of forms of consultation. The main differences concern who is consulted, how, and whether this is done within the accomplishment of a more or less formalized requirement. From the last viewpoint, consultation can be a choice of the public authority. For example, the Basel Committee often consults the regulated industry in order to ensure that the standards it proposes keep pace with technological developments in the financial services sector. The norms governing civil aviation, instead, impose on the International Civil Aviation Authority a duty to consult airlines' representative bodies. Another distinctive trait is that consulted stakeholders may include regulated businesses and also associations of consumers or other groups. The rules governing consultation may be more or less binding. Finally, while some rules make the obligation to consult the public a formal requirement, others lay down more specific obligations, such as hearing the opinion of the interested parties, making it public, or referring to it in their decisions.[40] The norms governing civil aviation impose not only a duty to consult airlines' representative bodies, but also the obligation to provide the grounds for its decisions. The second requirement reinforces the first, requiring the authority to justify its choices, and promotes a certain degree of fairness. In both cases, the basic idea is that regulators, insofar as they are called upon to equip themselves with adequate technical expertise, work in an environment where technological progress is very rapid.

In other cases consulting individuals and groups can be, and often is, less easy. If, for example, a railway is going to be built or technologically transformed or a coal power plant is susceptible of being converted into another using renewable energies,

[39] Alfred C Aman, *The Democracy Deficit*, 12; Mario P Chiti, *Partecipazione popolare e pubblica amministrazione* (Pacini, 1977).

[40] See, for example, Articles 22 and 33 of EC Directive n 22/2002 on universal service [2002] OJ L/108, 51. See also Article 16 of the Aarhus Convention and implementing guidelines, according to which procedures that enable access in environmental matters improve 'the quality of decision-making': UN ECE *Almaty decision II* (2005) 74.

the concerns expressed by residents' groups and environmental associations can be better met in open procedures, where evidence and arguments can be discussed. This method of reasoning shows, however, a sort of moral intellectualism, to the extent to that it presupposes that people will do what is 'right' as soon as they are provided with an opportunity to understand what is right.[41] Additionally, empirical studies point out that citizens' responses are often emotional or ideological.[42]

This does not mean, however, that their concerns can simply be ignored. Let us suppose again that an agency is carrying out a procedure to build a tunnel in order to modernize a railway. The question that arises is whether the agency undertakes an adequate technical assessment. Imagine that an association set up by some citizens were to present scientific papers attesting that the work presents risks to groundwater. Obviously, the agency is not obliged to accept their view, yet it cannot ignore the documents and evidence they have submitted. Otherwise, not only would the involvement of stakeholders be meaningless, but the agency would also be unlikely to reach an accurate decision on the substance of the case.[43] This does not imply that its decision is automatically void. However, the refusal to take those documents and evidence into account should be considered a symptom of the poor exercise of the power of choice and decision, reviewable by the courts, though their standards of review vary considerably.[44]

Citizens' participation through supervisory mechanisms

The point has already been made that administrative procedures do not always follow the adversarial logic that characterizes a trial, and which is replicated by quasi-judicial procedures such as those through which the European Union (EU) Commission ensures the respect of the rules that limit the issuing of State aid to public and private companies.[45]

The move away from the adversarial logic becomes evident, in particular, when considering participatory instruments in a transnational context.[46] The *Marlin Mining* case, mentioned in Chapter 5, is not an isolated case. Academic works concerning the procedures for the management of funds generated by the World Bank advance the theory that the rationales underlying such procedures are not

[41] From another viewpoint, Susan Rose-Ackerman, 'Regulation and Public Law in Comparative Perspective' (2010) 60 Un Toronto LJ 519, 528 notes that 'analysis cannot eliminate disagreement about values'.

[42] See Bruce B Clary and Michael E Kraft, 'Citizen Participation and the Nimby Syndrome: Public Response to Radioactive Waste Disposal' (1991) 44 Western Pol Q 299.

[43] An example is provided by the ruling of the ECJ, Case C-212/91, *Angelopharm v Freie Hansestadt Hamburg* [1994] ECR I-171.

[44] See Catherine Donnelly, 'Participation and Expertise: Judicial Attitudes in Comparative Perspective', in Susan Rose-Ackerman and Peter L Lindseth, *Comparative Administrative Law*, 359 (noting that the American framework 'appears to be strikingly participatory').

[45] Article 6, Council Regulation n 659/1999 of 22 March 1999 [1999] OJ L/83, 1.

[46] Thomas N Hale and Anne-Marie Slaughter, 'Transparency: Possibilities and Limitations' (2006) 30 Fletcher Forum of World Affairs 153, 161 (calling ombudsman 'information courts' and pointing out their dialogue with civil society).

only instrumental, but also non-instrumental, because the communities that are adversely affected by the works financed by the Bank's resources must be involved and their vulnerability is seen as an element which requires particular attention from policymakers. This participatory perspective is borne out by examples.

An interesting example is the World Bank funding of a highway project in Bombay, India. Completion of the work was said to imply significant benefits for the traffic and, ultimately, for businesses. But it required the dismantling of the existing buildings, including those where a significant number of artisans and merchants lived and worked. They tried to express their views, but to no avail. They did not even obtain access to certain documents held by the body that handled the funds. When their protest reached the World Bank's governing bodies, they ordered an inspection, to be carried out by the Inspection Panel.

Before illustrating its conduct in the *Mumbai* case, it is important to bear in mind some points about the Inspection Panel. First, the Panel enjoys autonomy and its role is the supervision of operational policies and procedures to which the procedures for the management of funds generated by the World Bank are subject, but it is not a court.[47] Secondly, its supervision regards the management of the World Bank's activities, not the activities of the States where the infrastructures will be built.[48] Thirdly, if the Inspection Panel finds that the operational policies and procedures have been infringed, it will neither quash the decision taken by the management nor hold it to be void. Rather, it will suggest that a different type of conduct should have been carried out. A revision of the guidelines followed may also be suggested. This is what happened in the *Mumbai* case. The Inspection Panel carried out its checks, found incomplete compliance with the internal guidelines issued by the World Bank, and documented it in of a series of reports.[49] The analysis and recommendations carried out by the Inspection Panel were taken into consideration by the management. More importantly for present purposes, interested parties were given access to the documents and were provided with an opportunity to express their grievances. In the light of this and other similar earlier cases,[50] we can reconsider both the distinction between instrumental and non-instrumental rationales and the argument that participation is either futile or perverse. The distinction between instrumental and non-instrumental rationales, though theoretically relevant, is sometimes practically less important. Bodies such as the Inspection Panel clearly serve primarily to ensure that available funds are used through

[47] For the thesis that the Panel's independence is a function of its 'advisory' role, see Daniel D Bradlow, 'International Organizations and Private Complaints: The Role of The World Bank Inspection Panel' (1993–94) 34 Virginia J Int'l L 553, 574.

[48] Ibrahim Shihata, *The World Bank Inspection Panel* (2nd edn, Oxford University Press, 2002) 85.

[49] Inspection Panel, *India—Mumbai Urban Transport Project*, Report n 34725 of 21 December 2005; *Management Response and Reconsideration in Response to the Inspection Panel Report*, 27 February 2006. Both documents are available at the site http://www.worldbank.org.

[50] For a survey of the initial practice of the Panel, see Dana Clark, Jonathan Fox, and Kay Treakle (eds), *Demanding Accountability: Civil-Society Claims and the World Bank Inspection Panel* (Rowman and Littlefield, 2003). The *Vlora* case is a more recent case: Inspection Panel, *Albania: Power Sector Generation and Restructuring Project* (IDA Credit No 3872 ALB), paragraph 50 (noting that preliminary investigations showed lack of information and involvement of the public).

adequate procedures and that management can be held accountable for its action or inaction.[51] But they may, secondarily, also serve to protect other rationales, such as dignity and respect for those who are affected by those procedures.

This brings us back to the argument that participation is either futile or perverse. A procedure based on the abstract equality of all affected parties may have favoured the economically stronger or the better organized in a certain institutional context. However, we cannot exclude that their influence could have been even greater in the absence of such procedure because other social groups had no informal way of being heard. It is a counterfactual hypothesis that common sense and research by social scientists justify.[52] In the *Mumbai* case, it was a procedure open to all stakeholders that ensured that the interests of the weaker were taken into account and could be afforded protection that they would not otherwise have received. The case thus shows how it is not at all clear that these processes disadvantage weaker groups. Indeed, a participative communitarian approach and an instrumentalist approach may coexist and interact, the latter promoting the former approach to the relationships between those who are entrusted with a power and those who are affected by their decisions. In this sense and within these limits, participation can serve as a corrective to the non-egalitarian characteristics of administrative procedure, seen as an instrument for taking unilateral decisions. Of course, this does not make the Inspection Panel a forum for cases brought by individuals. Still, its actions can give a voice to those who are affected by a procedure so that they can present evidence and arguments that could render a particular course of action inadvisable.

A detour: Third party participation in WTO dispute resolution proceedings

There is, however, another variant of the objection to participation that is based on the argument of perversity. It emerged in the *Shrimp* case with regard to the presentation of arguments and evidence by non-governmental organizations (NGOs) in the form of *amici curiae* briefs.[53] A quick recapitulation of the case might be useful. What was at issue was the decision taken by the US administration to limit the import of fish from some Asian countries on the grounds that their producers did not use fishing devices that could adequately protect sea turtles. Incidentally, it should be noted that the US administration had not negotiated with the governments of these countries, as it had done with the representatives of Caribbean countries, but this is a point to which we well return in the next chapter. Meanwhile,

[51] The new dimension of accountability was pointed out by the Inspection Panel's former President: see Richard E Bissel, 'Institutional and Procedural Aspects', in Gudmundur Alfredsson and Rolf Ring (eds), *The Inspection Panel of the World Bank: A Different Complaints Procedure* (Martinus Nijhoff, 2001) 109.

[52] Molly Beutz, 'Functional Democracy: Responding to Failures of Accountability' (2003) 44 Harvard Int'l LJ 387.

[53] *Shrimp II*. See also *United States—Imposition of Countervailing Duties on Certain Hot-Rolled Lead and Bismuth-Carbon Steel Products Originating in the United Kingdom* (AB Report WT/DS138/AB/R, 10 May 2000).

our focus is on a twofold choice taken by the AB. On grounds of substance, and as a matter of principle, the AB affirmed that the protection of natural exhaustible resources could provide a valid justification for limiting the import of products. But, before reaching this decision, the AB was confronted with a procedural issue—whether *amici curiae* briefs by NGOs could be admitted or solicited.

Since NGOs are not included among the World Trade Organization (WTO)'s contracting parties, they cannot initiate a dispute resolution procedure. Yet, this did not ineluctably prevent them from presenting *amicus curiae* briefs. At the least, the absence of any written rule concerning such briefs may be interpreted in either way. Indeed, while the panel interpreted it in the negative sense, the AB ruled that their briefs could be taken into account. It used the provision of the Understanding on dispute settlement procedures that confers upon it the power to acquire information, to request the submission of relevant documents, and to hear experts. It exercised this option, allowing the production of *amici curiae* briefs, and then lay down rules for the admission of statements by individuals and institutions protecting collective interests.[54] It is interesting to observe that the AB did not simply base this ruling on the inclusion of such briefs within the document presented by one of the contracting parties as the US administration had initially suggested. It held that the panel, and *a fortiori* the AB itself, had 'the discretionary authority either to accept and consider or to reject information and advice submitted to it, whether requested by the panel or not'.[55]

Such a ruling has clearly had an impact on evidence brought before dispute resolution bodies, to the extent that even unsolicited briefs may not be admitted. At the same time, its impact goes well beyond the procedural admissibility of evidence and the panel's access both to the facts and to the interests at stake. For it is clear that such procedural conditions do not serve only to resolve a dispute; they also have a broader impact upon the interests at stake and the holders of such interests. In national jurisdictions, admitting large aggregates of people, instead of individual litigants, has often changed the function of process itself. Battles on standing therefore became increasingly crucial. The AB seemed to follow the approach that emphasizes collaboration, in the sense that it allowed third party intervention because it made a helpful addition to the better understanding of the facts.[56]

There is, however, a considerable variety of opinions as to the legitimacy of this decision. This development can be particularly significant for those who criticize

[54] For further discussion, see David N Palmeter and Petros C Mavroidis, *Dispute Settlement in the World Trade Organization: Practice and Procedure* (2nd edn, Cambridge University Press, 2004) 223; Jorge E Vinuales, 'Amicus Intervention in Investor-State Arbitration' (2006–7) 61 Dispute Resolution J 72 (considering also North American Free Trade Agreement (NAFTA) and International Centre for Settlement of Investment Disputes (ICSID) cases).

[55] *Shrimp II*, paragraph 102. A completely different situation is that of an *amicus curiae* brief presented by another contracting party, admitted by the AB in the case of Morocco: *European Communities—Trade Description of Sardines*, WT/DS231/AB/R, adopted 23 October 2002 (EC regulation establishing standards for preserving sardines contested by Peru).

[56] See Robert Howse, 'Membership and its Privileges: The WTO, Civil Society and the Amicus Brief Controversy' (2003) 9 Eur J Int'l L 496, 508 (asserting that this choice has a sound legal basis in WTO law and in the practice of other international tribunals).

WTO dispute resolution processes because they are inadequately transparent and, participation being limited only to Member States, are not likely to be regarded as legitimate by those whose interests are not fully represented by State representatives.[57] For others, instead, the AB exceeded its powers in admitting this kind of *amicus curiae* brief. Still another point of view holds that this kind of intervention only benefits developed countries where most NGOs have been set up. NGOs would thus tend to maximize Western views about which interests should receive legal acknowledgment and protection, such as the environment. It is not denied here that this can be the case. However, this is not an argument against openness and participation, but an argument against their impact on intergovernmental processes.[58] It does not undermine, therefore, the usefulness of openness and participation in a decision-making process affecting a particular social group, as that of Mumbai traders. Even so, the argument against openness and participation in a transnational context such as that of the WTO fails to appreciate the advantages of a more open and inclusive procedure from the viewpoint of groups that aim at protecting other interests, according to the instrumentalist approach followed by the AB.[59] The reason is, as one commentator has observed, that 'the powerful interests in developed countries, such as corporate interests, have means of making their point of view known in dispute settlement circles that do not depend on *amicus* submissions'.[60] Finally, whether allowing NGOs to submit a brief can determine a shift in the way that substantive issues are considered is quite another matter.[61] In *Shrimp*, this did not happen. It was for precisely that reason that so many environmental activists contested the AB's final decision.

4. Conclusions

Looking back on the preceding discussion, some points deserve particular attention. Courts, arbitral bodies, and other public agencies such as ombudsmen do not conceive their review in narrow terms. Thus, for example, in reviewing governmental action that impinges on the exercise of rights and liberties, a court sympathetic to the tenets of procedural due process of law may prefer not to directly address the substantive policy choices made by a governmental body. That being

[57] Alfred C Aman, *The Democracy Deficit*, 5; Robert Howse, 'Adjudicative Legitimacy and Treaty Interpretation in International Trade Law: The Early Years of WTO Jurisprudence', in Joseph HH Weiler (ed), *The EU, the WTO and the NAFTA* (Oxford University Press, 2000) 35.

[58] For this remark, see Steve Charnovitz, 'Nongovernmental Organizations and International Law' (2006) 100 Am J Int'l L 348, 371.

[59] See James Crawford and Susan Marks, 'The Global Democracy Deficit: An Essay in International Law and Its Limits', in Daniele Archibugi et al (eds), *Re-Imagining Political Community: Studies in Cosmopolitan Democracy* (Cambridge University Press, 1998) 72, 83 (for the thesis that NGOs may contribute to democratizing global decision-making processes).

[60] Robert Howse, 'Membership and its Privileges', 509.

[61] A related perspective is that of how governments, in the framework of the WTO, are influenced by private sector actors: see Gregory Schaffer, *Defending Interests: Public–Private Partnerships in WTO Litigation* (Brookings Institution Press, 2003).

the case, the court may prefer to ascertain whether there is any dysfunction in the decision-making process that accounts for its contrast with human dignity. This would not, however, inhibit the court from exercising its supervisory function in order to control misuses and abuses of power by public authorities. Although a 'process jurisprudence' may appear centred on the enforcement of specifically procedural remedies, a closer look reveals that this is not the case. Neither national and international courts nor other bodies use a strictly positivist approach that focuses uniquely on the text and on legislative intent. They use, instead, a more principled approach that makes sense of broad clauses such as Article 6 ECHR.

One may be tempted, therefore, to view this 'process jurisprudence' as giving legitimate space for the development of conceptions of rights that are more extensive and that cohere with the increase of international legal and political documents aimed at protecting human rights. However, the reality is more complex. A question that arises is whether a conception of due process rights as 'absolute' rights is workable, or practicable, for the purposes of administrative life. A caveat is justified by the predisposition of the courts to recognize process values without using the language of absolute rights. Particularly when judges are confronted with 'hard cases' involving highly sensitive choices about interests, they tend to focus on the respect for existing procedures and requirements and, within this framework, to balance those interests with others, such as collective security.

A more nuanced view looks appropriate also with regard to 'participation'. There is no doubt that this is a fashionable word and one that echoes the ideals of democracy and individual empowerment. And it may be tempting to discern an evolution, if not progress, from administrative doctrines concerning the right of defence to participation, and thus a move away from the early twentieth century legacy where participation takes place in the political sphere, not in that of administration. But there is much to be said in favour of a more differentiated approach, from the perspective of both practicality and principle. Practically, involving individuals, groups, and other legal entities (undertakings and their umbrella organizations) entails costs that cannot be ignored, in terms of *lourdeur*. Moreover, on grounds of principle, different forms of involvement in the formation of policies coexist and rest on a variety of rationales, instrumental (in consultation) and non-instrumental (as far as individual dignity and participation are concerned). The next chapter will develop this line of reasoning from the angle of two rationales that are particularly important in the transnational arena: sound administration and cooperation between public authorities.

7

Sound Administration and Cooperation

In the previous chapter the analysis focused on procedural protections for the interests affected by the exercise of power by a public authority from the perspective of both dignity and participation. A distinction between participation, more narrowly intended, and consultation has emerged. When public authorities consult individuals and groups, the adversarial approach that characterizes right-based approaches is less appropriate. It is even less so when procedural requirements are justified by instrumental rationales such as sound administration, a concept that is increasingly important in the reform agenda of international sites of governance, including the EU, the OECD, and the World Bank. A related, but distinct, rationale is cooperation between public authorities. Although this is a traditional concern of international law, new forms of cooperation have emerged that affect directly administrative procedure and raise important questions concerning process rights.

1. Sound Administration

Even a quick look at the ways in which the concept of 'good' or 'sound' administration is used in many official documents shows that it is a loose term. Its usefulness lies in its potential adaptability to many situations, as well as to many needs.[1] Analytically, we will distinguish them, proceeding in stages. For expository clarity, there will be a focus on three aspects: compliance with predefined rules, consistency of the final decision with the outcome of the preparatory work, and soundness of that decision from a scientific or technical point of view.

Compliance with predefined rules

The first meaning of sound administration, compliance with predefined rules, may seem obvious. However, it must not be forgotten that it can be justified in many ways. The demand that the predefined procedure is respected and conforms to basic requirements of due process is a basic feature of the idea of the Rule of Law.[2] This

[1] See Deirdre Curtin and Ramsel A Wessels, *Good Governance: The Concept and Its Application by the European Union*, in Deirdre Curtin and Ramsel A Wessels (eds), *Good Governance and the European Union. Reflections On Concepts, Institutions and Substance* (Intersentia, 2005) 20.

[2] David Resnick, *Due Process and Procedural Justice*, in J Roland Pennock and James W Chapman (eds), *Due Process: Nomos XVIII* (New York University Press, 1977) 209.

is particularly important because public administrators are required to achieve the goals set by policymakers. Another justification is equality, in the sense that respect of established rules of procedure is necessary to prevent partiality and arbitrariness in exercises of power by public authorities.[3] In a slightly distinct sense, it can be suggested that a public authority is constrained in its conduct by its guidelines and past practice, following the logic of estoppel,[4] which is not too distant from that which inspires the maxim *tu patere legem quem ipse fecisti*.

The need to respect predefined rules in the achievement of government policies is particularly important in the work of agencies that dispense public money. The reason is not only that their administrators use a resource—money—that is scarce by definition, given that it can be assigned to alternative uses. It is also that administrators must be accountable to stakeholders. These reasons justify the checks carried out by the Inspection Panel. As observed before, if its assessment reveals irregularities or procedural anomalies, the Inspection Panel informs the executive directors. It is they who inform individuals and groups of their findings and the initiatives taken and who take the measures necessary to remedy any dysfunctions. If the policies and standards of the Bank are not respected, payment may be suspended.

Two consequences follow from this. First, the Inspection Panel works as a watchdog, ensuring that the policies and procedures of the World Bank are respected. Secondly, and consequently, the justification for its supervisory function is essentially an instrumental one, though representatives of 'civil society', such as environmental associations or ethnic groups, no longer play the part of a simple impulse and stimulus to activate controls, but can make their voices heard.

Consistent decisions

Although the need to respect the requirements of procedural due process of law can be justified by referring to their nature of legal standards, this only tells us that a certain requirement must formally be respected. There is another important reason why legislators set out procedural requirements and the courts and other public agencies ensure they are followed. The reason is that an administrative procedure serves to assure that decisions, especially when they adversely affect someone, have an appropriate basis from the point of view of ascertaining the relevant facts and weighing the interests at stake. In this sense, procedural propriety serves to achieve a certain degree of consistency and objectivity.

There is no such thing as a Decalogue, from which one may draw operational guidance in relation to the facts legally relevant to public decisions. Nevertheless, from experience and existing literature it is possible to find some general guidance. More specifically, three requirements can be individuated. First, if a public

[3] Albert V Dicey, *Introduction to the Study of the Law of the Constitution* (10th edn, MacMillan, 1956) 328.

[4] See Bin Cheng, *General Principles of Law as Applied by International Courts and Tribunals* (Cambridge University Press, 2006) 141 (illustrating the maxim *allegans contraria non est audiendus*).

authority may use a certain procedure only if certain circumstances arise and certain conditions are met, it must demonstrate their existence. Secondly, if it is obliged to take some steps, in particular to gather or accept evidence and documents, it cannot fail to fulfil such obligations. Finally, if it gathers or accepts evidence in the course of the procedure, it cannot ignore its relevance when taking a decision.

The field of public procurements provides several examples of the first requirement. If an agency intends to negotiate directly with a provider of goods or services, it must follow a certain procedure and give adequate reasons for its choice. A rubberstamp motivation, in the guise of referring to compelling reasons of public interest, will have few chances to be regarded as being acceptable by the courts. Nor will they easily accept an apodictic assertion of 'urgency' as the justification for the agency's decision to keep the same provider, without a selection process, when the contract expires.[5]

The norms aiming at preserving the environment furnish examples of the second requirement, that is, the duty of consideration of the evidence gathered within the administrative procedure. The Aarhus Convention requires, in particular, national authorities to publish the facts and the studies considered relevant in forming the main proposals relating to the environment and to enable individuals to express their point of view.[6] The duty of consideration is affirmed in a more stringent way by European Union (EU) law. In particular, Directive n. 97/11 requires national authorities to carry out an assessment of the environmental impact. This is not simply a formal duty, but requires an overall assessment of the relevant facts. What must be ascertained is not only the environmental impact of the projects, but also the use of the infrastructure that is going to be built. For example, if an airport or a railway is to be constructed, it is also necessary to take into account the volume of traffic and air pollution, or the noise levels it will produce.[7] Seen in this light, the requirement to carry out an environmental assessment is an important step in securing that decisions are appropriate and consistent. It is equally important for giving a voice to those who have an interest to assert or a protest to express, if the procedure is open to them. However, the drawbacks that can arise are far from negligible. The procedure for assessing any environmental impact is long and costly. The risk it entails is to penalize more complex works, which are precisely what modern societies need more of. The assessment of environmental impact also often leads to litigation, and to increasing costs and delays as a result. Hence the reluctance of administrators to carry it out, if not the overt repudiation of all requirements of this type, even of a milder nature.

This brings us to the third obligation, which requires decision-makers to take evidence previously gathered into account. The ruling of the European Court of Human Rights (ECtHR) in *Taskin* provides an interesting example of this requirement.[8] The Turkish government granted a multinational company the

[5] Florian Linditch, *Droit des marchés publics* (Dalloz, 2002) 19.

[6] Aarhus Convention, Article 5, § 7, letter a).

[7] ECJ, Case C-227/01, *Commission v Spain* [2004] ECR I-8253. Directive n. 97/11, of 3 March 1977 [1977] OJ L77/36.

[8] Eur Ct HR, judgment of 10th November 2004, *Taskin and others v Turkey* (case n 46117/99) [2004] ECHR, X.

concession to operate a goldmine. Only afterwards did they carry out a procedure to assess the impact of this activity on the health of the inhabitants and on the natural environment. Because of the serious risks from the use of explosives and, above all, cyanide, some residents challenged the concession before the administrative court. After various vicissitudes, the Turkish Supreme Court annulled it.[9] But the administration was slow to implement this ruling and a contrary decision was issued by the central government. It recognized the risks to the environment and to human health, but it considered them tolerable, balanced against the interests of economic development and employment. This decision was enforced, though it was not published in the official gazette or made public in any other way.

An action was then brought before the ECtHR. The applicants argued that the conduct of the Turkish government was detrimental to the citizens from the point of view of both the right to family life and the right to a fair trial. Guaranteeing the right to family life, from which the case law of the Court also drew the right to a healthy environment, does not clearly imply, however, the exclusion of economic activities. In a democratic society, it is the prerogative of politicians, elected and accountable to the people, to decide how to reconcile them. However, they cannot dispose arbitrarily of individual and collective rights.[10] The Court found it easy to argue that the actions of public authorities cannot be carried out by ignoring the existing rules of law. Digging and other mining activities had been authorized without a proper assessment of the risks associated with them. For this reason, the decision to authorize them was unfair and devoid of any legal basis.[11]

This discussion confirms that, although the existence of discretionary powers is simply a necessity, its exercise must be limited and structured. The action of government that may conflict with the interests of others must pass the test of non-arbitrariness. Governments must accurately assess all the issues of fact, weighing up all the interests at stake in order to ensure the legitimacy of the final decision.

In search of appropriate solutions: The contribution of science

Another source of legitimacy of administrative rules and decisions is increasingly found in the contribution of experts. Especially in highly technical areas, their influence is not only evident, but also decisive. What they do not recommend is not recommended. What they deem unfeasible or dangerous is hardly undertaken. The most radical solution is perhaps that of leaving monetary policy in the hands of central bankers. While this solution affects the structure of government, others are

[9] See Emre Oktem, 'Les rapports enigmatiques entre le droit international et le droit interne Turc', (2006) 18 Eur Rev Publ L 969 (arguing that Turkish administrative courts are more inclined than ordinary courts to acknowledge the importance of international treaties).

[10] On this concept, see Susan Marks, 'The European Convention on Human Rights and its "Democratic Society"'(1996) 66 Br Ybk Int'l L 222.

[11] See also the Eur Ct HR judgment of 27 January 2009, *Tătar v Romania* (case n 67021/01) (paragraph 93, referring to *Taskin*, and paragraph 110, where it is argued that national authorities failed to appreciate the risk to human health).

procedural in nature. Many regulatory regimes aim at ensuring that the decisions made by public authorities are objective and have a sound basis.

An interesting example is that of the Agreement on the Application of Sanitary and Phytosanitary Measures (SPS Agreement). It governs the application of sanitary measures within the World Trade Organization (WTO). To prevent them from being used to introduce arbitrary or unjustifiable discrimination, various obligations are imposed on the contracting parties. They must ensure that the measures are introduced for the sole purpose of protecting health or other public interests and apply them only as necessary, that is, proportionally. Additionally, public authorities are required to base their decisions on scientific principles and not uphold them without sufficient scientific evidence. Finally, they must develop an approach that allows them to find the most appropriate solutions.[12]

This is not, however, always an easy task. This was evident in the case that arose some years ago with regard to the fishing of a protected species, the Southern Bluefin Tuna, in the Pacific Ocean. In the last two decades of the twentieth century, concerns grew about the depletion of global fish stocks. Faced with doubt about the seriousness of the risk, Australia, New Zealand, and Japan agreed on special rules. Their fisheries policies would take a restrictive stance. The trend of the stock, which had become largely negative, seemed to reverse. According to the Japanese government, it regained a positive value. The governments of the other countries disputed both those estimates and the choice of the Japanese government to resume fishing, although to a limited extent and for scientific purposes. The dispute moved from diplomatic talks to dispute resolution bodies. The first decision was issued by an arbitral body[13] and was followed by that of the International Tribunal for the Law of the Sea (ITLOS). Urged by the applicants, ITLOS made an interim decision. It required compliance with the standstill clause, hence the obligation of the Japanese government to refrain from implementing its policy.[14]

This case shows the importance of a procedural perspective from two viewpoints. First, it furnishes an important example of how science can play a moderating role. Decision-making must be preceded by an adequate assessment of all the relevant facts and their potential consequences for the interests at stake. Adequate assessment of risk, in particular, is necessary. Only by carrying out an assessment of this kind can a public authority make decisions that may be considered as legitimate by the other partners, for example, a ban on the use of hormones,[15] unlike

[12] Articles 2, § 2; 5, § 1.

[13] First Arbitral Tribunal *Southern Blue Tuna Case between Australia and Japan and between New Zealand and Japan*, Award on Jurisdiction and Admissibility, 4 August 2000 (2000) 23 Rep Int Arb Awards, 1. For further details, see Cesare Romano, 'The Southern Bluefin Tuna Dispute. Hints of a World to Come ... Like it or Not' (2001) 32 Ocean Development & Int'l L 314; Sabino Cassese, 'Administrative Law Without the State? The Challenge of Global Regulation' (2005) 37 NYU J Int'l L & Pol 663.

[14] ITLOS, *Australia and New Zealand v Japan* (1999). For further remarks, see Mark E Evans, 'The Southern Bluefin Tuna Arbitration' (2001) 50 Int'l & Comp L Quart 447 (for the argument that the court erred in defining the relationship between the United Nations Convention on the Law of the Sea (UNCLOS) and the specific agreements reached at regional level).

[15] See the case concerning the health measures issued by Japan on imports of agricultural products: *Report of the Appellate Body* (1999) WT/DS76/AB/R, *Japan—Measures Affecting Agricultural Products*.

an *ipse dixit*. However, the *Southern Bluefin Tuna* case also shows that the contribution of experts is not without its deficiencies. Such deficiencies are not limited to the non-egalitarian connotations that a government of experts inevitably has and to experts' frequent 'tunnel vision'.[16] In fact, the previous example leads to the opposite conclusion, in the sense that it is not easy to reconcile divergent, if not conflicting,[17] scientific truths. What is relevant is, rather, the process by which evidence and arguments are discussed, that is, on the procedure as such.[18] Our analysis thus shifts to the methods of cooperation and negotiation between public authorities.

2. Cooperation Between Public Authorities

What was just observed brings us to the other instrumental rationale that underlies some requirements of due process of law—cooperation between public authorities. Analytically, it is useful to proceed in stages. As a first step, the gradual move away from coexistence to cooperation will be briefly mentioned. The next step will consist in highlighting the new form of cooperation that takes place within administrative procedure. Finally, the focus will be on the relation, a dialectic one, which exists between cooperation and process rights.

From coexistence to cooperation

The character of international relations has changed greatly since the 1970s. The proximate cause of the change has been the vast increase in joint attempts to regulate both economic and non-economic issues. Its immediate consequence has been the gradual shift from traditional diplomatic methods to cooperation between representatives of State departments and agencies. Another consequence has been the increasing importance of the law in managing conflicts between the interests at stake.

Although it is the second change that matters more for present purposes, it is useful to consider briefly the general context in which it has taken place. National rulers have stipulated a vast array of regulatory agreements to deal with problems as disparate as trade and climate change, as satellite communications and the use of chemical weapons. The reason is, simply, that in those fields and many others 'cooperation is necessary'.[19] There has thus been an increase—in their number, in

[16] Jerry Mashaw, *Due Process in the Administrative State* (Yale University Press, 1985) 17.

[17] Cesare Romano, 'The Southern Bluefin Tuna Dispute. Hints of a World to Come … Like it or Not', 609; Andrew Boyle, 'The Southern Bluefin Tuna Arbitration' (2001) 50 Int'l & Comp L Quart 452. The lack of technical evidence is expressly dealt with by Article 2, § 2 of the SPS Treaty: *Report of the Appellate Body* (2003) WT/DS245/AB/R, *Japan—Measures Affecting the Importation of Apples*.

[18] Marcos Orellana, 'Science, Risk and Uncertainty: Public Health Measures and Investment Disciplines', in Philippe Kahn and Thomas W Walde (eds), *New Aspects of International Investment Law* (Martinus Nijhoff, 2007) 675.

[19] See Vaughan Lowe, *International Law* (Clarendon Press, 2007) 2.

absolute terms, and typology—of international regimes[20] and, as a consequence, the importance of membership has grown remarkably.

There is, however, a variety of opinions about the nature and significance of this change. In contrast with the belief that a growth of regulatory agreements implies a corresponding diminution in the power of national governments, as though this were a zero-sum game in which losses must always offset gains, some academics argue that their power has grown in another respect. It is the capacity to influence the decisions that are taken within common processes and institutions and to secure their compliance by partners in a variety of ways. They thus emphasize cooperation, as distinct from coexistence.[21] Other commentators observe that States may have greater incentives to comply with some treaties than with those stemming from other treaties.[22] A different critique comes from commentators who argue that, despite apparent fragmentation of regulatory regimes, they are conceived and used by some nations in order to exercise hegemony over other nations.[23] The criticism is sometimes echoed extra-academically by policymakers afraid of being bound by global standards.

A related, but distinct, question is that of the increased importance of law. Many have welcomed the growing use of legal procedures to secure the enforcement of common rules, while others have raised a doubt as to whether this is really a good thing, an increased adversarial style and the resulting complexity of negotiations being the negative side of the coin.[24]

Cooperation in standard-setting

National and international officers are involved in such a vast array of networks that in many fields much of the regulatory agenda is now written at these new sites of authority rather than in the national capitals. They are asked to define technical standards about food safety and electronic communications, elaborate and enforce standards of private conduct (for instance, with regard to insurance providers),[25]

[20] For this concept, see Stephen D Krasner (ed), *International Regimes* (Cornell University Press, 1983); Andreas Hasenclever, Peter Mayer, and Volker Rittberger, *Theories of International Regimes* (Cambridge University Press, 2007). But see also, for critical remarks, Martti Koskenniemi, *The Politics of International Law* (Hart, 2011) 319–20.

[21] Abraham Chayes and Victoria Handler Chayes, *The New Sovereignty. Compliance with International Regulatory Agreements* (Harvard University Press, 1995) 229; Anne-Marie Slaughter, *A New World Order* (Princeton University Press, 2004).

[22] Harold Hongju Koh, 'Review of Abraham Chayes and Victoria Handler Chayes, The New Sovereignty. Compliance with International Regulatory Agreements' (1997) 91 Am J Int'l L 389, 390 (observing that States may have greater incentives to comply with some treaties than with those stemming from other treaties).

[23] See Bhupinder Chimni, 'Co-option and Resistance: Two Faces of Global Administrative Law' (2005) 37 NYU LSJ Int'l L & Pol 799 and 'International Institutions Today: An Imperial Global State in the Making' (2004) 15 Eur J Int'l L 1.

[24] Joseph HH Weiler, 'The Rule of Lawyers and the Ethos of Diplomats: Reflections on the Internal and External Legitimacy of WTO Dispute Settlement' (2001) 35 J World Trade 191 and Joost Pauwelyn, 'The Transformation of World Trade' (2005) 104 Michigan L Rev 1.

[25] See Maurizia De Bellis, 'Global Financial Standards and Regulatory Failure: Lessons for Reform', in Giacinto della Cananea and Aldo Sandulli (eds), *Global Standards for Public Authorities* (Editoriale Scientifica, 2012) 73.

and comply with standards regarding their own behaviour (an example is provided by the protection of the environment). In other cases, they do so autonomously, for example, the central banks' governors of some countries meet regularly within the framework of the Basel Committee, where they define and refine standards for banking supervision.[26]

We can, therefore, no longer think of our administrative systems as being characterized by an exclusive legal authority over economic and social forces. Standard-setting and adjudication are increasingly characterized by direct cooperation between governments and regulatory authorities. A 'governance by agreement' thus emerges[27] and, interestingly, it also affects dispute resolution, to the extent that norms such as Article 16(1) of the Convention for the conservation of Southern Bluefin Tuna urge parties to have their disputes resolved by negotiation and conciliation.

This arrangement is still controversial. It is one thing to accept that public administrators discuss and define technical standards about the quality of electronic communications and the patrimonial solidity of banking institutions. It may be another thing for parliaments to accept the idea that, once such standards have been negotiated and formalized, they can only accept or refuse them. Some fear that harmonization of standards will undermine important values traditionally associated with national sovereignty. Others point out that issues of legitimacy and accountability arise.[28] However, what is problematic is not only the shift of power from national to international sites of authority, but also the impact of regulatory regimes on national processes of formulation of policy. The following paragraphs explore this change from several angles.

Cooperation within administrative procedure

To begin with, a distinction can be drawn between the circumstances in which cooperation takes place on an ad hoc basis and a more institutionalized cooperation. For all its growth through recent years, the standardization produced by regional and global regulatory regimes is still partial, rarely occupying any field completely and, of course, it does not eliminate administrative discretion in individual cases. Precisely for this reason, regulatory regimes aim at achieving cooperation within administrative procedure.[29]

An interesting example is that of antitrust authorities. Since the last decades of the twentieth century most countries have enacted some form of competition law and have set up a more or less independent authority to ensure its respect. And an

[26] David Zaring, 'International Law by Other Means: The Twilight Existence of International Financial Regulatory Organizations' (1998) 33 Tex Int'l LJ 281.

[27] Sabino Cassese, *The Global Polity* (Global Law Press, 2012) 32.

[28] Robert P Delonis, 'International Financial Standards and Codes: Mandatory Regulation Without Representation' (2004) 36 NYU J Int'l L & Pol 563.

[29] Javier Barnès, 'Towards a Third Generation of Administrative Procedure', 353 points out that third-generation procedures allow collaborative processes between regulators.

international competition network has existed since 2001. Well before its creation, the OECD defined some guidance for its members, including duties of notification, coordination, and cooperation.[30] Notification to another member country is deemed necessary when a national antitrust authority undertakes a procedure that may affect its major interests, and it should be carried out during a phase that would facilitate comments or consultation. When two or more antitrust authorities proceed against an anticompetitive practice in international trade, they should endeavour to coordinate their action. Finally, a more institutionalized cooperation should be sought, through consultation or otherwise, in developing or applying measures that are 'mutually satisfactory'.

These requirements clearly mark a transition from a mere refraining from intervention, in application of the principle of comity, to an institutionalized form of cooperation, based on mutual assistance.[31] There is also another difference separating these devices from other forms of cooperation. The difference may be described as one between a generic duty of cooperation and a set of specific requirements that affect exercises of power by public authorities within administrative procedure. If this analysis is correct, an administrative procedure ceases to be the instrument for balancing individual and collective interests from a national perspective. It becomes an instrument for ensuring that balancing exercises take the transnational dimension of such interests into account.

Multilateralization of domestic procedures

Probably the best way to highlight this change is to consider a circumstance in which the transnational dimension is imposed on a recalcitrant administration.

Consider again the WTO dispute about shrimps and sea turtles. In 1999 the WTO meeting in Seattle faced strong opposition from hundreds of discontents, many of whom wore turtle masks. It would be wrong to dismiss this protest as if it were a simple manifestation of malcontent about globalization.[32] It is important to inquire into the reasons for this rather controversial record of arbitral intervention. The most common explanation is that WTO dispute resolution bodies did not take the protection of the environment seriously. But we saw earlier that the AB solicited *amici curiae* briefs from non-governmental organizations (NGOs) with the intent to reach a more accurate decision. It also dissented from the panel in that it held that preserving sea turtles, a natural exhaustible resource, could in the

[30] Organization for Economic Co-operation and Development (OECD), *Revised Recommendation of the Council Concerning Co-operation between Member Countries on Anticompetitive Practices Affecting International Trade*, 28 July 1995, C(95)130/FINAL. For further analysis, see Ernst-Ulrich Petersmann, 'International Competition Rules for Government and for Private Business' (1996) 30 J World Trade 5.

[31] For this distinction, see Mitsuo Matsushita, 'International Cooperation in the Enforcement of Competition Policy' (2002) 1 Wash Un Global Studies L Rev 470.

[32] See Julien G Ku, 'The Delegation of Federal Power to International Organizations: New Problems with Old Solutions' (2000–2001) 85 Minn L Rev 71, 72 (holding that 'the inchoate range of the Seattle protesters has greater constitutional substance than most academic commentators would like to admit').

abstract justify limits on imports. Whatever merit this view may have on grounds of substance, the AB found that those limits were arbitrary on grounds of process. The first problem lay in the fact that the US government had introduced those limits after negotiating with only some exporting countries, rather than all of them. Another problem was that the interests of Asian producers were not treated fairly in the course of the regulatory procedure.

From the first point of view, the AB recalled the principle requiring the contracting parties to reconcile their respective interests through bilateral or multilateral negotiations.[33] One may object that WTO agreements do not intend to eliminate the possibility of treating partners differently, for example, through preferential regimes.[34] Not only the US but also other contracting parties have widely used this option. But, according to the AB, the US administration abused it when it negotiated only with its neighbouring countries. The underlying assumption is that all contracting parties must be given 'similar opportunities to negotiate'.[35] By contrast, the US had failed to engage in serious negotiations and Asian countries had been denied an equal opportunity to negotiate. Negotiation processes, the AB clarified, need not be identical, but must be comparable in the light of the principle of good faith.[36] It was not irrelevant, in this respect, that the US ban included all shrimps coming from countries classified as 'non-certified', even though they had been caught in nets that met the US requirements. In sum, the principle of fairness limits the partners' freedom of manoeuvre, though it does not oblige them to reach an agreement.

Fairness also limits exercises of power in another guise, internally and with regard to administrative procedure. As observed before, the AB reached the conclusion that the US administration, which neither provided Asian nations with an opportunity to be involved in its regulatory procedure nor stated reasons for the measures it issued, failed to respect two basic requirements of procedural fairness. For the US this might be seen as a political defeat, but with long-term institutional gains, because such basic requirements must be respected by all partners.

The gist of *Shrimp*'s holding thus lies not in ruling that there can be good reasons of public policy for limiting trade, but rather in formulating an approach to the elaboration of the standards of due process of law. This approach, though leading the AB to criticize the conduct of the US government, has much in common with the due process jurisprudence of US courts, with its emphasis on openness, participation, and transparency. However, these instances of good governance do not underlie the use of procedural requirements in favour of individuals or

[33] Panel Report, WT/DS58/AB/R, 12 October 1998 (*Shrimp II*) paragraph 166.

[34] See Gregory Shaffer and Yvonne Apea, 'Institutional Choice in the Generalized System of Preferences Case: Who Decides the Conditions for Trade Preferences? The Law and Politics of Rights' (2005) 39 J World Tr 1000.

[35] Panel Report, WT/DS587AB7RW, 22 October 2001 (*Shrimp III*), paragraphs 115 and 122.

[36] See Bin Cheng, *General Principles of Law*, 136 (interpreting good faith as imposing a duty to notify a change in policy).

groups, as would have been the case for Asian producers, but their use in favour of Asian countries. The assumption on which the arbitral award is based is rather that WTO law obliges national governments to exercise their powers fairly, internally and externally, in order to foster cooperation, keeping open the channels of political negotiation and providing partners with adequate opportunities to make their case.

There is, however, growing concern as to whether, by granting participation not only to private parties (affected persons or NGOs aiming at protecting collective interests) but also to national governments or other public entities, global regulatory regimes overemphasize 'negotiated understanding'.[37] A more radical critique is that the policies of regional and global authorities 'leave us with a diminishing sense of what the law is'.[38] Whatever the ability of regulatory regimes to allow negotiations, there is a growing sense that they not simply accentuate the instrumental dimension of some procedural requirements, but also may 'pervert' them. Those requirements, so the argument goes, have an important non-instrumental dimension, which gets lost when they are not used to empower individuals and groups, but to promote dialogues between public officers that have become detached from the logic of the 'public interest' and are insulated from electorates. There is undoubtedly some truth in this, but it is, at best, a partial diagnosis. While it is certainly true that governments have a strong incentive in elaborating and negotiating standards of conduct in a relatively opaque manner, it is not obvious how we should cope with it, as enhancing transparency can be a good solution in many cases, but not in all. Nor is it obvious how we can balance the need to expand regulatory reach, by creating the conditions that are essential for long-term cooperation (only trust permits a regular exchange of information and the development of similar—not uniform—approaches to common problems), with the procedural requirements that were developed in several States over the last two centuries.

Interest balancing within administrative procedure

The importance of a fair representation and weighing of interests in *Shrimp* raises a further question. Since judgments about process adequacy always involve trade-offs between goals or interests,[39] we may ask ourselves whether the rationale of cooperation leaves some room for a consideration of the collective interests protected by governmental action. The procedural due process jurisprudence endorsed by *Shrimp*, if I interpret it correctly, implies neither a rejection of the margin of discretion enjoyed by national policymakers nor a prohibition of disadvantageous treatment. Indeed, should it turn out, on the basis of a well-grounded analysis, that

[37] Eric Posner, *The Perils of Global Legalism* (Chicago University Press, 2009).

[38] Simon A Roberts, 'After Government? On Representing Law Without the State' (2005) 68 Modern L Rev 23.

[39] Jerry Mashaw, *Due Process in the Administrative State*, 47.

certain characteristics of the goods or services provided by foreign producers are contrary to compelling reasons of public interest such as public order and health, neither panels nor the AB should view governmental action without suspicion.

As proof of this, consider another award of the AB, concerning gambling and betting services.[40] In this case, the US government invoked the exception regarding morals in order to limit gambling via the Internet. Serious and specific concerns were expressed regarding the possibility that adolescents could be involved in betting. Another reason for concern was about the recycling of unlawfully accumulated capital. This time there was no doubt that these were the real reasons inspiring governmental action. What was at issue was, rather, whether the measures taken were necessary. The attempt to demonstrate such necessity failed due to the failure to consider possible alternatives that the other partner would have accepted after appropriate consultations. The underlying assumption is that trade limits can be lawful if based on accurate knowledge of the relevant facts and that such knowledge can be obtained through consultation. There is more than a mere assonance, in this respect, with the instrumental justification for consulting individuals and groups. However, in this case the rationale for procedural requirements is the need to avoid ripping the delicate fabric of multilateralism, the *raison d'être* of the WTO. It implies that States must be treated with the same consideration not in relation to the final decision, but the procedure that must be followed in issuing it.[41]

Cooperation within domestic administrative procedure thus assumes a very different meaning from an axiological viewpoint. Where the interests of several countries are at stake, it serves to allow those interests to be considered through the discussion of solutions in a formal negotiating context. Thus, cooperation is the end and a simulated multilateralism is the means used to achieve it.[42]

3. Conflicting Rationales of Due Process

The analysis of interest balancing sheds some light on a related, but distinct, question. What is at issue here is not so much the relative weight that a court or an arbitral body should give to the collective interest served by a certain procedural requirement and to the interests of private parties. It is, rather, the potential conflict between the instrumental rationale of cooperation between public authorities and the non-instrumental rationales of due process.

[40] Report of the Appellate Body, WT/DS285/AB/R, 20 April 2005, *United States—Measures Affecting the Cross-Border Supply of Gambling and Betting Services.*

[41] See Alfred C Aman, 'Proposals for Reforming the Administrative Procedure Act: Globalization, Democracy and the Furtherance of a Global Public Interest' (2001) 6 Indiana J Global Legal St 397; Richard B Stewart, 'The Global Regulatory Challenge to U.S. Administrative Law' (2005) 37 NYU J Int'l L & Pol 695, 703.

[42] See Armin von Bodgandy, 'Law and Politics in the WTO—Strategies to Cope with a Deficient Relationship', in Stefan Griller (ed), *International Economic Governance and Non-Economic Concerns* (Springer, 2003) 613.

Cooperation and *raison d'état*

The conflict between individual rights and cooperation between public authorities is, for example, at the heart of a group of cases judged by the ECJ with regard to WTO law. Given the innovative role played by the EU—a non-State entity—in the framework of the WTO and the frequency of issues concerning the free movement of goods and services, the importance of litigation involving WTO law before EU courts is not surprising. Indeed, litigation concerning WTO law was the main field in which EU courts dealt with the relationship between EU law and international law before more recent cases regarding the antiterrorism measures taken by UN institutions.

The earliest dispute was *Portugal v Council*. The case involved the validity of the Council's decision to conclude Memoranda of Understanding with India and Pakistan on market access for textile products.[43] Portugal argued, among other things, that the Memoranda were inconsistent with the 1994 General Agreement on Tariffs and Trade (GATT 1994). What was at issue was, therefore, whether WTO law had direct effects within the legal order of the European Community (EC), the predecessor of the EU. The Court split the question into two parts. It referred to its 'settled case-law' to affirm that, although given their nature and structure, the WTO agreements are not in principle among the sources of law in the light of which the Court reviews the legality of the measures issued by EC institutions,[44] in particular cases it can do so. This is the case, the Court held, when an EC measure refers expressly to some particular provisions of WTO law.[45] However, this did not imply that such provisions of WTO law could have any direct effect, in the sense of being justiciable.

The Court's approach in this case and in similar cases, such as *Van Paris*,[46] was criticized for its methodological weakness and for its impact on the right to effective judicial protection.[47] It would be wrong, however, to look at this judicial policy as a manifestation of the tendency, common to government representatives and bureaucrats, to wriggle out of monitoring, particularly judicial monitoring.[48] There is a distinctive trait regarding the more intense need for cooperation between public authorities. The Court began by asserting that in order to allow the EC to participate as an equal in the construction of world trade, it was essential that it could enjoy no less autonomy than that enjoyed by its partners in the course of negotiations. Otherwise, there would be a lack of reciprocity, which would risk introducing an anomaly into the application of WTO rules. It followed from this that the

[43] Council Decision 96/386/EC of 26 February 1996 [1996] OJ L/156, 47.

[44] ECJ, Case C-149/96 *Portugal v Council* [1999] ECR I-8396, paragraph 47.

[45] ECJ, Cases C-149/96, *Portugal v Council*, paragraph 49 and C-93/02, *Biret International v Council* [2003] ECR I-10487, paragraph 53.

[46] ECJ, Case C-377/02, *Léon Van Parys NV v Belgisch Interventie- en Restitutiebureau (BIRB)* [2005] ECR I-1465.

[47] See Patricia Egli and Juliane Kokott, 'Comment on Case C-149/96, *Portuguese Republic v. Council of the European Union*' (2000) 94 Am J Int'l L 740.

[48] Eric Stein and Joseph Vining, 'Citizen Access to Judicial Review of Administrative Action in a Transnational and Federal Context' (1978) 70 Am J Int'l L 219.

institutions of the EC had a discretionary power with regard to the gradual adaptation of EC law to the provisions of the WTO.[49]

In this sense, *Van Paris* especially can be regarded as being both a reiteration of the courts' traditional concern for *raison d'état* and a paradigmatic example of pragmatic concerns about cooperation. In other words, a functional type of explanation can be proposed: the Court had to balance conflicting interests and the balance of enhanced cooperation over the effectiveness of the rights enjoyed by private parties. As a result, they can invoke before the courts neither WTO rules nor the findings of WTO dispute resolution bodies.[50]

Cooperation v process rights

The functional criteria used by EU courts are helpful in understanding another problematic aspect of cooperation between public authorities. It has already been suggested that this use of due process requirements is not immune from weaknesses. Indeed, procedural requirements such as the right to be heard and the right to have access to the reasons for a disadvantageous distinction are historically based on non-instrumental rationales. We may wonder, therefore, whether the use of such procedural requirements in a completely different legal context constitutes an abuse or a perversion of their original rationale.

This question looks problematic, in particular, when considering whether the need to assure cooperation between public authorities has an adverse impact on procedural due process of law. Consider again the measures taken against suspected members or supporters of transnational terrorist groups. While some procedures are directed towards freezing their funds and other assets, others limit their movements (the 'no fly' lists). Such procedures thus impinge on property and liberty respectively. As a consequence, issues of procedural fairness and propriety arise. However, the courts sometimes hesitate to enforce procedural requirements on the grounds that they could undermine the capacity of each government to protect human lives and goods. This argument has been used, for example, to affirm that suspected members and supporters of terrorist groups should not be informed that a procedure targeting them has begun, otherwise their funds would swiftly be sent elsewhere.[51] Similarly, it has been suggested that the giving reasons requirement should be tempered in order to preserve the confidentiality of sources of intelligence.

The governments that are most committed to cooperation against transnational terrorism are also the ones that most emphatically stress the unacceptable costs of disclosure. Their argument is not simplistically that to reveal the sources of certain pieces of information would jeopardize national security. It is, rather, that national

[49] See Case C-149/96, *Portugal v Council*, paragraphs 42–3.

[50] See Francis Snyder, 'The Gatekeepers: The European Courts and WTO Law' (2003) 40 Com Mkt L Rev 313.

[51] See Christian Tomuschat, *Comment* to CFI, Case T-315/01, *Yassin Abdullah Kadi v Council and Commission*, 539 (arguing that 'ordinary logic dictates' this).

security can no longer be adequately protected without intergovernmental cooperation. This, in turn, requires the parties to exchange mutual promises to keep their sources secret before they exchange the information in their possession. As a consequence, each individual government is not only answerable to the others regarding the honouring of the commitment undertaken but is also equally exposed to the risk of no longer being included in the exchanges of information that may be vitally important for its security. It is a risk that neither a court nor any other public agency, such as an ombudsman, can easily disregard.[52]

What all this suggests is not simply that openness and participation are not without costs in administrative procedure and that as a result they are subject to limitations. It is, rather, that in some cases the utilitarian connotation of some procedural due process requirements has the effect of contradicting the dignitarian foundation of process rights aiming at protecting individuals and groups from governmental interference.[53] Hence the need for an even more complex balancing exercise, in the sense that what is at stake is not only an issue of legal technique, but also an issue of values.

In a similar vein, we may wonder whether cooperation between public authorities justifies limitations to transparency with regard to trade negotiations. The question has both a pragmatic and an axiological side. Pragmatically, this used to be an area in which decisions were taken by negotiators during confidential meetings, the results of which remained 'largely invisible to the public'.[54] Of course, negotiations could have failed but, actually, this did not happen. Subsequently, instead, with the increase in the number of members and the resulting difficulty in preserving confidentiality and informality, negotiations reached a stalemate. The reason is the low propensity of negotiators to accept compromises that may appear unsatisfactory to public opinion. Axiologically, if procedural requirements can be tempered in order to preserve the confidentiality of sources of intelligence when a governmental authority interferes with liberty or property (and, *a fortiori*, with the integrity of the human body or life), it may be argued that the rationale of cooperation ought to be given even more serious consideration when public authorities negotiate. However, this is at odds not only with the theories that emphasize the importance of publicity, but also with the growing concern for openness and transparency,[55] especially when multilateral negotiation regard the interests of all, as happens when national

[52] Cooperation also impinges on confidentiality: see James Rill and Calvin S Godman, 'Confidentiality in the Era of Increased Cooperation Between Antitrust Agencies', in Leonard Waverman et al (eds), *Competition Policy in the Global Economy. Modalities for Cooperation* (Routledge, 1997) 152.

[53] Jerry Mashaw, *Due Process in the Administrative State*, 47 (observing that, 'as a constitutional theory, this brand of utilitarianism has the defect of its virtues').

[54] Robert O Keohane and Joseph S Nye, 'The Club Model of Multilateral Cooperation and Problems of Democratic Legitimacy', in Roger B Porter et al (eds), *Efficiency, Equity and Legitimacy: The Multilateral System at the Millennium* (Brookings Institution, 2001) 264.

[55] This sometimes justifies national norms urging States' representatives to seek to promote procedures: see the United States Code, Title 19, Chapter 22, Paragraph 3536 (according to which the 'Trade Representative shall seek the adoption by the Ministerial Conference and General Council of procedures that will ensure broader application of the principle of transparency').

and international civil servants discuss the release of GMOs or the marketing of new pharmaceutical products.

4. The Next Steps

At the beginning of Part II, it was suggested that history and comparative analysis show that the origin of some requirements of due process of law is a set of moral and political assumptions about freedom and authority. Coherently with their history, within and beyond the States, such requirements serve non-instrumental values: dignity and participation.

However, procedural requirements serve other purposes as well. This becomes increasingly evident when passing from national legal systems to modern regulatory regimes. Whether regional or global, such regimes serve to minimize conflict and maximize complementarity and make the trade-offs more evident. Various procedural requirements are justified by instrumental rationales, such as sound administration and cooperation. For example, the conduct of accurate preliminary fact-finding activities can be and often is justified not only by the requirements of good administration but also by the need to foster cooperation between one public authority and another.

The existence of a plurality of rationales, both instrumental and non-instrumental, raises the question of the relations that exist between them. Sometimes they coexist, for example, the accuracy of a procedure serves also to protect the interests that can be adversely affected by its outcomes. However, this is not necessarily the case. Both potentially and not infrequently, in reality, there are also collisions or conflicts. Whether this can be relevant when considering administrative due process of law on a more conceptual level is the question that will be examined in Part III.

PART III

A THEORY OF ADMINISTRATIVE DUE PROCESS BEYOND THE STATE

8

Administrative Due Process

A Conceptual Analysis

While the analysis carried out in the first part highlighted the common and distinctive traits that characterize the requirements of due process with regard to administrative procedure in the national and transnational arenas, the remarks made in the second part supported a theory of due process that takes both instrumental and non-instrumental rationales into account. It remains to be seen whether such theory is conceptually adequate. A few words can be helpful to clarify the argument that will be made in the following pages. An attempt will be made to identify some characteristics of procedural due process of law that permit us to distinguish it, conceptually, from other principles with which it is often associated—such as non-arbitrariness, legality, and the prohibition of denial of justice—in academic works, in the official documents of multilateral organizations, and in judicial and arbitral decisions and operationally, because its requirements are distinct and more suitable to administrative action.

1. Conceptual Clarity and Operational Standards

It should be stated at the outset that these concepts—due process of law, on the one hand, and non-arbitrariness, legality, and the prohibition of denial of justice, on the other—are neither clarified nor defined by legal provisions, which is not surprising in light of the old maxim that in law every definition can be dangerous because of the opposite risks of under-inclusiveness or over-inclusiveness. Nor do the courts or arbitral bodies define and refine such concepts except in very few circumstances. As a result, the exact meanings and scopes of application of such concepts are not precise, despite the extensive literature that exists on them.

An attempt to shed some light on their distinctive traits is, however, important both theoretically and practically. To be acceptable theoretically, a doctrine of due process must not run counter to the common-sense conviction that certain conduct of public authorities infringes the values of justice and fairness that underlie all such

Due Process of Law Beyond the State. First Edition. Giacinto della Cananea.
Published 2016 by Oxford University Press.

concepts.[1] However, if a theory of procedural due process of law acknowledges this common background and at the same time specifies its distinctiveness, we may more easily follow it and reject our less convincing 'common-sense' judgments where the implications of such a theory are partially different, for example, with regard to 'subjective' aspects such as bad faith.

There is also a practical side to the distinction. Not only in academic studies, but also in the 'official' documents elaborated by public institutions,[2] as well as in judicial and arbitral decisions, due process of law is often associated with concepts such as non-arbitrariness, legality, and (the prohibition of) denial of justice. However, if we consider due process of law and non-arbitrariness or denial of justice more closely, it soon becomes evident that we cannot speak of an effective identity. Indeed, not only are such concepts far from being identical, they are also based on different standards, which impose different obligations on public authorities.

A final caveat concerns the purposes and limits of this stage of our inquiry. The topics covered in this and the next chapter are only a sample of the variety of topics related to due process of law. There is not the space for an exhaustive analysis of the subject. The emphasis will be on how due process of law influences and shapes administrative procedure and, thus, the conduct of institutions involved in the business of government.

2. Beyond Non-arbitrariness

Due process of law and non-arbitrariness are often associated. This way of looking at due process is, in particular, a central feature of the oft-cited ruling of the Arbitral Chamber of the International Court of Justice (ICJ) in *ELSI*,[3] which was mentioned at the beginning of Chapter 1. Since this case is particularly important for understanding the difference between two different visions of due process, it is helpful to recall briefly the terms in which the question was raised and, subsequently, to focus on its weaknesses.

[1] See *Merrill & Ring Forestry v Canada*, (United Nations Commission on International Trade Law (UNCITRAL), International Centre for Settlement of Investment Disputes (ICSID) Administered Case, Award of 31 March 2010), § 211 (positing that 'the [FET] standard protects against all such acts or behavior that might infringe a sense of fairness, equity and reasonableness'). See also Albert V Dicey, *Introduction to the Study of the Law of the Constitution* (10th edn, MacMillan, 1956) 42 (arguing that the Rule of Law 'means in the first place the absolute supremacy or predominance of regular law as opposed to the influence of arbitrary power, and excludes the existence of arbitrariness').

[2] See, for instance, OECD, *Fair and Equitable Standard in International Investment Law* (2003) 26 (considering due process together with non-denial of justice and lack of arbitrariness).

[3] *Elettronica Sicula Spa (ELSI) United States v Italy* (1989). According to the Yale Law School database, at the end of 2014 there were sixteen citations made by ICSID awards to this award. Among them there are *Middle East*, paragraph 143 and *Bywater Gauff v Tanzania* (ICSID Case No ARB/05/22), Award of 24 July 2008, paragraph 531. For further details, see Stephen A Kubiatowski, 'The Case of Elettronica Sicula S.p.a.: Toward Greater Protection of Shareholders' Rights in Foreign Investments' (1991) 29 Colum J Transn'l L 215.

A case of 'ordinary' injustice: *ELSI*

In the late 1960s, a US company producing electronic components (ELSI) was going to close its plant in Palermo (Italy) in spite of the efforts made by local and national authorities to save hundreds of jobs. The Mayor of Palermo reacted by issuing an order (taking immediate effect) requisitioning ELSI's plant and related assets for six months. Sixteen months later, an administrative appeal brought against the order in the administrative courts—as distinct from an action seeking legal remedies available in the ordinary courts—still had not been decided by the Prefect of Palermo. The appeal was based on the argument that the Mayor had exceeded his powers and that the requisition had therefore been unlawful. The lower Italian court endorsed this argument. In the meantime, however, the plant had been unoccupied, production had ceased, and ELSI had been purchased at a low price by a subsidiary company of the State-controlled economic holding (IRI). An action for damages resulting from the requisition, initially dismissed by the Tribunal of Palermo, was later upheld by the Court of Appeal, but only for a small portion of the claim. The Court of Cassation eventually upheld the latter decision in 1975.

The US government brought the case to the ICJ, claiming that Italy was responsible for several alleged violations of the Treaty of Friendship, Commerce and Navigation concluded in 1948. The five-judge Arbitral Chamber of the ICJ rejected this claim. It affirmed that the existence of the 'constant protection and security' requirement in the Treaty did not imply that an Italian governmental entity, such as the municipality of Palermo, lacked the power to issue the requisition order. Moreover, and more importantly for present purposes, the majority interpreted the Treaty's provision that the nationals and corporations of the parties 'shall not be subjected to arbitrary … measures'[4] as meaning in this case that the 'minimum international standard' had not been violated by a sixteen-month delay in the domestic proceedings. In other words, although the administrative act (the requisition order) had been found unlawful, this did not imply that it was, as a result, arbitrary.

The dissenting opinion of Judge Schwebel sharply criticized this reasoning. On the basis of his reading of the *travaux préparatoires* and preamble to the Supplementary Agreement to the Treaty of 1948, he disagreed that the relevant standard should be the minimum one. He suggested that such standards should be drawn from the principle of equitable treatment and should limit the discretionary powers exercised by public administrations. He concluded that the requisition order had deprived the owner of its right of control over its properties.[5]

Weaknesses of the *ELSI* doctrine

This brief description of the case can help us understand why, although *ELSI* is often referred to, its importance must not be overestimated. Given the natural tendency

[4] See the Treaty's Supplementary Agreement, Article 1.
[5] Dissenting Opinion of Judge Schwebel [1989] ICJ Reports 94.

of lawyers to cite cases having similar facts, especially in the field of investment arbitration where there is a relatively limited number of cases, the search for the canons that should govern the conduct of public authorities easily becomes a search for case precedents closely related to the case at hand. However, a closer look at *ELSI* reveals that it is but an example of the traditional, indirect, protection that investors could obtain through their home countries.[6] By contrast, more recent bilateral investment treaties (BITs) provide investors with direct protection through arbitration. The same applies, *a fortiori*, when fully fledged courts are entrusted with the task of adjudicating disputes between individuals and business, on the one hand, and public authorities, on the other hand. From this point of view, although *ELSI* and the later cases that cite it have in common the fact that they are concerned with governmental interference with the property of foreign investors, the later cases cite this earlier case as if they were institutionally similar, but they are not.

There is, however, a more fundamental reason why the importance of *ELSI* should not be overestimated. In *ELSI* the majority affirmed that the 'minimum international standard' had not been violated because national measures were unlawful, but not arbitrary. It defined arbitrariness as 'not so much something opposed to a rule of law, as something opposed to *the rule of law*.... It is *wilful disregard of due process of law*, an act which shocks, or at least surprises a sense of judicial propriety'.[7]

Interestingly, the *ELSI* doctrine brought foreign investors under the protection of the Rule of Law, as distinct from the respect for the rules of law. So far, so good. But when we look at how the majority constructed the canons of conduct that must be respected by public authorities, it soon becomes evident that it defines arbitrariness in a negative way and vaguely. Moreover, the *ELSI* doctrine referred to a subjective element, the 'wilful disregard' of due process of law, whose relevance is questionable. Both aspects deserve critical analysis.

The prohibition of arbitrariness is not simply a vague standard, but it also refers to 'extreme' circumstances. It is infringed by conduct attributable to a public authority and harmful to the claimant only if such conduct is arbitrary, grossly unfair, idiosyncratic, 'or involves a lack of due process leading to an outcome which offends judicial propriety—as might be the case with a manifest failure of natural justice in judicial proceedings or a complete lack of transparency and candor in an administrative process'[8] or, still, if the decisions taken by the host State are characterized by a 'lack of due process or other characteristics that shock the conscience ... [or] defy ... elemental fairness'.[9] This is really a 'minimum standard' in the sense that such a high threshold is susceptible of being reached only in cases of blatant injustice, and thus of being applied in a very limited range of cases. The *ELSI* ruling was thus criticized

[6] Jan Paulsson, *Denial of Justice in International Law* (Cambridge University Press, 2005) 3; José Alvarez, *The Public International Law Regime Governing International Investment* (Brill/Nijhoff, 2011) 203.

[7] *Elettronica Sicula Spa (ELSI) United States v Italy*, paragraph 128 (emphasis added).

[8] *Waste Management Inc. v United Mexican States* (ICSID Case No ARB(AF)/00/3), Award of 30 April 2004, paragraph 98 (emphasis added).

[9] *Unglaube v Republic of Costa Rica* (*Unglaube*) (ICSID Case No ARB/08/1), Award of 16 May 2012, paragraph 246.

for its failure to 'condemn acts which, for instance, on the ground of administrative excess or *détournement de pouvoir*, the legal systems of civilized nations consider illegal'.[10] In sum, *ELSI* failed to articulate specific standards of justice.

To the contrary, though open, procedural due process of law is a standard that aims at ensuring protection against a broader spectrum of conduct. It is precisely because it does not target only grossly arbitrary and capricious conduct, but all that which infringes basic elements of fairness, that due process of law is a much more workable standard and is increasingly used by arbitrators. Several recent decisions show a common concern; that is, that foreign investors may suffer from the negative consequences of how a procedure is shaped, or, more simply, by the lack of a procedure in the proper sense. The same applies to the other two requirements of which arbitrators seek to ensure respect: that investors whose interests are likely to be adversely affected by a public decision have a meaningful opportunity to be heard before it is taken and that the reasons supporting such decision are made known. In all these respects, due process of law is not only a standard less ambiguous and imprecise than non-arbitrariness, but, as a NAFTA tribunal has held, due process of law provides arbitrators with 'more rigorous standards for evaluating what governments do to people and companies'.[11]

The *ELSI* doctrine also suffers from another weakness, to the extent that a connection was established between arbitrariness and the 'wilful' disregard of due process of law.[12] In theory the protection that the law offers against intentional harm is certainly capable of encompassing injuries suffered by investors, but in practice it is hard to demonstrate such intention. Conversely, neither the FET standard[13] nor, *a fortiori*, the BITs' specific clauses governing expropriation require such a subjective analysis. In other words, there is no need to prove that the host State acted in bad faith or 'wanted' to deprive the foreign investor of its process rights.

Other instructive cases

Two more recent cases concerning other fields of law and distinct legal situations confirm the distance that separates due process of law from non-arbitrariness. The first is the World Trade Organization (WTO)'s *Shrimp* dispute, the other is the ruling of the ECJ in *Kadi*.

In *Shrimp*, like in *ELSI*, the complaining parties were the States acting on behalf of the importers who felt discriminated against.[14] In fact the US ban was against

[10] Francis A Mann, 'Foreign Investment in the International Court of Justice' (1992) 86 An J Int'l L 90. Another comment pointed out *ELSI*'s partial contribution to defining the concept of arbitrariness: Kurt J Hamrock, 'The ELSI Case: Toward an International Definition of "Arbitrary" Conduct' (1992) 27 Tex Int'l LJ 837.

[11] *Pope & Talbot v Canada*, Award in respect of damages of 31 May 2002, paragraph 64.

[12] See, for instance, *OKO Pankki Oyj and others v Republic of Estonia* (ICSID Case No ARB/04/6), Award of 19 November 2007, paragraph 367.

[13] *PSEG Global Inc. v Republic of Turkey* (ICSID Case No ARB/02/05), Award of 19 January 2007, paragraph 256 ('even if the conduct … were to comply with good faith').

[14] For further details, see Chapter 3, Section 4, p. 53.

imports from countries that did not impose the use of turtle-excluding devices, with a view to preserving this type of exhaustible natural resource. In itself the ban did not target Asian countries. However, according to the Appellate Body (AB), the ban was 'arbitrary and capricious' because of the modalities through which the US administration had acted. On the one hand, whilst negotiating a transitional period with Caribbean countries, it had failed to do so with Asian countries. On the other hand, the US administration had adopted administrative guidance without any notice and comment requirements having been observed. Nor was there any transparent and predictable process for issuing certifications with the indication of reasons.

The legal literature is replete with excellent articles illustrating and criticizing the substantive agenda that was undertaken by WTO dispute resolution bodies. But this does not inexorably lead to the conclusion that the decision taken by the AB makes sense as part of a substantive arbitral programme to promote free trade at the expense of other interests. Indeed, the reasoning followed by the AB, especially where it was argued that the chapeau of Article XX of the General Agreement on Tariffs and Trade (GATT) 1994 justifies limits to trade in order to protect and promote other interests,[15] runs in the opposite direction. It creates the conditions that are necessary for interest balancing. Moreover, the AB's search for procedural fairness is confirmed by an exquisitely procedural decision it took to solicit *amici curiae* briefs.

In *Kadi* the complainant reacted against the targeting of suspected terrorists and supporters of terrorism carried out by United Nations (UN) and European Union (EU) authorities. In the course of deciding that the targeted physical and legal persons were entitled to 'some kind of hearing' and to an effective judicial review, the ECJ dissented from the lower court's holding that 'the principle of Community law relating to the right to be heard cannot apply in such circumstances, where to hear the person concerned could not in any case lead the institution to review its position'.[16] The ECJ did not simply reassert the importance of human rights within the legal order of the EU, and the related unacceptability of a generalized immunity from jurisdiction.[17] It argued that a more satisfactory use of interest balancing was needed, affirming that:

> it is ... the task of the Community judicature to apply, in the course of the judicial review it carries out, techniques which accommodate, on the one hand, legitimate security concerns about the nature and sources of information taken into account in the adoption of the act concerned and, on the other, the need to accord the individual a sufficient measure of procedural justice.[18]

Unlike the ICJ's award in *ELSI*, which was rather vague even with regard to what administrators should not do, this statement of the ECJ relies on its precedents and adds or specifies something important for present purposes. The pioneering

[15] *United States—Import Prohibition of Certain Shrimp and Shrimp Products*—Report of the Appellate Body of 21 October 1998 (*Shrimp II*) paragraph 124.

[16] CFI, Case T-315/01, *Kadi v Commission and Council*, paragraph 259.

[17] ECJ, Joined Cases C-402/05 and C-415/05, '*Kadi*' and '*Yusuf and Al Barakaat*', paragraph 297.

[18] ECJ, Joined Cases C-402/05 and C-415/05, '*Kadi*' and '*Yusuf and Al Barakaat*', paragraph 344.

cases—*Alvis* and *Transocean*—referred to due process as a general principle of law, which must be enforced even absent particular rules. All this sounds like the English concept of 'natural justice'. But the concept of due process is used to assess the conduct of a public authority in the exercise of non-judicial powers. And the Court clearly uses the language of interest balancing. This is evident not only in its choice to refer to both individual rights and 'legitimate security concerns', but also in the point that is made about the need to ensure 'a sufficient measure of procedural justice'. We may doubt whether it is all that simple, especially with regard to the assessment of 'sufficiency' or 'adequacy'. But three things are clear: a hearing, by its very essence, demands that reasonable advance notice be given, that the possibility to contradict allegations and evidence be provided, and that the measure issued by the public authority takes these into account. Other requirements that are deemed essential in judicial proceedings may be dispensed with and even the time at which the hearing takes place may be postponed if overriding reasons of public interest so require. To the extent that the Court was ready to accept that a hearing could take place after the decision adversely affecting *Kadi* was taken, it was far from following a sort of idealized approach to procedural justice. However, by its very essence, the right to be heard implies that everyone must have an opportunity to answer the case against him or her. Without any hearing at all—and without any sort of information about the grounds on which he had been targeted—Kadi's treatment was not simply arbitrary, it was evidently contrary to the due process of law.[19]

Interestingly, from the perspective of public authorities, the three cases just discussed differ. Functionally *ELSI* involves an executive function close to expropriation, but distinct from it, that of requisition; *Shrimp* is a trade law case; and *Kadi* involves the exercise of powers that impinge not only on the use of assets, but also on the free movement of capital. These cases also differ in that the first two are concerned with the conduct of State officers, while the last one reveals the growing interaction between national, international, and supranational authorities. The interplay between legal systems thus plays a part and shows conflicting views about justice. However, each of these cases suggests that an important dimension of justice is the respect of certain requirements of procedural due process of law. Although ensuring due process certainly serves to prevent or correct arbitrary—not simply discretionary—decisions, the methodology of procedural due process is specific in a twofold respect. First, it imposes an order in administrative decision-making, instead of setting limits concerning substance. Second, if a decision is taken by an agency without observance of procedure required by law or of particular requirements, and thus it fails to assure an ordered decision-making process, then the courts or other bodies can hold agency action unlawful. In conclusion, due process is not just conceptually distinct from non-arbitrariness, but it also provides more rigorous and workable indicators of justice.

[19] Martti Koskenniemi, *The Politics of International Law* (Hart, 2001) 254 (noting the risk that 'individuals will continue to find themselves blacklisted and embargoed without being heard or given effective remedy').

3. Due Process and Legality: A Distinction

As the arbitral and judicial practice with respect to governmental interference with the interests of individuals suggests that due process of law is a much more workable standard than non-arbitrariness, so too practice shows that, as a legal standard, it is distinct from legality and operates differently.

Due process as an inference of legality

Some decades ago, the sense of this distinction was almost lost in the OECD Draft Convention on the Protection of Foreign Property. It opened with the statement that 'it is a well-established general principle of international law that a State is bound to respect and protect the property of nationals of other States'. It also referred to due process of law in the context of the taking of property. A note to this provision added that 'in essence, the contents of the notion of due process make it akin to the requirements of the Rule of Law ... or *Rechtsstaat*'.[20]

Arguably, not only was this an oversimplification, because the Rule of Law and *Rechtsstaat* have distinct institutional and theoretical underpinnings,[21] but bringing due process of law under the former (or the latter) does not help us much. There is no doubt that due process of law draws inspiration from the Rule of Law ideals of the necessity for a shield against arbitrariness and unjustified discrepancies in treatment.[22] However, the issues that are raised are distinct, including whether the decision has been reached through a fair process and for reasons that have been clarified during such process. Putting the emphasis on due process marks an important shift away, in particular, from the traditional approach to the use of administrative power, under which the exercise of this kind of power was reviewable only on the question of whether the power existed (because it was provided by a specific norm), and not as to the fairness or propriety of its exercise. Moreover, for all the importance of the emphasis on individual rights, there are other potentialities of due process that must not be forgotten. Such potentialities can be achieved either in consultation procedures that give voice to social groups or in the exercise of supervisory powers, as the *Mumbai* and *Marlin mining* cases show.

Due process as a shield against expropriation

The field of foreign investment provides some interesting examples of the distinction between legality and due process. Instead of looking, as is often done, at arbitral practice, it can be interesting to devote attention to the treaties that set out the

[20] OECD, Draft Convention on the Protection of Foreign Property (1967).

[21] Jurgen Habermas, *Law and Morality—The Tanner Lectures on Human Values* (Sterling M. McMurrin ed, 1988) 273.

[22] For a discussion of the ways in which the Rule of Law is shaped beyond the State, see David Dyzenhaus, 'The Rule of (Administrative) Law in International Law' (2004) 68 Law & Cont Probl 127.

standards which arbitrators must respect. A sample analysis shows that some BITs, especially in Latin America, request an expropriation to be carried out in respect of either existing legislation or the principle of legality.[23] Other countries—in Europe, Latin America, and Asia—introduce into their BITs a more specific clause which obliges the host State to exercise its powers 'in accordance with the procedure established by the legislation'.[24] There is still another way to protect the rights of investors, chosen by some BITs as well as by NAFTA and CAFTA, when expropriation is deemed admissible only if it is carried out with respect to 'due process of law'.[25] Interestingly, it is the third way that is increasingly chosen by both traditional and new important capital-exporting countries, such as Germany[26] and China.[27]

Bearing in mind the distinction just drawn between the three models (legality, respect of existing procedures, and due process), let us now look at arbitral practice. It is not difficult to understand why arbitrators are reluctant to endorse claims about the lack of an adequate legal basis for the activities carried out by the host State. Such claims call into question the goals that elected officials have established. Arbitrators have at least three means for not making merit judgments of this type. The first is to deny that the claim relates to an interest that merits protection because it is unrelated to the transnational situations covered by the BIT. The second is to emphasize their limited scope of review and necessary deference to the autonomy of national policymakers. The third is to take a procedural approach. Sometimes arbitrators have endorsed the claimants' argument that the final decision taken by the State was based upon evidence not in the record or upon evidence which the recipient had no opportunity at all to test by cross-examination (or that was even undisclosed). In other cases, they found that such final decision was based on elements that were virtually immune to adversarial procedures. Sometimes, there was no reason at all, for example, if a licence to provide gambling services was revoked without justification, let alone an adequate or sound one.

From (administrative) power to its exercise

The distinction between legality and due process emerges more clearly when considering the traditional concerns about legality and the traits that characterize a process jurisprudence. Concerns about legality focus on the existence of a certain power, the respect of the conditions that legitimize its exercise, and the respect of

[23] See, for instance, the Mexico–Germany BIT and Argentina's BITs with Ecuador and Mexico.

[24] See Italy's BITs with Argentina, Egypt, and Mexico, as well as with Albania, Libya, Lithuania, and Turkey, while the BIT with Saudi Arabia refers to legality and that with Tunisia neglects this issue. See also Mexico's BITs with the UK and Uruguay, as well as those of Egypt with Russia and South Korea.

[25] This is an invariant of US BITs, as noted by Christoph Schreuer, 'Fair and Equitable Treatment in Arbitral Practice' (2005) 6 J World Trade 125, 128. It characterizes the US Model BIT and its BITs with several countries (including Argentina, Congo, Croatia, Estonia, Georgia, Jamaica, Jordan, Lithuania, Mongolia, and Ukraine).

[26] See the German Model BIT, Article 4(2).

[27] China's BITs often refer either to due process or to existing procedures in the context of expropriation: see those with Botswana, Cameroon, Myanmar, North Korea, Poland, and Syria.

the limits established by legislation or custom. If a public authority exceeds such limits, and thus acts *ultra vires*, its action is invalid. If, instead, it does not respect the procedure it had followed in similar cases or does not pay attention to the evidence and arguments provided by those who are adversely affected by its measures or does not provide reasons that are related to the facts it has adduced and the legal norms it has referred to, then the claim that can be made is that the government function has not been exercised fairly and properly.

This distinction can be discussed in the light of a traditional power of the State, expropriation. The concept of legality includes the public authority's competence and the payment of compensation. It may also refer to the fair value of the assets expropriated if legislation and treaties so specify. For instance, the Treaty between the US and Italy that was at the heart of the *ELSI* case referred to 'just and effective compensation'. Procedural due process of law adds requirements that are completely independent from those concerning the power to carry out an expropriation and its fair value. It requires public authorities to comply with duties of procedural propriety in decision-making, as well as to respect foreign investors' process rights, such as the right to be heard before the final decision concerning the expropriation and its compensation is taken. It permits judges and arbitrators to carry out an accurate review of the decision-making process without contesting the choices made by the public authority. A judge or an arbitrator can thus refrain from considering whether the expropriation of the right concerning a certain property is 'just',[28] whilst not hesitating to ascertain whether due process has been respected.

Consider, now, regulation. Suppose that, as happened in *Lemire*, a State is going to issue a certain number of telecommunications licences without establishing a procedure and defining the aspects that must be considered within it. Although this way of regulating scarce resources is clearly quite distant from the ideals of equality and predictability that lie at the root of the Rule of Law,[29] it can hardly be regarded as outrageous. A failure to define a procedure and to specify the elements of fact that must be considered therein can, however, influence negatively all of its outcomes, especially if so many facts enter into the decision to grant a licence that it would be hard to tell which factors could be and have been decisive. A situation like this would hardly meet the narrow standard of non-arbitrariness. Nor, as a related but distinct weakness, could the arbitral tribunal object to the State having anything different from a 'manifest' lack of reasons. Under the FET standard, instead, the mere absence of a given procedure can be regarded as being 'symptomatic' of procedural unfairness and thus of treatment that is unjust and inequitable.

We can read the AB's decision in *Shrimp* in the same way. The starting point is, again, the assumption that the need to protect environmental resources could justify the US ban on shrimp and shrimp-related products coming from nations

[28] A controversial case was that of expropriation of foreign properties in Iran in 1951, which gave rise to litigation in other countries: see, for instance, the Italian Tribunal judgment n 3906/1953 and the comment in (1954) 48 Am J Int'l L 259.

[29] See Josef Raz, *The Authority of Law* (Clarendon Press, 1979) 210.

that did not oblige producers to use turtle-excluder devices. The AB had made it clear that the results of the US rules and decisions might have been valuable in this respect, but the process was bad, as a *process*. According to the AB, that process did not pass the test aimed at avoiding arbitrary and capricious discrimination. Discrimination against foreign producers emerged, among other things, from the failure to respect two basic due process requirements, that would have permitted a sort of interest representation and would have made the reasons known.

There are some differences between these cases about investment and trade and the *Tysiac* case adjudicated by the European Court of Human Rights (ECtHR),[30] but there is also an important common thread. The first difference is, obviously, that the former dealt with economic rights, such as freedom of trade, while the latter covered a variety of rights and liberties. Another difference is that the European Convention on Human Rights (ECHR) laid down a provision on fair trial, Article 6, which provided the Strasbourg Court with an important basis for emphasizing fundamental fairness ideas, especially when dealing with criminal (and quasi-criminal) procedural and evidentiary standards. However, in *Tysiac* the ECtHR did not draw from Article 6 additional unenumerated protections for familial integrity, nor did it engage in interest balancing in order to assess whether Poland had correctly appreciated Tysiac's personal interest against the collective interest. It followed what could appear to be a more humble approach, to the extent that it took as an undisputed premise that the new Polish legislative framework had limited the margins for exercising the right to abortion. However, it held, if those margins existed and had to be taken seriously within the administrative procedure set out by the State, then such procedure had to be applied properly. Public officers, therefore, could neither deny the woman a meaningful opportunity to be heard before decisions so adversely affecting her life and health were taken, nor comply with this fundamental procedural requirement only formalistically.

The unifying thread in this set of cases is the belief that what is legally relevant is not only the existence of a range of powers aiming at achieving a certain set of ends, but also the propriety and fairness of the legal processes that they set out and follow. It is in the light of this unifying thread that the development of procedural protections is justified.

4. Due Process of Law as Distinct from Denial of Justice

The prohibition of denial of justice is well established in international law. Several studies, some recent and accurate, examine this concept from several perspectives. The analysis that follows makes no pretense at being a complete survey of these differing approaches. It makes an attempt, rather, to address the subject in a way that is coherent with our focus on due process of law and that is

[30] Josef Raz, *The Authority of Law*, Chapter 6, p. 103, paragraph 2.

somewhat under-theorized.[31] The central issue is, therefore, whether a distinction can be drawn between due process of law and denial of justice, although such concepts are often associated in the two subsidiary sources referred to by Article 38(1)(d) of the Statute of the ICJ; that is, scholarly works and judicial decisions.[32]

The structure of the analysis will be as follows. As a first step, the conceptions of denial of justice that emphasize its connections with due process of law will be illustrated. The next step will be to point out some elements that support the thesis of a clear distinction between the two concepts. The third and final part will consider whether there is some middle way between the adoption of a conception of denial of justice that overlaps with due process and another that separates them. In other words, a distinction can be of crucial importance in determining the nature of the specific requirements that apply to an administrative procedure and a judicial process respectively, but we do not need to assume that all such requirements are exclusive either of the former or of the latter.

Denial of justice and due process as overlapping concepts

Two arguments can be made to point out the connections between due process of law and the prohibition of denial of justice. While one is based on history, the other follows from the procedural conception of denial of justice.

Historically, neither the fundamental rule of natural justice which is expressed by the maxim *audi et alteram partem* nor the giving reasons requirement are peculiarly requirements of administrative procedure. In fact both requirements were initially developed in the context of the judicial function. Only more recently have such requirements been imposed in the context of administrative procedure.

The other argument suggests that the concept of denial of justice does not designate only a court's unjustified abstention from the obligation to render justice, an obligation that is affirmed by the positive norms of most modern legal systems. It also includes any circumstance in which the judicial branch of a State 'administers justice to aliens in a fundamentally unfair manner'.[33] Once the focus is placed on the administration of justice it is easier to affirm, in contrast with the less recent opinion that theorized the existence of substantive denial of justice,[34] that the manifestations of injustice that are relevant under this concept are always procedural. They include both outside interference with the administration of justice, such as the manipulation of a court's composition by the State and its failure to execute judgments, and the conduct that is imputable to the decision-maker, such

[31] Thomas W Wälde, 'Denial of Justice: A Review Comment on Jan Paulsson, *Denial of Justice in International Law*' (2006) 21 ICSID Rev 449, 457.

[32] See, for instance, Christopher F Dugan, Don Wallace, Noah Rubins, and Borzu Sabahi, *Investor-State Arbitration* (Oxford University Press, 2008) 525–6.

[33] Jan Paulsson, *Denial of Justice*, 4.

[34] Alwyn Freeman, *The International Responsibility of States for Denial of Justice* (Longmans, Green and Co, 1938).

as unjustified delays,[35] lack of due process, and judicial corruption. The conclusion that is inferred from all this is that 'international responsibility arises as a result of the failure of a national legal system to provide due process'.[36]

Contrasting due process and denial of justice

Two main arguments can be brought against the equivalence between (the prohibition of) denial of justice and procedural due process of law. On the one hand, obviously, if one does not agree with the idea that denial of justice is eminently procedural, but thinks that it also has a substantive component, then there are reasons to affirm that the two concepts may overlap, but not entirely.[37] There is, in other words, a missing part of the story. On the other hand, even if one accepts, instead, the procedural conception of denial of justice, four elements can support a distinction between this concept and due process of law.

First, on grounds of legal theory, according to one school of thought, the executive and judicial functions of government differ, among other things, because the former consists in the exercise of discretionary powers and thus is connoted by adaptability to a certain end, the second by a constrained character.[38] One aspect that can be regarded as exemplary for the activities of the executive branch of government is that policymakers enjoy wide (though not unlimited) powers to modify the content and conditions of their decisions and can thus amend, revoke, or withdraw them, so long as they respect the relevant procedure. Conversely, the principle of *res judicata*[39] strictly limits the reviewability of judicial decisions. All this confirms the opinion of Justice Frankfurter that 'differences in origin and function preclude wholesale transplantation of the rules of procedure and review that have evolved from the history and experience of the courts'.[40]

Secondly, and consequently, there can be significant differences concerning the threshold of due process requirements. This line of reasoning can provide a reasonable justification for the cases in which requirements that are essential in strictly judicial proceedings[41] may be dispensed with in the courts of administrative procedure. For instance, if overriding reasons of public interest so require, a hearing may take place after a certain measure has been taken and reasons can be reduced

[35] Jan Paulsson, *Denial of Justice*, 178 (noting that defendant States' defences based on 'reference to overcharged dockets' were unsuccessful).

[36] Jan Paulsson, *Denial of Justice*, 36.

[37] Andrew Newcombe, 'Review of Jan Paulsson, Denial of Justice in International Law' (2006) 17 Eur J Int'l L 17 692, 693.

[38] Rudolf von Jhering, *Law as a Means to an End* (Isaac Husik (tr), Boston Book Company, 1913) 290.

[39] See the arbitral tribunal's award in *Helnan International Hotels A/S v Arab Republic of Egypt* (ICSID Case No ARB/05/19), Award of 3 July 2008.

[40] *FCC v Pottsville Broadcasting Co*, 309 US 134 (1940).

[41] Occasionally, and questionably, also the standards of judicial process are relaxed: see *The Loewen Group, Inc. and Raymond L. Loewen v United States of America* (Case No ARB(AF)/98/3), Award of 26 June 2003, paragraphs 119 and 189.

to what is essential to understand why such measure was taken. The practice of investment arbitration and the contemporary debate about antiterrorism measures reveal that, although the indicators of the process that is 'due' are more or less the same, their intensity differs. A different intensity in the application of indicators of the process that is due has emerged, for example, with regard to the maxim *audi alteram partem*.[42] This impinges on the criterion for egregiousness or significant materiality of dysfunctions or anomalies in the conduct of public authorities.[43]

Thirdly, whatever the intellectual soundness of procedural or substantive conceptions of (the prohibition of) denial of justice, this designates a fundamentally unfair manner of administering justice to aliens.[44] Its scope is, therefore, more limited than administrative due process of law, from a subjective viewpoint; that is, one that focuses on the classes of subjects who are entitled to avail themselves of them.

Finally, the concept of denial of justice is often used to designate the more systemic shortcomings of a judicial system. It is under this heading, for example, that an arbitral tribunal may be called upon to assess whether a State has failed to fulfil the obligation stemming from international law, that is, the obligation to create a system of justice within which errors in the administration of justice can be corrected.[45] A denial of justice, properly intended, thus arises only if there is no 'reasonably available national mechanism to correct the challenged action'.[46] An important practical implication of this is that the requirement to exhaust local remedies is not, in itself, a denial of justice, though justice delayed is often justice denied. Another more questionable implication is that a limitation upon access to justice, in other words an immunity, is not necessarily contrary to international law if it is not discriminatory.[47]

Accordingly, most of these elements support the view that denial of justice, though often associated with concerns about due process of law, should be regarded as referring essentially to the judicial function. It should not be used, instead, to designate governmental interference with private property.[48] However, the second element opens the path to a more nuanced view, which will now be developed.

Common and distinctive traits

Another way to look at the relationship between denial of justice and due process of law is to observe that they have some important common elements, especially if one accepts the view that both concepts are essentially concerned with process. In other words, they are not concerned with whether the decision taken by a judicial or administrative authority is a good one or a bad one, provided that certain legal

[42] See *Bosh International, Inc and B&P Ltd Foreign Investments Enterprise v Ukraine*, ICSID Case No. ARB/08/11, Award of 25 October 2012, paragraph 200 ('and in any event, the Respondent argues that the due process requirement in the context of administrative decisions is lower than the judicial').

[43] Thomas W Wälde, 'Denial of Justice', 457.

[44] Jan Paulsson, *Denial of Justice*, Chapter 1; Thomas W Wälde, 'Denial of Justice', 455.

[45] Jan Paulsson, *Denial of Justice*, 109.

[46] Jan Paulsson, *Denial of Justice*, 100.

[47] Eur Ct HR, *Fogarty v United Kingdom* (Application no 37112/97), judgment of 21 November 2001, Reports, 2001, IX-157 (excluding violations of Articles 6 and 14 ECHR).

[48] See Muthucumaraswamy Sornarajah, *The International Law on Foreign Investment* (2nd edn, Cambridge University Press, 2004) 330.

requirements were respected. But such requirements are not always the same and, even when they are substantially the same, their thresholds differ, in the sense that the threshold is higher for administrative adjudication and regulation. There is, in other words, more than a distinctive trait which justifies a conceptual distinction. This approach looks preferable to the formulations used by some practitioners, for example, the term administrative denial of justice.[49]

Let us discuss this distinction by way of an example concerning an administrative act planning financial cuts to hospitals in an Italian region. A dispute arose between a municipality, *Terlizzi*, and the broader territorial unit where it is located, the *Regione Puglia*. When it became known that the latter was going to issue a plan to transfer some sections of the local hospital elsewhere, the former tried to intervene in the decision-making process. When this attempt failed, it applied for judicial review before the administrative court. This was clearly an attempt to solve a political conflict by legal means. It was equally clear that the regional authority was interested in preventing such a course of action. What it did was to re-approve the contested administrative act, this time by way of a statute. The administrative court of appeal (*Consiglio di Stato*) dismissed the case without judging on the merits and without asking the Constitutional Court to review the constitutional legitimacy of the regional statute.[50]

Two aspects of this ruling are particularly problematic. First, there was evidence that the regional authority used legislation in order to sidestep the due process requirements attaching to administrative procedures. The *Consiglio di Stato* acknowledged that it did so on purpose, but apodictically denied that Article 6 ECHR had been infringed and even neglected to recognize that, under national constitutional law, an international treaty prevails over legislation. Second, once it had found that due process requirements had been sidestepped, it should have drawn the logical conclusions from this, bringing this case to the Constitutional Court. But it did not do so. This is all the more unacceptable because, if a legal provision stemming from a statute is in conflict with the ECHR, it must be brought before the Constitutional Court. It can be said, therefore, that the judge failed to render justice,[51] while the regional authority had disregarded due process of law.

5. Two Lines of a Theory of Due Process

In this chapter, I have sought to look at administrative due process of law from a conceptual point of view. My intent was not to seek to define an abstract concept. It

[49] See *Thunderbird Gaming Corporation v United Mexican States*, UNCITRAL Award of 26 January 2006, paragraph 197.

[50] *Consiglio di Stato*, VI, judgment of 20 January 2004 n 1559, available at https://www.giustizia-amministrativa.it.

[51] For this remark, see Franco G Scoca, 'Condizioni e limiti alla funzione legislativa nella disciplina della p.a. Riflettendo sul pensiero di Aldo M. Sandulli', in *Aldo M Sandulli (1915–1984). Attualità del pensiero giuridico del Maestro* (Giuffrè, 2004) 188.

was, rather, to place due process in the context of concepts that are used by administrators, judges, and arbitrators. This attempt had a twofold purpose. First, for the sake of conceptual clarity, whilst seeking to set the framework for our consideration of what due process and other concepts with which it is often associated have in common, in particular the concern for misuses and abuses of power, its distinctive traits have been pointed out. Second, it has been argued that administrative due process of law is not only distinct from those other concepts; it also provides a set of indicators for procedural fairness and propriety that are partially distinct from the indicators that are used to assess both the legality of administrative action and (non) denial of justice, properly intended, and are more rigorous for assessing the conduct of public authorities than the generic and loose concept of non-arbitrariness.

This has also set the framework for our consideration in the chapters that follow of two lines of a theory of due process. One line suggests that, whilst being a much more workable standard than equity or non-arbitrariness, due process of law is a variable standard and can thus be conceptualized as a general principle of law. Another line suggests that, within the sense and the limits specified in this inquiry, administrative due process of law can be regarded as a 'global' principle of law. In the discussion that follows a distinction is thus made between 'generality' and the global reach of due process of law, though sometimes in academic literature such aspects are conflated.

9

Administrative Due Process as a General Principle of Public Law

In Chapter 8 it was suggested that administrative due process of law is distinct from other concepts and provides more indicators that are distinct from those related to legality and denial of justice and at the same time are more rigorous standards than non-arbitrariness for assessing the conduct of public authorities. This chapter adds that administrative due process must be viewed as a general principle of law. The structure of the argument is as follows. The first section points out the importance of general principles in the national and transnational arenas. The focus of the argument then shifts to a consideration of the role that due process of law plays. The second section explains in which sense it can be viewed as a general principle of law and discusses the implications that follow from this. Next, the possibility of a complementary and corrective role, which is a recurring theme amongst specialists of international law, is considered. But the enquiry also focuses on a different role, which is not simply complementary and corrective, but foundational. The fourth section thus presents this view, drawing on the analysis carried out in earlier sections and on examples taken from previous chapters. It is followed by some concluding observations.

1. General Principles of Law in the National and Transnational Arenas

Our focus on the general principles of law deserves some preliminary discussion, first of all historically and comparatively.

General principles of natural and positive law

For a long part of the history of Western legal thought, in an arena that was 'transnational by definition',[1] general principles of law were largely derived from natural law. At the beginning of the nineteenth century, the French Civil Code was a turning

[1] Raoul C van Caenegem, *European Law in the Past and the Future. Unity and Diversity over Two Millennia* (Cambridge University Press, 2002) 13.

point.[2] It was the expression of legal positivism. Yet, as a reaction to what was perceived by many citizens and lawyers as arbitrary behaviour by old tribunals (*parlements*), the Code not only prohibited denial of justice, but it also sanctioned it.[3] What followed from this was a duty to render justice, though not a duty to define a rule that did not exist. However, judicial discretion was not fully eliminated.

Other civil codes made explicit reference to the principles of natural law. The best known is the Austrian Civil Code of 1811. Its structure was clearly of a positivist stamp and thus gave priority to the text of the law. It recognized the importance of the similarity of cases decided according to the law, and the 'tenets of similar laws'. But it took care to avoid *non liquet*, by providing that, in a 'doubtful case', the judicial decision was to be made in accordance with the 'principles of natural law'.[4] These principles were subsidiary to positive rules, the only ones that could be interpreted by analogy. However, the existence of two sources of norms, positive law and natural law, rather than only one, ensured a healthy dialectic. It allowed legal rules to be integrated without leaving too much room for the discretion of the court. The same solution was followed by other European and Latin American codes.[5]

The same question—how to allow judges to find solutions for problems not dealt with by existing rules—was resolved differently by other codes. An interesting, though isolated, solution is that followed by the Swiss Civil Code, which gives the court the power to establish a rule as if it were the legislative branch of government.[6] A legitimate concern for the excessive discretionary powers of judges explains why the majority of modern codes contains a *renvoi* to the 'general principles of law', either to those of the State's legal system or to general principles *tout court*.[7] There is, of course, an important difference between the last two options. For instance, while the Italian Civil Code of 1865 entrusted the judge not only with the power to use interpretation by analogy but also with the power to use the 'general principles of the legal order', the Code of 1942 replaced this term with another, 'the legal order of the State', which was not simply narrower but was also inspired by a different conception of law and State.[8]

[2] Mario Ascheri, 'A Turning Point in the Civil-Law Tradition: From Ius Commune to Code Napoléon' (1996) 70 Tulane LR 1041.

[3] French Civil Code (1801), Article 4, which provides that 'judges who refuse to decide a case on the pretext of silence, obscurity or insufficiency of the law are liable to be prosecuted for a denial of justice'. See also the Spanish Civil Code (1888), Article 6.

[4] Austrian Civil Code, Article 7 ('If the case still remains in doubt, it shall be decided according to the principles of natural law, taking into careful consideration all the circumstances of the case').

[5] See the Chilean Civil Code (1855), Article 24 (referring to 'the general spirit of legislation and natural equity'), the Portuguese Civil Code (1867), Article 16 (establishing that if doubts persist 'regard shall be had to the principles of natural law'), and the Colombian Civil Code (1887), Article 4 (referring to the 'principles of *natural law*') (emphasis added).

[6] Swiss Civil Code (1907), Article 1 ('when no legal provision is applicable, the judge shall decide according to customary law and, in default of custom, according to the rules which he would lay down if he had himself to act as legislator'). For further remarks, see Alfred E von Overbeck, 'Some Observations on the Role of the Judge Under the Swiss Civil Code' (1977) 37 Louisiana LR 681, 687.

[7] See, for example, the Italian Civil Code (1942), Article 12(2), the Argentinian Civil Code (1896), Article 16, and the Peruvian Civil Code (1894), Article VIII.

[8] See the Italian Civil Code, Article 12 ('if the case still remains doubtful, it is decided according to the principles of the juridical system of the State') and, for further remarks, Guido Alpa, 'General Principles of Law' (1994) 1 Annual Survey of Int'l & Comp L 15.

Critics of these broad clauses point out that without some standard of decision the requirement that the judge be impartial risks becoming meaningless and the parties' contribution to the making of the judicial decision through reasoned argument loses much of its significance.[9] The constitutional requirement that the judicial decision be reasoned is also negatively affected by the lack of a previous standard. Codes have thus laid down broad clauses referring to 'good faith', 'equity', and 'fair practice'. But these are 'standards that any court could apply without the aid of a code'. [10]

In the field of public law, general principles are even more important. General principles emerged as unwritten, doctrinal constructions, institutionalized as case law. The most important principles materialized in judicial decisions, as more or less self-evident propositions. The courts of last resort, in particular, applied such principles as inherent, taken-for-granted constituent elements of their legal systems. The role of particular legal doctrines such as natural justice in the UK and the *principes généraux de droit sans text formel* in France can only be adequately assessed within such a framework. The case-by-case development of principles was by no means confined to these legal systems. Similar trends emerged in other legal systems of Europe and the Americas.

The emergence of the 'general principles of law recognized by civilized nations'

If we now move from the national to the international arena, we may note a shift to a positivist conception of law, which gradually excluded principles of natural law as a source of legal obligation, 'although vestiges of it survived in the references to moral principles' made by some scholars in their arguments.[11] Others developed arguments based on analogies with the principles of the major domestic legal systems. In the last decades of the nineteenth century arbitral practice furnished several examples of cases in which 'in default of any specific provision of law', arbitrators applied 'the corollaries of general principles ... so to find the solution of the problem' they were confronted with.[12] The existence of a common core was referred to by the Hague Convention of 1899 in reference to the 'legal conscience of civilized peoples'. Article 38 of the Statute of the Permanent Court of International Justice introduced a more precise category in 1920. This was the category of 'general principles of law recognized by civilized nations'.[13] Its inclusion in the Statute

[9] Lon Fuller, 'The Forms and Limits of Adjudication' (1978) 92 Harvard LR 353, 373.

[10] Lon Fuller, 'The Forms and Limits of Adjudication', 373.

[11] Vaughan Lowe, *International Law* (Clarendon Press, 2007) 34.

[12] See, for instance, the holding of the Arbitral Tribunal (Great Britain–United States) constituted under the Special Agreement of 18 August 1910 (1912) 6 Reports of International Arbitral Awards 114 ('International law, as well as domestic law, may not contain, and generally does not contain, express rules decisive of particular cases; but the function of jurisprudence is to resolve the conflict ... by applying, in default of any specific provision of law, the corollaries of general principles').

[13] In the debate that preceded the adoption of the Statute two positions emerged. The first referred to the *règles de droit international telles que les reconnait la conscience juridique des peuples civilisés*, and the second, which prevailed, referred to the *principes généraux de droit reconnus par les peuples civilisés*. For

had an important significance. Even for strict positivist lawyers, those principles were included within the norms that the Court had to follow during the course of its mission to resolve disputes.[14]

After 1945, the category of 'general principles of law recognized by the civilized nations' did not lose its importance. Quite the contrary, together with custom and treaties, it was included in Article 38(1)(c) of the Statute of the International Court of Justice (ICJ) as among the sources of law which the Court has to respect. There is considerable diversity of opinion concerning the meaning and status of this category. As often happens in public law,[15] description and prescription are not easily separated.

It can be helpful, therefore, to give a quick account of the evolution of this category, before analysing some different views about its significance. First, even though Article 38 specifically concerns the ICJ, it is traditionally regarded as an authoritative statement of the legal sources to which all international courts and other bodies, including arbitral tribunals, may resort.[16] Secondly, Article 38(1) envisages a variety of sources, each with its own form of legitimacy.[17] All such sources are distinct from judicial decisions, which constitute a subsidiary source together with academic works, and allow the ICJ to avoid pronouncing a *non liquet*. Thirdly, and more specifically, the way in which the category of 'general principles of law recognized by civilized nations' is constructed shows a distinction between two requisites that must be satisfied if the ICJ intends to apply a certain principle. On the one hand, such a principle must be 'general',[18] as distinct not only from the rules that govern particular conduct, but also from those that apply to a particular field of law, the 'polluter pays' in environmental law being a notable and increasingly important example of this. On the other hand, such a principle must be recognized by a plurality of legal systems, if not by all.

The persisting importance of general principles is confirmed by international and supranational legal systems. In the EC, general principles have been elaborated and

further remarks, see Frances T Freeman Jalet, 'The Quest for the General Principles of Law Recognized by Civilized Nations. A Study' (1962–63) 10 UCLA L Rev 1041.

[14] See Hersch Lauterpacht, *Private Law Sources and Analogies of International Law* (Longmans, Green and Co., 1927) 67.

[15] Paul Craig, *Administrative Law* (5th edn, Sweet & Maxwell, 2003) 3.

[16] See Vaughan Lowe, *International Law*, 35 (calling this 'the orthodox view').

[17] Article 38 of the Statute of the International Court of Justice states that:

1. The Court, whose function is to decide in accordance with international law such disputes as are submitted to it, shall apply:
   a) international conventions, whether general or particular, establishing rules expressly recognized by the contesting states;
   b) international custom, as evidence of a general practice accepted as law;
   c) the general principles of law recognized by civilized nations;
   d) subject to the provisions of Article 59, judicial decisions and the teachings of the most highly qualified publicists of the various nations, as subsidiary means for the determination of rules of law.

Statute of the International Court of Justice, Article 38(1), 14 April 1986.

[18] Frances T Freeman Jalet, 'The Quest for the General Principles of Law', 1046.

applied by the Court of Justice 'under the pressure of having to reach decisions in relation to matters not expressly covered by the Treaties', with the notable exception of the matter of non-contractual liability, for which the Treaty of Rome explicitly referred to the 'general principles of law common to the legal orders of the Member States'.[19] Another important development is the Statute of the International Criminal Court. Although its scope of application is that of criminal law, its general significance should not be underestimated. As regards applicable law, it refers to the 'general principles of law derived by the Court from national laws of legal systems of the world'.[20] This confirms the trend that was envisaged after the Nuremberg trials.[21] To the extent that the treaty lays down several individual principles including legality and *ne bis in idem*, it is evident that the *renvoi* to general principles has an autonomous function.[22]

Three views of the 'general principles of law recognized by civilized nations'

As observed before, there is a vast literature on general principles and it would be superfluous to seek to add to it here.[23] For our purposes, three views can be distinguished.

There is, first, a strand in international law that combines the emphasis put on Article 38 with a strong interest in comparative legal analysis. It found expression in an important academic writing by Bin Cheng, often referred to by parties and arbitrators.[24] He highlighted the fact that international judges and arbitrators have referred to a variety of general principles of law. Examples include the fundamental rules of natural justice, *nemo judex in cause propria* and *audi alteram partem*, as well as the principle of *res judicata*.[25] Following this line of reasoning, it has been argued that not only the investment field but also other fields of international law would benefit from a more principled approach based on comparative legal analysis,

[19] Treaty of Rome, Article 215(2). The quotation is drawn from Lord Justice Schiemann, 'The Application of General Principles of Community Law by English Courts', in Mads Andenas and Francis Jacobs (eds), *European Community Law in the English Courts* (Clarendon Press, 1998) 137, 141. For further analysis, see Paul Reuter, 'Le recours de la Cour de justice des Communautés européennes à des principes généraux de droit', in *Mélanges Rollin* (Pedone, 1964) 263.

[20] Statute of the International Criminal Court, Article 21(1)(c).

[21] Hans-Heinrich Jescheck, 'The General Principles of International Criminal Law Set Out in Nuremberg, as Mirrored in the ICC Statute' (2004) 2 J Int'l Crim L 38.

[22] See Antonio Cassese, 'The Contribution of the International Criminal Tribunal for the Former Yugoslavia to the Ascertainment of General Principles of Law Recognized by the Community of Nations', in Sienho Yee and Wang Tieya (eds), *International Law in the Post-Cold War World—Essays in Memory of Li Haopei* (Routledge, 2001) 43.

[23] For an account, see Giorgio Gaja, 'General Principles of Law', Max Planck Encyclopedia of Public International Law (1998) and Hermann Mosler, 'General Principles of Law' (1995) 2 Encyclopedia of Public International Law 511.

[24] See Bin Cheng, *General Principles of Law as Applied by International Courts and Tribunals* (2nd edn, Cambridge University Press, 2006) 383.

[25] *Helnan International Hotels A/S v Arab Republic of Egypt*, ICSID Case No ARB/05/19, Award of 14 June 2010.

especially from a public law perspective.[26] Judges and arbitrators have used this method in several cases, the dissenting opinion of Thomas W Wälde in *Thunderbird* being one of the clearest examples.[27]

In parallel to this theory, which seeks to bridge the gap between international law and the major legal systems of the world, runs a second strand that is perhaps majoritarian. Underlying this strand, there is a combination of legal positivism and a strong emphasis on national sovereignty that is susceptible of being limited only by express choices made by policymakers. Three important implications follow from this for the study of general principles. First, as Michael Reisman observed, there is a lower probability of acceptance of a supplementing decision taken by a court.[28] Secondly, and consequently, general principles can play only a supplementary and corrective role. Thirdly, those who adhere to this school of thought place a strong emphasis on the special nature of every field of international law[29] and do not see, therefore, why international lawyers should turn to domestic law, even though considered from a comparative point of view.[30] This theory underlies the arguments made by counsel of respondent States or arbitrators in circumstances where the doctrine of the intent of the contracting parties is used to make it illegitimate for arbitral tribunals to impose any kind of constraint on the States, outside those which they have explicitly agreed to.[31]

A third school of thought contends that, by virtue of Article 38(i)(c), genuine legal principles should be recognizable, and not a mere expression of the opinions of certain arbitrators, judges, and scholars. However, these principles would not belong to a distinct category, different from customary norms. Rather, they would be just a different way of describing custom.[32] Following another variant of this strand, the general principles of law would be a sort of modern repository for the

[26] Thomas W Wälde, 'The Specific Nature of Investment Arbitration', in Philip Kahn and Thomas W Wälde (eds), *Les aspects nouveaux du droit des investissements internationaux—New Aspects of International Investment Law* (Brill/Nijhoff, 2007) 100; Stephan W Schill, *International Investment Law and Comparative Public Law—An Introduction*, in Stephan W Schill (ed), *International Investment Law and Comparative Public Law* (Cambridge University Press, 2010) 10.

[27] Wälde formulated his dissent, focusing on the protection of legitimate expectations, in a North American Free Trade Agreement (NAFTA) case under the United Nations Commission on International Trade Law (UNCITRAL) Arbitration Rules: *International Thunderbird Gaming Corporation v United Mexican States*, Award of 26 January 2006 (denial of an authorization to operate a gaming facility).

[28] Michael W Reisman, 'International Non-Liquet: Recrudescence and Transformation' (1968–69) 3 Int'l L 770 (examining the various theories about *non liquet*).

[29] See José Alvarez, 'Beware: Boundary Crossings', NYU School of Law, Public Law Research Paper No 14–51 (available at http://papers.ssrn.com/sol3/papers.cfm?abstract_id=2498182##), in Tsvi Kahana and Anat Scolnicov (eds), *Boundaries of Rights, Boundaries of State* (Cambridge University Press, 2016, forthcoming).

[30] Christian Tamis, 'The Sources of International Investment Law', in Tarcisio Gazzini and Erik De Brabandere (eds), *International Investment Law: The Sources of Rights and Obligations* (Martinus Nijhoff, 2012) 319.

[31] See the dissenting opinion of El Mahdi in *Middle East Cement Shipping and Handling Co. S.A. v Arab Republic of Egypt* (*Middle East*), ICSID Case No ARB/99/6, Award of 12 April 2002 (a case in which the majority found that the State had disregarded due process rights to be afforded the investor in seizure and auction procedures).

[32] See Lassa FS Oppenheim, *International Law. A Treatise* (3rd edn, Longmans, Green and Co, 1921, edited by Ronald F Roxburgh) 20.

maxims and standards that lawyers, judges, and arbitrators have traditionally drawn from equity.[33]

There are, however, some problems with this view. First, even a quick look at Article 38(1) shows that general principles are an autonomous source of legal norms whose legitimacy as positive international law is simply not in question. In contrast, the third strand of thought fails to explain the existence of a distinct legal provision. Article 38(1) of the Statute of the ICJ distinguishes between the two categories of principles, deriving from custom and national laws. Whether this distinction ought to be ignored is, at the least, questionable. Moreover, when considering Article 38(1)(c), it is evident that the requisite of general practice is absent.[34] In addition, even if one accepts that there are nowadays no general principles recognized by civilized nations, it could not be said that this will be the case in the future.[35]

There is also another problem with this strand of thought: it juxtaposes general principles of law and equity, but this is not the case. This becomes evident when looking at the second paragraph of Article 38, which specifies that the three sources of law previously considered (custom, treaties, and general principles) do not prejudice the power of the ICJ to decide a 'case *ex aequo et bono*, if the parties agree thereto'.[36] Other treaties confirm this finding. For instance, the Vienna Convention on the Law of Treaties' reference to 'the principles of justice' does not mean that tribunals are normally empowered to judge *ex aequo et bono*. Similarly, when indicating the law that arbitrators must apply, the same Article of the International Centre for Settlement of Investment Disputes (ICSID) Convention that in the first paragraph refers to the 'rules of international law', in another—Article 42(3)—clarifies that such reference 'shall not prejudice the power of the Tribunal to decide a dispute *ex aequo et bono* if the parties so agree'. This provision, therefore, distinguishes between the rules of law and equity and makes their use compulsory for the former, optional for the latter.

Accordingly, a juxtaposition between general principles and equity must be excluded. We are left, therefore, with the other two strands, one that maximizes the role of general principles and another that assigns them only a supplementary and corrective role. The role that is played by administrative due process of law will be assessed in these terms.

Variable and non-variable standards

Thus far the salience of general principles has been considered mainly historically. It is now time to consider it systematically. Legal systems are often described as 'worlds of rules'. Rules, of course, are important in all fields of law, but they are neither the only nor the main element of legal systems. For instance, Hart has convincingly

[33] Hersch Lauterpacht, *General Rules of the Law of Peace*, in *Collected Papers* I (first published 1936; Cambridge University Press, 1993) I, 364.

[34] Bin Cheng, *General Principles of Law*, 24.

[35] See Rudolf Schlesinger, *Research on the General Principles of Law Recognized by Civilized Nations* (1957) 51 Am J Int'l L 734, 740.

[36] ICJ Statute, Article 38(2).

criticized the view that a legal system '*wholly*, or even *primarily*, consists of rules',[37] emphasizing another distinction between variable and non-variable standards. At the basis of such distinction there is again the observation that while certain legal standards aim at regulating specific human conduct, for a variety of purposes (to impose it, to make it legitimate, or to prohibit it), other standards have an undetermined extent. But there is also an additional element, which regards the role of the courts, or of other agencies entrusted with a supervisory function. Hart thus emphasized 'the open texture of law', which means that there are variable standards that must be developed by courts in the light of 'competing interests which vary in weight from case to case', while non-variable standards—or rules—regulate actions with only 'a fringe of open texture' and that do not, therefore, require from them a 'fresh judgment from case to case'.[38] In sum, bounded judicial discretion may be a realistic option in several cases, but not in all cases.

Both the distinction between principles and rules[39] and the critique to bounded judicial discretion are well established in legal theory. Some theorists link the distinction between rules and standards to 'values', which are more likely to be expressed by broad standards rather than rules.[40] Others emphasize the 'logic' of rules, which is 'binary' in the sense that if a measure taken by a public authority falls within the scope of application of a certain rule, either it is coherent with that rule (and then is valid) or is inconsistent with it (and then it is invalid).[41] There is still another theory that considers principles as 'optimization imperatives, in the sense that they can be fulfilled in varying degrees, while rules are precepts that can only be respected or disregarded.[42]

A serious challenge to the doctrine of bounded judicial discretion comes also from the works of the Israeli Supreme Court's Chief Justice Aharon Barak.[43] He holds that not only constitutional courts, but also other judges, occasionally find themselves confronted with—and must resolve—'hard cases', for which several lawful outcomes are possible. In such cases, literal and even systematic interpretation will have little to offer the courts or the scholars examining their work. An accurate application of existing legal rules will not suffice. The judge will have, literally, to create a new rule for solving the new problems. Principles provide fertile ground for this, due to their generality and 'weight', in the sense that they express values that are socially important.

[37] Herbert L Hart, *The Concept of Law* (3rd edn, Clarendon Press, 1994) 12.

[38] Herbert L Hart, *The Concept of Law*, 131–2.

[39] See Ronald Dworkin, *Taking Rights Seriously* (Harvard University Press, 1977) 24 (arguing that the distinction is logical) and Joseph Raz, 'Legal Principles and the Limits of Law' (1972) 81 Yale LJ 823 (for the converse argument that the distinction is the result of political choices).

[40] See Kathleen M Sullivan, 'The Justices of Rules and Standards' (1992) 106 Harvard L Rev 22 (pointing out the arguments in favour of rules, including fairness as formal equality, and standards, including fairness as substantive justice respectively).

[41] Ronald Dworkin, *Taking Rights Seriously*, 25.

[42] Robert Alexy, *A Theory of Constitutional Rights* (Julian Rivers (tr), Oxford University Press, 2002); 'Constitutional Rights and Proportionality' (2014) 22 Revus, 52.

[43] Aharon Barak, *Judicial Discretion* (Yadin Kaufmann (tr), Yale University Press, 1989) 40 calls this the 'objectivity test'.

This discussion is particularly important for present purposes for three reasons. First, while less recent ideas and thoughts about the law have raised doubts about both the existence of unwritten principles, which could be uncertain, and their content, which was not precise enough, the significance of general principles of law is well established in both jurisprudence and legal theory. Whether or not they are based on a text,[44] general principles are norms of conduct and must, therefore, be respected by public authorities.

Secondly, general principles are neither distinct from rules for their generality nor do they have simply an integrative role, when a particular rule is either lacking or is unclear. Their role is especially important from a dynamic viewpoint. General principles, it is claimed, 'lay down the essential elements of the legal order',[45] express the 'fundamental legal concepts and essential values of any legal system',[46] and legitimate 'all or any of the more specific [legal] rules in question'.[47] Their distinctive feature (*differentia specifica*) within the genus of legal norms is, rather, their foundational nature.[48]

Thirdly, precisely because of these features, general principles do not apply in an all-or-nothing fashion. This is neither irrelevant nor tangential to my central point, for I want to show that, though procedural due process of law is less abstract and generic than non-arbitrariness, it retains an important fringe of open texture, which explains why judges and arbitrators frequently resort to it in a transnational arena.

2. Due Process as a General Principle

It is time to focus on administrative due process, viewed as a general principle. Three aspects will be considered in more detail: its scope of application, the way in which it works, and the consequences for public authorities that deviate from the requirements of procedural due process.

A general scope of application

By 'generality', I refer to the scope of application of administrative due process, viewed as a general principle of law; that is, a principle that potentially applies in all

[44] Benoît Jeanneau, *Les principes généraux du droit dans la jurisprudence administrative* (Sirey, 1954) 185.

[45] Armin von Bogdandy, 'Founding Principles of EU Law. A Theoretical and Doctrinal Sketch' (2010) 12 Pravus 35.

[46] Meinhard Hilf and Goetz Goettsche, 'The Relation of Economic and Non-Economic Principles in International Law', in Stefan Griller (ed), *International Economic Governance and Non-Economic Concerns: New Challenges for the International Legal Order* (Springer, 2003) 9–10.

[47] Neil MacCormick, *Legal Reasoning and Legal Theory* (Oxford University Press, 1978) 152.

[48] Vezio Crisafulli, 'Per la determinazione del concetto dei principi generali del diritto' (1941) 21 Rivista internazionale di filosofia del diritto 15 (criticizing theories that exclude general principles from legal norms).

fields of law and to all issues that arise. There are, in this respect, two aspects that deserve attention.

There is, first, a similar development of administrative due process within a national and transnational context. With the notable exception of US public law, where due process was established by the Fifth and Fourteen amendments, in other national legal systems the principle is a judicial creation and has been generalized judicially. In both the UK and in other national legal systems, including Germany and Italy,[49] as well as in the context of international organizations, such as the International Labour Organization (ILO) and the European Union (EU), in staff disciplinary cases it was stated that, according to a general principle of law, a public authority acting as employer had to allow its employees the opportunity of replying to allegations before any decision adversely affecting them was taken. Sometimes this principle was affirmed on grounds of fairness. Sometimes the underlying rationale—an instrumental one—was instead that the judge or an authority exercising quasi-judicial powers ought to hear both parties, because otherwise a mistake could be made.[50] But the outcome was the same, in the sense that a decision taken *inaudita altera parte* was invalid and was annulled by the court. The courts' view of the status and importance of this requirement, as well of others such as the giving reasons requirement, has strengthened over the years. Gradually the observance of such requirements has been regarded, in all procedures that are susceptible of adversely affecting one or more individuals or groups, as a fundamental principle that must always be guaranteed, in short a *lex generalis*[51] which shapes the substantive areas of public law.

This brings us to the other aspect of administrative due process, viewed as a general principle of law: its relationship with particular rules of procedure. In the absence of particular rules (*lex specialis*) governing an administrative procedure, the *lex generalis* will have to be applied. If, instead, particular rules exist, then they will have to be applied consistently with the general principle. The content of procedural protection may vary from area to area. Viewed in this light, procedural fairness is—as Harlow and Rawlings have argued—a very flexible friend.[52] While the threshold is relatively high in cases concerning deprivation of office, withdrawing of benefits (including licences and concessions), and discipline, it is lower with regard to aliens, especially in cases concerning terrorism. However, no government action, from the collection of taxes to the distribution of benefits, may take place without regard to this principle. What due process of law prevents is the possibility that individuals and groups are subjected to treatment that affects the essence of certain basic requirements; but it does not exclude that the thresholds

[49] For further remarks on European legal systems, see John A Usher, *General Principles of EC Law* (Longman, 1998) 73–5.

[50] John M Kelly, 'Audi Alteram Partem' (1964) 1 Natural Law Forum 103.

[51] See Campbell McLachlan, Laurence Shore, and Matthew Weiniger, *International Investment Law. Substantive Principles* (Oxford University Press, 2007) 105 (noting that the FET standard 'gives expression to a general principle of due process').

[52] See Carol Harlow and Richard Rawlings, *Law and Administration* (3rd edn, Cambridge University Press, 2010) 495.

are different; nor does it exclude that a particular procedure may provide better treatment.

The principle's impact on exercises of power is thus huge. Consider again the dismissal of international civil servants by public employers, in cases such as *Alvis* and *Ferrecchia*, examined in Chapter 3. Although the power to dismiss them is undisputed, those civil servants may not be fired except for cause and as determined by the procedure provided by the law. Such procedure is necessary, first of all, to gather all necessary evidence and, second, even if the facts are undisputed, to provide the employee with a meaningful opportunity to be heard. Consider also the field of foreign investment, where the fair and equitable treatment (FET) standard can be, and has been, interpreted as requiring national authorities to hear investors before taking measures that will adversely affect them. Similarly, a giving reasons requirement makes an *ipse dixit* by public authorities, if not impossible, at least undefendable before the courts. Unless this requirement is intended in the sense that 'adequate' or even 'good' reasons must be provided, it retains its procedural character, but is a constraint on the exercise of governmental powers, especially when it is applied beyond traditional expropriation in the vast realm of regulation.[53]

Administrative due process of law as a variable standard

Another aspect of the way in which procedural due process works can be fully appreciated from the viewpoint of the distinction made before between variable and non-variable standards. In most cases the conduct of public administrators is regulated by particular rules—which Hart calls non-variable standards—that do not require from them a fresh judgment and, from a Weberian perspective, permit them to work efficiently. However, in other cases, more limited in number but highly significant, public officials act outside specific standards. They must, therefore, strike a balance between competing interests, whose weight may vary from one case to another.[54]

In order to show that due process is less abstract than non-arbitrariness, although it retains an important fringe of open texture, it is useful to compare a case we discussed before, *ELSI*, not with a more recent case but with a contemporary case, *Amco*. The reason is that it would not be unreasonable to conjecture that more recent cases reflect the changed importance of procedural due process of law or at least a changed perception by arbitrators. It was not possible to anticipate, at that time, what has turned out to be a growing concern over the last twenty-five years. Other cases demonstrate the predisposition, if not the willingness, of arbitrators to refer to less abstract ideas of justice and fairness. An interesting case is *Amco*,[55] where the arbitral tribunal considered in detail the administrative procedure through which

[53] Andrew Newcombe, 'The Boundaries of Regulatory Expropriation in International Law', in Philippe Kahn and Thomas W Wälde (eds), *Les aspects nouveaux du droit des investissements internationaux—New Aspects of International Investment Law*, 391.

[54] See Herbert L Hart, *The Concept of Law*, 135.

[55] See above, Chapter 3, Section 3, p. 51.

the national government had seized the property of a foreign investor. It was held that the revocation of the licence was unlawful, for Indonesian law provided that sanctions against foreign investors, including the revocation of a licence, could be adopted only after they had previously been given notice, which in this case had not been adequately provided.[56] According to the Tribunal, this was against both national law and the international principle of due process. How such principle could be identified and what it implied was not, however, clear and this led to criticism.[57] But even those who criticize the award affirm that providing due process is a 'rule of prudence' and that State interference with foreign investors is now admissible only if due process standards are met.[58]

Seen from this viewpoint, due process of law is much more helpful than the prohibition of arbitrariness because it does not target only extreme cases. However, it is not a non-variable standard, but a variable one. This can be seen by way of example in *Saluka*, concerning the indirect expropriation of the rights regarding a banking activity.[59] In a very well drafted award, arbitrators considered the claimant's argument that the agreement on encouragement and reciprocal protection of investment between the Contracting Parties placed the emphasis on the 'desirability' of the FET standard, with a view to stimulating the flow of capital and technology and economic development.[60] The Tribunal endorsed this view of FET as an autonomous standard. It was substantiated in several respects, including consistency, transparency, and even-handedness. When it referred to procedural fairness, the Tribunal observed that 'the host State must never disregard the principles of procedural propriety and due process'.[61]

What emerges from judicial and arbitral practice is, therefore, that there are—from a Hartian perspective—two aspects to the way in which due process of law works. First, it has a fringe of open texture, which permits it to work as a variable standard, or as a principle. Enforcing broad standards, such as FET, requires considering numerous facts and weighing them in any particular case. As a consequence, arbitrators may assign different weights to the values and finalities set by the contracting States in order to see whether their conduct has fallen below an acceptable standard. Second, precisely because FET is a broad standard, arbitrators have defined and refined some autonomous indicators for procedural fairness, including the requirement to carry out a procedure, the right to be heard, and the giving reasons requirement.

The term 'indicators' may seem loose, but the point I want to make is that due process does not work as a non-variable standard. For instance, in *Saluka*, it was

[56] *Amco Asia Corporation and others v Republic of Indonesia* (ICSID Case No ARB/81/1), Award of 20 November 1984, paragraph 202.

[57] For further analysis, see Michael W Reisman, 'The Breakdown of the Control Mechanism in ICSID Arbitration' (1984) 4 Duke LJ 739, 770.

[58] Muthucumaraswamy Sornarajah, *The International Law on Foreign Investment* (2nd edn, Cambridge University Press, 2004) 97, 165.

[59] *Saluka Investments B.V. v The Czech Republic,* UNCITRAL Award (partial) of 17 May 2006, available at http://www.italaw.com.

[60] *Saluka*, paragraph 299.

[61] *Saluka*, paragraph 376.

precisely because the Tribunal was enforcing a variable standard that it did not come to the conclusion that any deviation from those requirements implied an injury and, therefore, the State's responsibility.[62] In this sense, it can be said that the standard of due process is not of strict liability.[63] It is because under a bilateral investment treaty (BIT) the FET standard is an autonomous standard that it has not been conceived as a 'minimum' standard, applicable only to idiosyncratic or egregious conduct of the host State. But it is because the FET standard and the provision governing expropriation were interpreted as giving much more weight to procedural propriety and due process of law that the Tribunal could go beyond the 'minimum requirements' constituted by the two fundamental rules of natural justice, that is, impartiality of the adjudicator and the right to be heard. In conclusion, whilst producing more principled and more predictable decisions, administrative due process of law is a flexible standard.[64]

The test for review: Essential and non-essential procedural requirements

An analysis of due process can be helpfully completed by an attempt to devise how it works concretely. The test that I am proposing consists in the fulfilment of two steps that are distinct but not independent, in the sense that the second step takes place only if the first has been completed, though a possible derogation from the second step might be considered under the third.[65] The first step is to see whether the infringement of an 'essential' procedural requirement has occurred, while the second is to ascertain whether the infringement of the essential requirement of due process is manifest. The third step consists in considering the consequences of a public authority's failure to respect a pre-established procedure or to observe the requirements of due process.

The first step not only excludes any review of the substantive, as opposed to procedural, aspects of the conduct of public authorities. It also excludes that their measures are invalid if a non-essential procedural requirement has been infringed, which is the case when a simple irregularity has occurred. Most domestic legal systems, as well as that of the EU, follow an approach of this kind. The major legal systems of the world, if not all, keep distinct mere procedural irregularities or dysfunctions from infringements that can induce the courts to

[62] In *AES, Corporation v Argentina*, ICSID Case No. ARB/02/17, Decision on jurisdiction (April 26, 2005), available at http://www.italaw.com, paragraph 9.3.73, the Tribunal found that, although the administrative process was 'sub-optimal, it did not fall outside the acceptable range … of behaviour'.

[63] Campbell McLachlan, Laurence Shore, and Matthew Weiniger, *International Investment Law. Substantive Principles*, 241.

[64] Sanford L Kadish, 'Methodology and Criteria in Due Process Adjudication' (1974) 66 Yale L Rev 319, 325; George C Christie, 'Due Process of Law—A Confused and Confusing Notion', in Chaïm Perelman and Raymond Vander Elst (eds), *Les notions a contenu variable en droit* (Bruylant, 1984) 157.

[65] For a similar attempt, see Richard J Pierce, *Making Sense of Procedural Injury* (2010) 62 Admin L Rev 1.

quash an administrative measure.[66] Often they also construct a further class of 'anomalies' that justify the exercise of the *actio nullitatis*, that which may lead a court of law to come to the conclusion that the measure was so distant from any normative criteria that it must be regarded as being null and void in an absolute, as distinct from relative, sense. Similarly, Article 230 of the Treaty of Rome, establishing the EC,[67] entrusted the Court of Justice with the task of ensuring that the 'law' is respected in the interpretation and application of the Treaty having regard, among other things, to the 'infringement of an essential procedural requirement'. This provision reflected a concern common to the legal orders of the six Founding Member States, to avoid the excesses of formalism, by distinguishing between administrative procedures.[68] But also the UK system distinguished between mandatory and directory procedural requirements.[69]

Following this distinction, suppose that a national legal provision governing a procedure uses the word 'may' with regard to the consultation of an advisory body. Failure to consult would not result in unlawfulness, even though it is—once again—reasonable to affirm that a public authority should give the reasons, if not 'good' reasons, for not fulfilling such requirement. Or, as a variant of the previous case, suppose that before taking a decision adversely affecting the completion and management of a hotel in a touristic area, the decision-maker has not consulted a certain scientific body that may certify whether the area where the hotel is to be located has a specific cultural or environmental importance, but it has consulted another institution with an equivalent or better qualification. In a case like this, it is questionable whether the legal rule has really been infringed, but it is beyond doubt that, even that being the case, there is no serious negative consequence that derives from it. Or, to take another example, instead of sending a telegram to inform the foreign investor that, before taking any decision, the decision-maker will hold a hearing, the notice of the hearing has been provided with an equivalent, more modern technology, while other elements of the notice (the minimum delay of, say, five or three days and the indication of all the main elements of fact and law) are unchanged. There is no reason why the final decision should be regarded as invalid. Nor is there any reason to include necessarily in the test any consideration regarding discrimination, in the sense that an adjudicatory decision in breach of due process can raise the responsibility of the State even though it is

[66] See Pascale Idoux, *La contradiction en droit administratif français* (Faculté de droit de Montpellier, 2005) 5 (mentioning variable standards—an *échelle de contradiction*—with regard to the right to be heard); Kenneth C Davis, 'The Requirement of a Trial-type Hearing' (1956) 70 Harv L Rev 193 (pointing out that a trial-type hearing is not required in all administrative procedures).

[67] Now replaced by the Treaty on the European Union and the Treaty on the Functioning of the European Union, whose Article 262 reproduces the provision of 1957. See, for instance, CFI, Joined Cases T-79/89 et al, *BASF* et al. *v Commission* [1992] ECR II, 315.

[68] Eduard Laferrière, *Traité de la juridiction administrative et du recours contentieux* (2nd edn, Berger-Lavrault, 1896) II, 494–8 (discussing substantive and non-substantive formalities); Christian Autexier, *Introduction au droit public allemand* (Presses universitaires de France, 1997) 280; Georg Nolte, *General Principles of German and European Administrative Law* (1994) 57 Modern L Rev 197.

[69] Paul Craig, *Administrative Law*, 389.

not discriminatory, while unjustified discrimination may be a further symptom of injustice.

While the first part of the test focuses on the essentiality of the procedural requirement, the second aims at ascertaining whether there is an evident or manifest infringement of due process. The reason for emphasizing that the infringement must be manifest is that it corresponds to the widespread opinion, expressed by case law and scholarly literature, that to raise an international concern the threshold cannot be a low one. This is related to my claim that procedural due process of law requests neither that the infringement is 'shocking' nor that there is a wilful disregard by the public authority.

Consider, first, the right to be heard. Whether or not national rules governing an administrative procedure introduce the requirement that the affected parties have a reasonable opportunity to be heard is a fundamental requisite of procedural due process. Similar considerations would apply to process rights that are distinct, but related, such as receiving due advance notice and having access to documents and evidence relied upon by the public authority. However, this does not necessarily imply that an oral hearing must be held.

Consider also the giving reasons requirement. It can be argued that a complete lack of any reasons would be regarded as implying that the public authority has acted in an arbitrary and capricious manner. Suppose, then, that a public authority does not provide the reasons in the text of its decision. This can be regarded as a procedural irregularity, especially if national legislation (as happens in the US, Latin America, Europe, and in some Asian countries) lays down the giving reasons requirement. However, it is not necessarily a symptom of procedural unfairness if either the reasons can be inferred from other acts or documents (*per relationem*) or if the public authority provides them upon a request by the affected party, as is required by South African legislation.[70] Similarly, the conciseness of the motivation would not necessarily be regarded as an infringement of this transnational standard of due process, while an inherent contradiction in the reasoning or within the reasoning and the final decision taken by the public authority would amount to an evident failure to respect due process of law.

Finally, the consequences of the infringement must be taken into account. This does not only mean, of course, that an undertaking may not reasonably raise a claim against a measure that is not adversely affecting its interests. It means also that an exception to the second element of the test could be admitted if, as some arbitral awards have affirmed: (a) there is a plurality of procedural dysfunctions or anomalies and, even though none of them, considered in isolation, is sufficiently serious, (b) considered as a whole, they can be regarded as symptoms of the fact that the conduct of the public authority did not respect procedural fairness, as specified by one or several 'essential' requirements of the due process of law.

[70] See above, Chapter 4 Section 2, p. 67. See also Resolution No (77)31 issued by the Committee of Ministers of the Council of Europe, whose Article IV provides that reasons can be given 'by communicating them, at his request, to the person concerned in writing within a reasonable time'.

3. A Complementary and Corrective Role

After explaining in which sense administrative due process can be considered as a general principle of law and which implications follow from this, we may now turn to the first two strands of thought concerning general principles. While the former emphasizes the role of general principles, the latter views it simply as a complementary and corrective role. Arguably, this diversity is not simply a product of a different interpretation of Article 38 of the ICJ Statute. Both approaches are founded upon a particular vision of international law, if not of law *tout court*. None of these are right or wrong in some absolute sense. All require an adequate understanding in terms of their justifications, implications, and deficiencies. This explains why, in addition to subjecting various interpretations to rational scrutiny, they will be subject to inquiry both normatively and in respect of the outcomes of empirical analysis.[71] Normatively, the crucial question is whether judges and arbitrators must use general principles of law only to justify gap-filling, when existing rules and procedures are determined to be inadequate or incomplete. Empirically, the crucial question is whether the way in which judges and arbitrators behave coincides with the assertion that general principles only have a complementary and corrective role or whether there are at least some cases that do not fit with this theory. That being the case, either the theory must be refined or a new theory must be formulated.

An exemplary case: *Klochner*

Even though one cannot know how desirable a theory is without evaluating its normative basis, sometimes considering the doctrinal answers that the background theory gives to the issues or cases with which lawyers deal can be preferable to a high level of abstraction. The investment field provides a helpful starting point in this sense, through two of the earliest ICSID cases, *Klochner* and *Amco*.

In *Klochner* the arbitral tribunal was requested to check whether the applicant, a multinational enterprise based in Germany, was entitled to recover the whole of the contract price from the respondent State, Cameroon. Without entering into the details of the dispute, one finding of the arbitral tribunal is particularly interesting. Due to the fact that the civil law principle *exceptio non adimpleti contractus* (in a reciprocal contract it allows a party to withhold its own performance until the other party has performed its obligation) was reflected in both English and international law, such principle could be invoked by the tribunal.[72] Being dissatisfied with the award, Cameroon invoked the application of the remedy provided by the ICSID Convention. Such remedy is not an appeal, but the institution of an ad hoc Annulment Committee. When the award was annulled, the Committee endorsed

[71] For this approach, see Martin Loughlin, *Public Law and Political Theory* (Clarendon Press, 1992) 36.

[72] *Klochner industry v Republic of Cameroon*, ICSID Case No ARB/81/2, Award of 21 October 1983.

the appellant's argument that the tribunal had exceeded its jurisdiction.[73] However, it acknowledged that 'arbitrators may have recourse to the "*principles* of international law" after having inquired into and established the content of the law of the State party to the dispute'.[74]

Two aspects of the Committee's reasoning are particularly relevant for our purposes: the reference to Article 42(1) of the ICSID Convention and the dual role that it assigned to principles. As observed before in this chapter, Article 42(1) concerns the law that arbitrators must apply. It includes both national law, either that of the parties or the law of a third country, and the 'rules of international law'. Although some versions of the same provision refer to 'rules' and others to 'principles',[75] the Committee found that it could be read as referring to the latter. The Committee also held that Article 42 gives the principles of international law as may be applicable a dual role, that is, complementary or corrective.

This was not an isolated decision, as *Amco* shows. In *Amco*, there was a seizure of a hotel by Indonesia's police and armed forces and the foreign investor's licence to manage the hotel was revocated. The investor held that this caused prejudice and that it was the responsibility of the host State to compensate for such prejudice. Another cause of action was the unjust enrichment of the national government. While the Tribunal rejected this claim, it endorsed the others. Interestingly, the Tribunal's starting point was that international law was applicable in a both 'supplemental and corrective' fashion.[76] The latter role implied, it added, that even if the host State has laid down more or less detailed precepts governing an administrative procedure, such precepts must be interpreted in the light of international law.

As far as Amco's second claim was concerned, the Tribunal observed initially that the licence was not alien 'to the general concept of contract'. Nor was it alien to general principles of law.[77] But there are significant differences between a contract and a licence, in the sense that a State is entitled to withdraw its consent for reasons of public interest that could not be invoked by a private entity, including the disregard of certain conditions agreed by the other party. However, to be lawful, the revocation must meet procedural requirements and be punctual. In both respects, the Tribunal found that the action of Indonesia was unlawful. The fact that a notice had been sent to the licensee literally minutes before the seizure was regarded as

[73] See Christoph Schreuer et al, *The ICSID Convention. A Commentary* (Cambridge University Press, 2008) 610 (observing that the *Klockner* Ad Hoc Committee took the initial award's insistence on general principles, without any evidence, as a reference to equity).

[74] *Klockner* Ad Hoc Committee's Decision of 3 May 1985 on Annulment of the Award of 21 October 1983, §§ 68–70. For further remarks, see Jan Paulsson, 'The ICSID Klockner v. Cameroon Award: The Duties of Partners in North-South Economic Development Agreements' (1984) 1 J Int'l Arb 145.

[75] See Emmanuel Gaillard and Yas Banifatemi, 'The Meaning of "and" in Article 42(1), Second Sentence, of the Washington Convention: The Role of International Law in the ICSID Choice of Law Process' (2005) 18 ICSID Review 376, 378 (providing examples of many BITs that confirm the Convention's option). But see also W Michael Reisman, 'The Regime for Lacunae in the ICSID Choice of Law Provision and the Question of its Threshold' (2001) 15 ICSID Rev 362, 373 (calling for a restrictive interpretation of Article 42).

[76] *Amco*, Award on the Merits (1984), paragraph 148.

[77] *Amco*, paragraph 188.

being contrary to, if not the letter, then the spirit of national legislation, as well as the international principle of due process.[78] Similarly, the allegation of the licensee's failure to respect certain terms of the agreement that preceded the issuing of the licence did not satisfy the giving reasons requirement.

Critics have argued that the Tribunal unduly underestimated the justification provided by the host State, in particular because *Amco* had not met its full requirement of foreign capital.[79] But this critique misses the point. Even if there was evidence of a disregard of a substantial condition of the licence, Indonesia had, under its own law, to follow the predefined procedure and to provide the investor with a meaningful opportunity to be heard. It was precisely because national requirements were improperly applied that the Tribunal found that the due process principle had been infringed. It can be said that the Tribunal's reasoning may have been an attempt not to hurt 'sovereign sensibilities'.[80] But, that being the case, this would not be a mistake, especially for those who think that States are the principals of arbitrators. In any case, *Amco* illustrates a way in which due process can play an integrative role by excluding some interpretations of national law that are unreasonable and that are incompatible with instrumental (avoiding errors) and non-instrumental (protecting rights) rationales of due process.

Normative foundations

A proper understanding of the normative foundations of this approach embraces two distinct, but related, issues: the prohibition of *non liquet* and the delimitation of the power of judges and arbitrators.

At an intuitive level, the requirement that a judge must always render justice, and may not abstain from so doing on grounds of either absence or obscurity of the law, is appealing. It can ensure the fulfilment of several values acknowledged by modern legal systems, including equality and legal certainty. Such values are protected also by international regimes. As observed before, both the Statute of the ICJ and the ICSID Convention prohibit the ICJ and arbitral tribunals, respectively, to incur in a *non liquet*.[81] The appeal of the solution envisaged by Article 38(1) of the ICJ Statute goes, therefore, beyond simple intuition. It is coherent with the solution provided by many modern legal systems to a twofold practical problem; that is, how to deal with the problems to which the rules of law offer no solution at all whilst at the same time not conferring an excessive discretionary power on those who judge.

It is in this respect that this strand of thought makes an important claim. It argues that the use of general principles of law may well be suited to a domestic arena, but is likely to be much less suitable for the international or transnational

[78] *Amco*, paragraph 192 (referring to 'procedural requisites', 'as set up by the applicable law and which have to be in accord with the *fundamental principle of due process*') (emphasis added).

[79] Muthucumaraswamy Sornarajah, *The International Law on Foreign Investment*, 117, 165.

[80] W Michael Reisman, 'The Breakdown of the Control Mechanism in ICSID Arbitration', 772.

[81] Julius Stone, 'Non Liquet and the Function of Law in the International Community' (1959) 35 Brit Yb Int'l L 124.

arenas.[82] The reason is that the discretion of judges and arbitrators is not unlimited, but depends on the wider institutional context. In the international arena, their discretion is inevitably more limited than in the domestic arena because there is a lower probability of acceptance of a supplementing decision taken by a court.[83]

This reasoning must be subjected to critical scrutiny in two respects. First, one thing is that international courts and tribunals must exercise great caution in order to avoid being accused of judicial overreach, which is an argument of expediency; another thing is to come to the conclusion that recourse to general principles is allowed only within very strict limits.[84] Secondly, and consequently, there is nothing wrong in emphasizing the gap-filling function of general principles.[85] But the phrase 'gap-filling' should not be invoked in order to disguise the extensive law-making that judges and arbitrators actually generate when they 'fill gaps' in general principles. Last but not least, Article 38(1)(c) is itself incomplete in that it does not indicate how general principles, left unenumerated, are to be identified, let alone applied. In sum, if something—the concern for the affront to our dignity and legal interests that would derive from 'the blind alley of *non liquet*'[86]—has led several legal systems to pursue this fundamental requirement to render justice, this should not be valued only for its own sake. It remains to be seen whether this reflects more general ideas and thoughts about the law, and in particular about due process of law.

4. A Foundational Role

After examining the theory that assigns to general principles only a complementary and corrective role, the other theory must be subjected to the same kind of critical scrutiny. This requires more than the general articulation of concepts such as due process, reasonableness, proportionality, and the like. If the call for procedural principles is to be taken seriously, then this necessitates specific delineation of the underlying normative foundations.[87] Next, I will proceed to the second stage of the enquiry, which is of an empirical nature.

[82] Michael W Reisman, 'International Non-Liquet' (1969) 3 Int Lawyer, 770, 774.

[83] Michael W Reisman, 'International Non-Liquet', 774.

[84] Wolfgang Friedmann, 'The Uses of "General Principles" in the Development of International Law' (1963) 57 Am J Int'l L 279, 280 (agreeing with Hersch Lauterpacht).

[85] Rudolf Dolzer and Christoph Schreur, *Principles of International Investment Law* (2nd edn, Oxford University Press, 2012) 18 (pointing out that 'general principles in the sense of Article 38(1) have received increasing attention in recent practice ... especially in the case of lacunae in the text of treaties'); Lucien Siorat, *Le problème des lacunes en droit international. Contribution à l'étude des sources du droit et de la fonction judiciaire* (LGDJ, 1959) 253 (distinguishing between the systematization of particular provisions and the elaboration of abstract notions).

[86] ICJ, *Advisory Opinion on the Threat or Use of Nuclear Weapons* (1996) ICJ Rep 323 (Schwebel J, dissenting).

[87] For a similar remark about international custom, see Jack Goldsmith and Erik Posner, 'A Theory of Customary International Law' (1999) 66 U Chi L Rev 1113, 1117. See also Francis Mann, 'Reflections on a Commercial Law of Nations' (1957) 33 Br Y Int'l L 20, 35 (excluding 'any tendency to state general principles in general terms').

A normative analysis

To begin with, it must be recognized that, compared to the international system of the 1950s, the legal world has been transformed in two main respects. There is a connection between the proliferation of international courts and the increase of justiciable individual claims brought against States and other public authorities. However, the role of general principles is not simply a function of the role which any theory prescribes or indicates for courts and other supervisory bodies. This is too narrow a focus. Not only does it tend to overemphasize the power of the judiciary, but it also neglects the more complex relationship that emerges between rules and principles, in the sense that the latter constitute the central structures of legal orders. I shall thus start from this.

As Chaim Perelman observed, if after 1945, alongside principles that even the exegetic school might have recognized, courts have increasingly frequently resorted to unwritten general principles of law,[88] the reason is not simply that the Nuremberg trials revealed the intrinsic limits and excesses of legal positivism. For instance, since 1944 the French *Conseil d'État* has enforced general principles in order to ensure that the legislation enacted by the Vichy régime complied with constitutional values. A few years later, in the UK the revival of natural justice reflected a changing perception of individual rights against public authorities. During the same period the procedural clause laid down by the Indian Constitution was reinterpreted. The Indian Supreme Court might not have reached the conclusion that a particular interest was immune from interference, but still protected it on the assumption of the existence of a constitutional obligation which government was bound to respect. At the most basic level, therefore, the traditional approach fails to provide a convincing explanation of the role that general principles can, and do, play within national legal systems.[89]

The institutional premises about the way in which courts and other bodies performing a supervisory function must operate in a transnational arena are also questionable.[90] The idea that the transnational arena must be governed essentially by the rules dictated by political authorities and that, therefore, judges and arbitrators should only intervene when such rules either do not exist or are unclear may be appealing. But it is questionable. As observed initially, compared to the international system of the 1950s, the legal world has been transformed. International courts and arbitral institutions have proliferated,[91] and the domain of justiciable individual claims against States and other public authorities has massively expanded. These

[88] Chaïm Perelman, *Logique juridique. Nouvelle rhétorique* (Dalloz, 1979) 67.

[89] For a discussion of this 'foundational dimension', see Paul Craig, *UK, EU and Global Administrative Law. Foundations and Challenges* (Cambridge University Press, 2015) 167.

[90] This section draws on the arguments developed elsewhere: Alec Stone Sweet and Giacinto della Cananea, 'Proportionality, General Principles of Law, and Investor-State Arbitration: A Response to Alvarez' (2014) 46 NYU J of Int'l & Pol 911.

[91] Jenny Martinez, 'Towards an International Judicial System' (2003) 56 Stanford L Rev 429; Ruti Teitel and Robert Howse, 'Cross-Judging: Tribunalization in a Fragmented but Interconnected Global Order' (2009) 41 NYU J Int'l L & Pol 959.

two factors have increased the demand, on the part of all users of the system, for general principles. Put differently, whatever the status of custom, international law can no longer be understood merely as State-to-State contracting.[92]

Perhaps most importantly, States have proved unwilling or unable to produce treaties that are relatively 'complete' contracts that could potentially constrain judicial lawmaking.[93] Instead, an example being the FET standard in the investment field, States routinely leave crucial terms undefined. Nor do they set out detailed codes of procedure. As a result, the need to circumscribe and structure the powers of public authorities is certainly not less intense in a transnational context. Judges and arbitrators are thus required to develop general principles in order to resolve disputes effectively; yet, in doing so, judges render more 'complete' the treaty law they apply. When sovereigns do not subsequently override this judicial lawmaking, they at least indirectly legitimize it. And virtually all general principles can be deployed to promote coherence and order in systems beset or threatened by fragmentation, as well as to help judges adjust the law dynamically in the face of external shocks or changing circumstances.

An empirical analysis

The traditional theory according to which general principles of law can play only a complementary and corrective role is not only questionable on normative grounds. It has a further problem: this is simply not the way in which judges and arbitrators behave. An incremental but expansive jurisprudence of general principles has served to construct (and reconstruct) the normative foundations of several legal systems, national and international, and due process has played an important part in this respect.

The general principles of law supplement the national constitution or important legislation, such as that regulating administrative procedure. They thus substitute for the absence of any basic text that would govern the work of the courts. This method has rapidly diffused to other jurisdictions across Europe and globally. It is no exaggeration to say that much of European and Latin American public law has been constituted by the development of general principles. While some of them concern the order that must be respected by public authorities in the course of a procedure, an idea that is increasingly shared by other countries of the world, others provide administrators with instruments for interest balancing. For instance, the principle of proportionality provides an analytic procedure for reconciling opposing values and interests, or resolving conflicts between two sets of norms.[94] Accordingly, it is no exaggeration to say that general principles have a foundational dimension.

92 Christopher A Ford, 'Judicial Discretion in International Jurisprudence: Article 38 (1) (c) and "General Principles of Law"' (1994–95) 5 Duke J Comp & Int'l L 35.

93 Anthea Roberts, 'Power and Persuasion in Investment Treaty Interpretation: The Dual Role of States' (2010) 104 Am J Int'l L 179.

94 See Alec Stone Sweet and Jud Mathews, 'Proportionality Balancing and Global Constitutionalism' (2008) 47 Colum J Transnat'l L 73 (discussing the global use of proportionality analysis).

Non-State courts have not hesitated to refer to administrative due process of law. They have done so not simply when a problem has arisen for which existing rules of law simply provided no answer at all, but also when a legal provision was susceptible of a variety of interpretations or when it could lead to an outcome that was contrary to the changes occurring in the interests or values that were acknowledged or protected by the law. What follows is an illustration of the foundational role that due process of law can play in the context of administrative adjudication and regulation. Two cases already examined, *Shrimps* and *Transocean*, provide the main focus. These are not, of course, the only significant administrative due process cases. However, they are clearly distinguishable from cases in which no procedural requirement at all was provided by legislation or secondary rules. Moreover, they are cases in which arbitrators and judges fulfilled their duty to enforce due process of law. By contrast, in a more recent case, *Terlizzi*, a national court did not do so. Precisely for this reason, it is also interesting to look at this case, to show that it is not a counter-example. Quite the opposite, it confirms the foundational importance of administrative due process of law.

As observed before, when approving World Trade Organization (WTO) treaties States did not contract a code of procedure, leaving the details to be worked out by dispute resolution bodies themselves. The panels and the Appellate Body did so with regard to their own procedures, thus meeting the contracting parties' demand to be treated equally and fairly. They did so likewise with regard to the constraints imposed on the contracting parties. Sometimes the Appellate Body (AB) broadly interpreted particular treaty provisions. In other cases it developed procedures and due process as general principles outside any textual basis, but with clear analogies with the requirements set out by most national legal systems. The most important WTO ruling in this respect is the AB's ruling in *Shrimp-Turtles II*.[95] The AB found the process through which the U S had taken the measure had violated procedural norms, and was thus arbitrary and unjustifiable under the General Agreement on Tariffs and Trade (GATT). Not only had the US not consulted with many countries whose industries would be affected prior to the rule's entry into force, but it had adopted the rule without observing basic notice and comment requirements. Further, the Americans had failed to put into place a transparent and predictable certification procedure, or to ensure that reasons would be given for the rejection of applications for certification. The informality of these processes therefore failed to protect the rights of the shrimp-exporting nations and their individual exporters to 'basic fairness and due process'.[96]

Consider now the ruling of the ECJ in *Transocean Marine Paint Association*.[97] The problem with which the ECJ was confronted was typically the lack of a specific provision about the hearing of the undertaking adversely affected by a

[95] See above, Chapter 7, Section 3, p. 129.

[96] *United States—Import Prohibition of Certain Shrimps and Shrimps Products*—Report of the Appellate Body of 21 October 1998 (*Shrimp II*) paragraph 18.

[97] See above, Chapter 3, Section 4, p. 55.

Commission's decision to impose certain conditions with a view to preserving free competition. This problem was exacerbated by the fact that in other cases the same Regulation provided for a hearing. This provided the Court with an opportunity to solve such problem as a national court would have done in one of the legal systems that favour interpretation by analogy to similar cases. But this is not what the Court did. Rather, it followed its Advocate General, Werner, who had carried out a comparative analysis of the legal systems of the (then) six Member States, finding that there was 'a rule embedded in the law of some of our countries' and that could, thus, be included among the rules of law which the Court had to respect. This rule was that, before exercising power that could adversely affect a particular person, a public authority had to provide such person with an opportunity to be heard, as required by the maxim *audi alteram partem*.[98] Interestingly, the AG emphasized the 'general' nature of this requirement of due process. He specified that, for this reason, the rule had to be applied even if the *lex specialis* governing an administrative procedure did not expressly require it. However, he added, the rule applied 'in general' because it was 'subject to exceptions, as are most legal principles'.[99] It ought to be added that due process, proportionality, and other general principles played an important role in the 'constitutionalization' of the EC, conceived initially as an international regulatory regime. The judicial elaboration of general principles served to ensure its legitimacy when national courts criticized the lack of safeguards equivalent to those of national laws. There is not only a striking similarity but also a connection between this judicial development of due process and the jurisprudence of the European Court of Human Rights. The unifying thread in these judicial doctrines is the idea that the effects of process on persons, groups, and organizations must be considered in judging the legitimacy of public decision-making processes. Due process values are thus an essential part of Europe's common legal patrimony.

Thus far then, we have illustrated two ways in which an arbitral body and a fully-fledged court have imposed the observance of due process. Apart from the distinct nature of these institutions, both cases point towards the same result. What my argument comes to is this: national judges, international judges, and tribunals have little choice but to construct indicators of procedural fairness through a jurisprudence of general principles. It is in the light of such principles that the validity of the measures taken by public authorities must be assessed. This is confirmed, though in a negative way, by the dispute, illustrated in Chapter 8, that arose between an Italian municipality, *Terlizzi*, and the broader territorial unit where it was located, the *Regione Puglia*. The latter disregarded the former's process rights. It ultimately enacted retrospective legislation, giving legislative form to the content of the plan that had been issued in the form of an administrative act. The administrative court acknowledged this, but did not bring it to its logical conclusions. Nor did it refer the case to the Constitutional Court, as it should have done, given that the regional

[98] Opinion of Advocate General Werner, Case 17/74 [1974] ECR 1082, 1087.
[99] Opinion of Advocate General Werner, 1088.

legislation was clearly contrary to Article 6 of the European Convention on Human Rights (ECHR).[100]

5. From the Generality of Due Process to its Global Reach

This chapter has drawn on history of law and legal theory to justify the assertion that general principles of law do not simply play a complementary and corrective role, but are the 'building blocks of the legal order'.[101]

The courts and arbitral bodies that act in the transnational arena, including the Appellate Body of the WTO, the European Court of Justice, and the ECtHR have gone beyond building due process guarantees into the procedures governing their activities. They have also developed a host of general principles that apply to the governmental organs whose measures are under their review. Such principles constitute the foundation for core precepts governing administrative action. They thus provide guidance to public authorities. Accordingly, if a State 'acts against the law', the institutional machinery existing for ensuring that the law is enforced must be applied. Courts, arbitral tribunals, and other agencies are simply part of this institutional machinery under review. General principles also mitigate the concern for judicial discretion. This function is captured well by the words of an English constitutional lawyer, Trevor Allan, according to whom 'in the absence of principle, legal control depends on judicial instinct alone, employed in the manipulation of an undefined discretion'.[102]

There is, however, another ground for concern that must be considered. This regards the extent to which judges, arbitrators, and other public officers refer to ideas and thoughts about public law that are not peculiar to a certain legal culture or tradition. The question that thus arises, and which will be examined in the last chapter, is whether and in which sense due process can be said to be a global principle of law.

[100] For the broader argument that disregard of general principles of law undermines the acceptance of a legal order, see Bin Cheng, 'Epilogue: Nature and Sources of International Law', in Bin Cheng (ed), *International Law: Teaching and Practice* (Stevens, 1982) 218, 221.

[101] Martin Loughlin, *Public Law and Political Theory*, 209.

[102] Trevor C Allan, 'Pragmatism and Theory in Public Law' (1998) 104 LQR 422, 431.

10

Administrative Due Process as a Global Principle of Public Law

The last chapters have suggested two lines of a doctrine of administrative due process of law beyond the State: it is distinct from other concepts; it is a general principle of law and, as such, performs not only a complementary and corrective role, but also a 'foundational' role. A third line of reasoning will be developed in this chapter. It will be argued that administrative due process of law is—*de lege lata*, not *de lege ferenda*—a 'global' principle of law; that is, a principle that public administrators must abide by in the transnational arena. Because this is a claim over which others disagree on both normative and empirical grounds, both will be considered. I will, first, make some general remarks about the theories concerning the existence of 'invariable laws'. Secondly, I shall explain why administrative due process of law should be regarded as a principle that is common to most, if not to all, legal systems of the world, as well as to several regional and global regulatory regimes. Thirdly, two objections that emerge in recent literature will be subject to critical scrutiny. Finally, it will be argued that, while all this does not imply that due process must be regarded in the same manner by all legal systems, as a sort of 'global fifth amendment', it is very important for legal interpretation.

1. Variety of Views About Invariable Laws

Whether legal systems are characterized not only by variables, but also by invariable laws is a vexed question. Because much has been said about this in the history of ideas, the analysis will focus only on certain aspects. Three approaches will be outlined and discussed. While the first emphasizes the analogies between legal systems on the underlying assumption that they are coherent with 'reason', the second approach points out that not only do innumerable differences exist, but also that they are the inevitable outcome of history and culture. There is still another approach that seeks to reconcile unity and differentiation mainly at the level of general principles. It ought to be stated at the outset that my intent is neither to describe two mutually exclusive approaches, or opposites, only to reject them,[1] nor to include them in a sort of Hegelian dialectic that ends up with a (necessary)

[1] Inga Markovitz, 'Playing the Opposites Game: On Mirjan Damska's "The Faces of Justice and State Authority"' (1989) 41 Stanford L Rev 1313.

Due Process of Law Beyond the State. First Edition. Giacinto della Cananea. © Giacinto della Cananea 2016. Published 2016 by Oxford University Press.

synthesis. This section has the more modest purpose of setting the intellectual framework for examining our topic in more depth.

Ex ante invariants between reason and the 'nature of things'

For a long part of the history of Western legal thought, general principles were not seen from the perspective of a separation between law and reason. Even Grotius and Vattel, who distinguished natural law and *jus gentium*, acknowledged the relationship between law and reason. Much time and energy has thus been devoted to 'the effort of pure reason to work out a complete body of detailed precepts of universal validity—applicable to all men at all times and in all places'.[2] The problem with this approach was not only, intellectually, the confusion between the observed regularity of nature and the rules of natural law,[3] but also, practically, that its stabilizing side could preclude any social change,[4] which was regarded as being contrary to the legal order of nature. This explains the struggle against this idea during the nineteenth century by Benthamite utilitarianism.

The possibility and desirability of invariable laws received a slightly different justification from the father of comparative analysis of legal institutions, Montesquieu.[5] He was fully aware of the existence of innumerable differences between the countries of the world. But he thought that differences did not always originate in entrenched convictions and value judgments, but also regarding other factors, including asymmetries of information that can be overcome in time. He thus suggested a dynamic perspective for legal institutions[6] and devoted attention to best practices. One such practice was due process of law. Montesquieu began by observing that in ancient Rome criminal laws were far from being perfect in this respect. He added that in French criminal law the maxim *audi alteram partem* had been codified several centuries earlier. He provided two plausible reasons for its codification, namely that a different practice had existed in certain particular cases or elsewhere in less civilized legal cultures.[7] Interestingly, although Montesquieu thought that the contrary practice, that is to say judging accused persons without giving them a prior hearing, was unacceptable to a civilized nation, he conceded that, at least in some cases, things had

[2] Roscoe Pound, 'Introduction', in Giorgio Del Vecchio, *General Principles of Law* (first published 1942; Felix Forte (tr), Boston University Press, 1956) X. See also Martti Koskenniemi, 'The Advantage of Treaties: International Law in the Enlightenment' (2009) 13 Edinburgh L Rev 54 (referring to 'law in accordance with reason—*Vernunftrecht* as the Germans like to call it').

[3] Herbert L Hart, *The Concept of Law* (3rd edn, Clarendon Press, 1994) 187.

[4] For Grotius, natural law was so immutable that not even God could amend it: *Le droit de la guerre et de la paix* (first published 1625; P Pradier Foderé (tr), Presses Universitaires de France, 1999) I.I.X, § 5 ('le droit naturel est tellement immuable, qu'il ne peut pas méme etre changé par Dieu').

[5] Montesquieu, *De l'esprit des lois* (first published 1748; Flammarion, 1997). On Montesquieu as a comparatist, see Eric Stein, 'Uses, Misuses—and Nonuses of Comparative Law' (1978) 72 Nw U L Rev 198 (discussing the views of Otto Kahn-Freund and Alan Watson).

[6] For further remarks on this, see Robert Howse, 'Montesquieu on Commerce, Conquest, War and Peace' (2006) 31 Brooklyn J Int'l L 693, 708.

[7] Montesquieu, *De l'esprit des lois*, Book XII, Chapter II.

gone differently even in France. Instead of making a claim to universal truth, he thus referred to the 'nature of things'.[8]

A distinct approach emerged in Adam Smith. After explaining why casuistry had to be rejected, he argued that 'every system of positive law may be regarded as a more or less imperfect attempt towards a system of natural jurisprudence, or towards an enumeration of the particular rules of justice', and added that 'those rules are, in general, intended to coincide with those of natural justice'. However, he was aware that this is not always the case. Systems of law could not, therefore, be regarded as reproducing the rules of natural justice.[9]

An even clearer move away from the concept of natural justice characterized, after the decline of what he called the *Jus Publicum Europeum*, the approach of Carl Schmitt. He proposed an interpretation of due process of law that deserves analysis. He distinguished *jus gentium* in the sense of a *jus inter gentes* from a 'general common law extending beyond the borders of the self-contained *gentes* (peoples, states, empires)'.[10] Interestingly, when Schmitt used the term 'general common law', he was referring neither to the common law of Anglo-Saxon countries, nor to customary law, but to a set of precepts that were founded either on a shared constitutional standard or a minimum of presupposed international organizations; and the main point of such precepts was 'a generally recognized right of free men to property and due process of law extending beyond the borders of states and peoples'.[11] There was, in this, an evident deviation from theories of natural rights.

Yet, something is missing in this approach. It is unclear whether Schmitt's concept of 'general common law' is based on the assumption that there are concepts and principles that are immutable, notwithstanding the passing of time. There is another aspect of this concept that is, to say the least, controversial. It is possible that, like Montesquieu, Schmitt thought that, with the gradual progress of law and government, there is a consequential improvement of legal institutions, which more or less inevitably goes in the direction of due process, which is questionable.[12] The underlying assumption, that a set of common principles in a variety of societies exists and can be used to guide governmental action, has been contested by the strand of legal thought that emerged in Germany in the nineteenth century.

The divide between domestic and international law

This new school of historical jurisprudence, founded by Savigny and Puchta, did not simply challenge the intellectual premises of natural lawyers, claiming that the law is

[8] For this remark, see Maurice Hauriou, *Principes de droit public* (Dalloz, 1910) 10. See also Benoît Jeanneau, *Les Principes généraux du droit dans la jurisprudence administrative* (Sirey, 1954) 133 (noting that often general principles of public law are based on the 'nature of things').

[9] Adam Smith, *The Theory of Moral Sentiments* (first published 1790, Liberty Classics, 1976) Section VII.4.36.

[10] Carl Schmitt, *The Nomos of the Earth in the International Law of Jus Publicum Europaeum* (Gary L Ulmen (tr), Telos Press, 2003) 211.

[11] Carl Schmitt, *The Nomos of the Earth*, 212.

[12] Gunther Frankenberg, 'Critical Comparisons: Re-thinking Comparative Law' (1985) 26 Harvard Int'l LJ 411, 438 (criticizing functionalist approaches to comparative law).

embedded in every society and must be coherent with its 'spirit'. It also fiercely criticized the idea that the law could be founded on the commands of a politically legitimated authority, as held by the positivists. Neither reason nor politics could provide an adequate basis for conceptualizing legal principles. As these lawyers understood law as the unique product of each nation's cultural and ideal patrimony, they contested the plausibility of any attempt to transfer legal institutions from one country to another. There was more than a simple assonance between this way of conceiving the law and the metaphysical jurisprudence of Hegel,[13] which became dominant in Germany. Both Savigny and Hegel widely used the concept of *Volksgeist*, but it had different meanings for them: while the former emphasized the role of jurists, the latter focused on the role of the State. This also explains why, unlike Savigny,[14] Hegel was not an enemy of codification, for its potentiality of rationalization, as well as for legislation, was ultimately in the hands of the monarch.

Hegel's conception of the State[15] is the basis of his thesis that there is a divide between the two great provinces of public law, internal and external to the State. The fact that each individual State has its own particular law[16] was obvious, almost axiomatic, for Hegel. The following step was to argue that there is a completely different law within and outside the State. Hegel asserted that the reality of internal public law changes when the relationships between States are involved, that is to say in their external law. Such relationships are subject to the State's external law. Accordingly, two legal orders exist, not only independent, but also reciprocally isolated, due to their different foundations. It is fair to add that Hegel acknowledged the need to respect the duties stemming from the treaties agreed by the States. But he emphasized that such relationships were based on the sovereignty of each State. Since there is not a higher source of authority and power, the States' autonomy might be exercised above individual treaties.[17] Hence, the sharp contrast with the Kantian cosmopolitan ideal[18] and the critical remarks of those who consider his work to be an apology for the use of force.[19]

The idea of a divide between internal and external public law ought not to be simply dismissed as a product of a distorted metaphysics or political doctrine. It is this conception that provided the framework for the school of thought of which Heinrich Triepel has been one the leading figures.[20] According to this school of

[13] Roscoe Pound, 'Introduction', III.

[14] Friedrich Karl von Savigny, *Vom Beruf unserer Zeit für Gesetzgebung und Rechtswissenschaft* (Mohr und Zimmer, 1814) § 2 (contrasting the customs of a people with the arbitrariness of a legislator).

[15] Georg F Hegel, *Grundlinien der Philosophie des Rechts* (first published 1821, Holzinger, 2013) paragraphs 257–8.

[16] Georg F Hegel, *Grundlinien der Philosophie des Rechts*, paragraph 259.

[17] Georg F Hegel, *Grundlinien der Philosophie des Rechts*, paragraph 330.

[18] Georg F Hegel, *Grundlinien der Philosophie des Rechts*, paragraphs 332–3. For further remarks on Kantian ideas, see Martti Koskenniemi, *The Politics of International Law* (Hart, 2001) 325. Alec Stone Sweet, 'A Cosmopolitan Legal Order: Constitutional Pluralism and Rights Adjudication in Europe' (2012) 1 Global Const 53

[19] Léon Duguit, 'The Law and the State' (1917) 31 Harvard L Rev 95, 97.

[20] Heinrich Triepel, *Volkerrecht und Landesrecht* (C.L. Hirschfeld, 1899) 11. For further analysis, see Walter Rudolf, 'Incorporation of Customary Law into Municipal Law', in Grigory I Tumkin and Rüdiger R Wolfrum (eds), *International Law and Municipal Law* (Duncker und Humblot, 1988) 24

thought, international law is not simply separated from internal public law, but is built on completely different foundations. The Hegelian legacy manifests itself also with regard to the use of comparative legal analysis. Hegel did not provide any extensive discussion on this, simply because of his ideas that the borders of the State, of each State, looked like Hercules' columns. Together with the idea that treaties only bind States, this is the intellectual foundation on which it has been claimed that each treaty (for instance, a bilateral investment treaty (BIT)) must be regarded as a self-contained regime, with the result that comparative legal analysis is of limited use.[21] A more radical variant holds that, beyond the manifest diversity of innumerable rules of national laws, there is a deeper difference of mindset, as a result of which only in very few cases can legal institutions be meaningfully compared.[22]

This is not the place for a structured survey of the deficiencies of the Hegelian theory of law. Rather, three aspects of the separation between two provinces of public law deserve critical scrutiny. At the most basic level this approach is flawed because it is not fully coherent with its premises. As for its abstract way of proceeding from logical premises, it faces the same difficulty faced by theories of natural law that Hegel vigorously contested. In other words, a divergence between national legal orders ought not to be taken as an axiom or an article of faith.[23] The question whether there are some similarities is, rather, a question of fact and can, therefore, have different answers in different contexts and epochs. Secondly, as observed by Carl Schmitt,[24] Triepel and other followers of the model of separation neglected the existence of a commonality of values and principles. Of course, we may discuss whether such commonality still exists in a much more differentiated world but, again, this is a question of fact. Thirdly, the divide between domestic and international was an intellectual representation of reality (not without normative intents) and reality has changed. Many legal processes are not in fact channelled through the State. Transnational processes determine a growing need for legal regimes and these give rise to litigation. The divide between the two great areas of public law is simply unsustainable in a world in which the International Court of Justice and other courts must solve transnational disputes and can refer, in addition to custom and treaties, to the general principles of law.[25] The model of separation may thus retain its value as a critique of old, taken-for-granted analogies between domestic laws and international law, but not in relation to its constructive side.

(noting that, while Triepel considered municipal law and international law using the metaphor of 'two circles tangent to each other', Anzilotti and others conceived them as 'two intersecting circles').

21 See José Alvarez, 'Beware: Boundary Crossings', NYU School of Law, Public Law Research Paper No 14–51 (available at http://papers.ssrn.com/sol3/papers.cfm?abstract_id=2498182##), in Tsvi Kahana and Anat Scolnicov (eds), *Boundaries of Rights, Boundaries of State* (Cambridge University Press, 2016) 21, 54.

22 Pierre Legrand, *Le droit comparé* (PUF, 1999) 14, 64.

23 See Maurice Hauriou, *Principes de droit public*, XXXV.

24 Carl Schmitt, *The Nomos of the Earth*, Part IV, Chapter 2.

25 Arnold McNair, 'The General Principles of Law Recognized by Civilized Nations' (1957) 33 Brit Ybk Int'l L 1, 4; Rudolf Dolzer and Cristoph Schreuer, *Principles on International Investment Law* (2nd edn, Oxford University Press, 2012) 12.

The quest for *ex post* invariants

Thus far, we have seen that the alternative positions face the same problems from an epistemological point of view, in addition to other problems that are distinct for each. We may thus be tempted to seek to turn to another approach that emerged after 1950 and draws its inspiration from Article 38(1) of the ICJ Statute. But I will argue that, though such an approach seems to be the most promising because it faces less serious problems, two serious weaknesses remain.

This approach was premised on the third legal source referred to by Article 38(1) of the ICJ Statute, the 'general principles of law recognized by civilized nations'. Rudolf Schlesinger's seminal article on this category, arguing that '[t]he concrete determination and formulation of the general principles of law recognized by civilized nations is a task hardly begun [but] … the task is important, perhaps more important than any other to which' comparative law can be devoted.[26] His project, epistemologically, was not based on the assumption that general principles of law exist *ex ante*, as suggested by the old 'science of legislation'. An adequate answer to the question whether invariable laws exist must thus be given *ex post*. It also connected the use of the comparative method (*Rechtsvergleichnung*) with international law.

However, because this approach uses Article 38(1) simply as a legal basis it focuses only on national law. It does not devote adequate attention to the vast array of non-State sources, including treaties, the legal norms issued by international and supranational institutions, and the other precepts that they set out.[27] These sources are particularly important to the extent that many standards of conduct for national authorities de jure or de facto emanate from them.[28] A related, but distinct, problem is whether the focus on national laws allows an adequate individuation of the solutions that are appropriate for exercises of power by such international and supranational institutions. A revision of this approach is, therefore, necessary to make it suitable to the challenges of global law.

2. Due Process of Law as the Closest Thing to an Invariant

Some defects of the three theories concerning unity and differentiation of law have been presented above. Criticism is, of course, an important task, but because less recent theories, in addition to being more or less intrinsically flawed, have lost their heuristic capacity due to the changes that have occurred, it is important to try to make sense of such changes. The *pars destruens* should, therefore, be followed by

[26] Rudolf Schlesinger, 'Research on the General Principles of Law Recognized by Civilized Nations' (1957) 51 Am J Int'l L 734. See also, for a retrospective and a prospective, Mauro Bussani and Ugo Mattei, 'The Common Core Approach to European Private Law' (1997) 3 Columbia J Eur L 339, 340.

[27] For this remark, see Mathias Reimann, 'The Progress and Failure of Comparative Law in the Second Half of the Twentieth Century' (2002) 50 Am J Comp L 674, 680.

[28] Paul Craig, *UK, EU and Global Administrative Law. Foundations and Challenges* (Cambridge University Press, 2015) 9.

a more constructive critique. To begin with, the intellectual foundations of due process, viewed as a global principle of law, will be revealed and assessed. This does not mean that legal realities have a relative importance but, rather, that they must be ordered in some manner before they acquire relevance for law and significance for an attempt to explain them.[29] State practice will thus be considered from three points of view that are particularly apt for showing the increasing global reach of administrative due process of law: first, parallel developments and cross-fertilization processes; second, the standards set out by international and supranational regimes; third, judicial and arbitral practice. A later stage of the analysis, in the following section, will be devoted to a consideration of two objections against such arguments and evidence, along with my responses to them.

Intellectual foundations of due process, viewed as a global principle of law

A common element of some academic works is that due process of law is taken for granted, as if it did not require a specific justification. But a closer look reveals an important distinction in the way due process is conceived. Some conceive it as a sort of 'immanent' principle; that is, one that no legal system may fail to recognize. A second conception of due process builds upon the first in the following way. It is regarded as a variable standard that is 'inherent' in the exercise of these supervisory functions. A third way to look at due process comes closer to the idea of the 'nature of things'.

The first conception is well rooted in the tradition of thought that assigns to due process of law a paramount importance, with a view to ensuring the protection of the interests that can be adversely affected by exercises of power. I am referring to the Anglo-Saxon tradition that emphasizes the 'moral roots' of due process of law,[30] though it does not exclude the importance of instrumental rationales, such as the avoidance of errors and the search for efficient exercises of power. In this account, the requisites of administrative due process seem to have an intuitive or self-evident appeal, in a line of reasoning that echoes Fuller's argument about law.[31]

The second conception of due process draws more specifically upon legal theories of adjudication, as well as of review of administrative action. Such theories differ in many respects, but they are often based on two underlying assumptions. One is that a review of administrative action, unlike an appeal, does not contest the merit or substance of the choice made by the competent public authority, but looks at the process that it has followed. The other assumption is that, if the courts and other public agencies are to carry out such a review, they must 'naturally' impose respect for certain standards of legality, fairness, and propriety that are designed to

[29] Martin Loughlin, *Public Law and Political Theory* (Clarendon Press, 1992) 57.

[30] See Robert P George, 'The Natural Law Due Process Philosophy' (2000) 69 Fordham L Rev 2301.

[31] Fuller included several elements of procedural due process, such as the right to be represented by counsel, the right of cross-examination, and the right to appeal an adverse decision to a higher tribunal: Lon Fuller, *The Morality of Law* (2nd edn, Yale University Press, 1967) 141. For a recent appraisal

prevent the misuse or abuse of power by public authorities *stricto sensu*, as well as by the plethora of quasi-public or private bodies that perform public functions in the transnational arena. It is in this sense that administrative due process of law is conceived as a sort of 'inherent' standard of review.[32] A problem with this approach is, therefore, the substantially unlimited discretionary power that is left to judges and arbitrators. Possible remedies for this problem include a solution that could have a certain appeal for moderate positivists, namely that, when lacking a clear rule, courts will exercise discretion to determine not what is procedurally fair, but what is unfair.[33] Another remedy is the idea that judges, when interpreting broad standards of justice, should look at common practices.

There is still another way to look at administrative due process of law. It is close to the approach followed by Montesquieu when he delineated the status and significance of the right to be heard and seemed to assume that it corresponded to the 'nature of things'. The growing importance of regional and global regulatory regimes that promote not only free trade, but also collective interests such as the preservation of exhaustible resources, can be regarded as implying the acceptance of basic elements of procedural fairness. It is from this perspective that, according to some commentators, old and new questions concerning the exercise of authority can be assessed and answered in the light of general principles of law, such as due process, proportionality, and transparency.[34]

These intellectual foundations provide us with important insights in order to understand the role that due process of law can play in the current state of international law and law *tout court*. It can be helpful to consider such role in the light of the ideas and thoughts of a prominent international lawyer, Martti Koskenniemi. He has argued that law 'comes first' in founding a public sphere.[35] Once the constitutive dimension of law has been recognized, the next step is to seek to understand how it can be achieved. An initial solution was elaborated by the international lawyers who emphasized the role of international courts and tribunals. For them, lacking international legislation, judges and arbitrators had to elaborate international law using 'general principles and domestic law analogies'.[36] This was but a temporary solution, however. As Koskenniemi has observed, international legislation fails

of Fuller's argument, see Gianluigi Palombella, 'The Rule of Law, Democracy and International Law: Learning from the US Experience' (2007) 20 Ratio Juris, 456, 476.

[32] Eduard Laferrière, *Traité de la juridiction administrative et du recours contentieux* (2nd edn, Berger-Lavrault, 1896) xiiii; Paul Craig, *UK, EU and Global Administrative Law*, 19. For a discussion of a specific court, see Friedl Weiss, 'Inherent Powers of National and International Courts: the Practice of the Iran-US Claims Tribunal', in Christina Binder et al (eds), *International Investment Law for the 21st Century: Essays in Honour of Cristoph Schreuer* (Oxford University Press, 2009) 185.

[33] Herbert L Hart, *The Concept of Law*, 132.

[34] Benedict Kingsbury, Nico Krisch, and Richard B Stewart, 'The Emergence of Global Administrative Law' (2005) 68 Law & Cont Probl 15; Benedict Kingsbury, 'The Concept of "Law" in Global Administrative Law' (2009) 20 Eur J Int'l L 23, 29–30 (for a discussion of what he terms the qualities 'immanent' in public law).

[35] Martti Koskenniemi, 'Constitutionalism as Mindset: Reflections on Kantian Themes About International Law and Globalization' (2007) 8 Theoretical Inquiries in Law 29.

[36] Martti Koskenniemi, 'International Legislation Today: Limits and Possibilities' (2005) 23 Wis Int'l LJ 61, 67.

to assure adequate coherence. The reason for this is related, first, to the fragmentation of international law and the emergence of multiple levels of governance[37] and, second, to the fact that the main contemporary style of international legislation fails to provide adequate normativity.[38] Even though the 'global public realm' has a low level of institutionalization and is fragmented, Koskenniemi's view is that this should not be seen as 'overly problematic'.[39] The reason is that the absence of a legislator does not imply that there can be no Rule of Law. Notwithstanding the concern for norms that have not been elaborated and approved by politically elected or otherwise legitimated authors, the general principles of law can play a role. In particular, 'no lawyer will ... ask for evidence for the rule *audiatur et altera pars* merely because the immediately applicable law is silent about such matters'.[40]

Evidence from State practice: Two issues of method

State practice, in the form of customary law and treaties, is normally regarded as the main object of research, despite the increasing importance of the decisions taken by international courts and tribunals and the attention that scholars devote to the works of their colleagues. It is nonetheless important to be mindful of two issues of methodology. One concerns the meaning and salience of general practice; the other is whether a practice is only relevant if it is shared by all nations.

An easy starting point is to observe that it is only with regard to international custom that Article 38 refers to practice, where custom is defined as 'evidence of a general practice accepted as law'. Though such provision might more properly refer to a 'general practice' as evidence of an international custom,[41] its meaning is clear. Custom is identified by the two traditional requisites: general practice and *opinion juris*, though sometimes the latter is assessed on the basis of the former,[42] which is more relevant here. It must be intended in the sense that a customary norm arises when a certain practice among nations is extensive and virtually uniform.[43] But this is a requisite for custom, not for general principles of law,[44] even though the line of demarcation is not always easily discernible and the latter may evolve into the former.

37 See Martti Koskenniemi and Paivi Leino, 'Fragmentation of International Law: Postmodern Anxieties' (2002) 15 Leiden J Int'l L 553. See also the report by the UN International Law Commission, *Fragmentation of International Law: Difficulties Arising from the Diversification and Expansion of International Law* (2004) and, in the increasingly burgeoning literature, Bruno Simma, 'Fragmentation in a Positive Light' (2003–4) 25 Mich J Int'l L 845.

38 Martti Koskenniemi, 'International Legislation Today', 78.

39 Martti Koskenniemi, 'International Legislation Today', 92.

40 See Martti Koskenniemi, 'Constitutionalism as Mindset', 19; 'General Principles: Reflexions on Constructivist Thinking in International Law' (1985), in Martti Koskenniemi (ed), *Sources of International Law* (Aldershot, 2000) 359.

41 Vaughan Lowe, *International Law* (Clarendon Press, 2007) 36.

42 Jack Goldsmith and Erik Posner, 'A Theory of Customary International Law' (1999) 66 U Chi L Rev 1113, 1117.

43 See Anthea Roberts, 'Traditional and Modern Approaches to Customary International Law: A Reconciliation' (2001) 95 Am J Int'l L 757, 762 (underlining descriptive accuracy).

44 Bin Cheng, *General Principles of Law as Applied by International Courts and Tribunals* (2nd edn, Cambridge University Press, 2006) 24.

It is in the light of the conclusion just reached—that is, generality of practice is required by Article 38(1) only with regard to international custom—that the other issue can be better assessed. There are, not surprisingly, differing views as to the significance and implications of the standard of civilization set out by Article 38(1)(c). Some commentators see the reference to 'civilization' as a legacy of Western cultural imperialism.[45] Others take a different view, seeing a broader significance in the 'standard of civilization', in the sense that it reveals the search for standards that could be shared by all peoples that have reached a certain degree of development,[46] There is still another view, which attributes simply a functional meaning to the word 'civilized'. It has thus been suggested that the reference to 'civilized nations' was introduced in order to prevent the risk of arbitrariness[47] and that it would thus serve to exclude only primitive peoples.[48] That being the case, it can be argued that all nations that are members of the UN are, by virtue of this fact, to be regarded as civilized. However, this solution leaves unresolved the question of whether the general principles to which Article 38 of the ICJ Statute refers must be common to all jurisdictions of the world or to most of them. The first option might be appealing, for it is based on the idea that general principles of law must possess some kind of 'universality'. It can also avoid questionable, if not arbitrary, uses of general principles. But this interpretation of Article 38(1)(c) is not satisfactory. If judges and arbitrators were allowed to resort only to principles shared by all legal systems, such provision would be of little use.[49]

A more systematic interpretation of Article 38 also supports an alternative view. The essence of the argument can be conveyed quite simply. In addition to setting out the three sources of law (custom, treaties, and general principles of law), Article 38 entrusts the ICJ with the power to apply the rules of law that emerge from 'judicial decisions of different nations of the world'.[50] If the ICJ is empowered to do so with regard to a subsidiary source, then *a fortiori* it can do so with a primary source of law.[51] Additional support for this line of reasoning can be found in the Statute of the International Criminal Court. As regards applicable law, it refers to the 'general principles of law derived by the Court from national laws of legal systems of the world'.[52] The ICC may thus refer to particular national legal systems, not necessarily to all.

[45] For critical remarks, see Martti Koskenniemi, *The Gentle Civilizer of Nations: The Rise and Fall of International Law 1870–1960* (Cambridge University Press, 2002) 134–5.

[46] See Gerrit W Gong, *The Standard of Civilization in the International Society* (Oxford University Press, 1984) and Hedley Bull, 'Preface', iii–iv; David P Fidler, 'The Return of the Standard of Civilization' (2001) 2 Chi J Int'l L 137, 147 (asserting that in the post-1989 world liberalism provides the only standard of civilization on a globalized scale).

[47] Bin Cheng, *General Principles of Law*, 290.

[48] Bin Cheng, *General Principles of Law*, 25.

[49] Emmanuel Gaillard, 'Use of General Principles of International Law in International Long-Term Contracts' (1999) 27 Int'l Business Lawyer 216.

[50] Statute of the ICJ, Article 38(1)(d).

[51] Louis B Wehle, 'Comparative Law's Proper Task for the International Court' (1951) 99 U Pa L Rev 13, 24.

[52] Statute of the International Criminal Court, Article 21(1)(c).

Empirically, the idea that judges and arbitrators should refer only to norms that are common to all jurisdictions of the world is not consistent with the way in which they work. Consider, for instance, how the CJEU has interpreted a similar provision, that concerning 'the general principles of law common to the legal systems of the Member States' in the field of non-contractual liability. Specialists of EC law have noted that the Court has, when developing general principles of law, not normally demanded that the principle should be present in all Member State legal systems: thus proportionality and legitimate expectations were read into EC law even though they were not independent principles of judicial review in all national legal systems.[53] More generally, even though courts and arbitral bodies have rarely made explicit reference to the 'general principles of law', they have not refrained from developing standards of administrative due process of law in order to ensure that 'justice' is rendered to individuals and businesses. There is not simply a growing predisposition of judges and arbitrators to refer to due process of law, but also to give weight to a series of factors or indicators of procedural fairness that manifestly correspond to the types of procedural dysfunctions and anomalies that have been elaborated in the major legal systems of the world.

What these arguments thus suggest is that, under Article 38 of the ICJ Statute, the ICJ, and by extension other international tribunals, can have resort to general principles of law common to most modern legal systems or, as others have suggested, to those of the major municipal legal systems. The preceding line of reasoning was nevertheless based upon an important implicit premise. Comparative legal analysis must be taken seriously. If legal discourses require the use of evidence and persuasion, lawyers, judges, and arbitrators cannot be satisfied with little more than a quick look at the practice of a few States, even though they can rightfully be regarded as the major legal systems of the world.[54] For all the importance of regional custom, an attempt to ascribe a certain norm to the general principles of law that can be transposed from the national to the transnational arena requires, at the least, consideration of practice in different regions of the world. Moreover, the use of such principle to solve a particular dispute should be avoided if it is seriously contrary to the laws or public policies of one of the parties. This condition has the advantage of safeguarding equality of the parties.

The implications of the preceding discussion can be summarized as follows: although due process of law might be regarded either as a principle that is morally or logically necessary in the field of international law—that is, a norm of *jus cogens*[55]—or as

[53] Paul Reuter, 'Le recours de la Cour de justice des Communautés européennes à des principes généraux de droit', in *Mélanges Rollin* (Pedone, 1964) 273; Koen Lenaerts and Kathleen Gutman, 'The Comparative Law Method and the Court of Justice of the EU', in Mads Andenas and Duncan Fairgrieve (eds), *Courts and Comparative Law* (Oxford University Press, 2008) 158.

[54] Vaughan Lowe, *International Law*, 47.

[55] That is, a fundamental norm of international law from which no derogation is admitted, by virtue of Article 53 of the Vienna Convention on the Law of Treaties. See Alfred Verdross, 'Jus Dispositivum and Jus Cogens in International Law' (1966) 60 Am J Int'l L 55 (distinguishing norms that do and do not admit exceptions). For instance, in *Kadi*, the CFI (Case T-315/01, paragraph 238) decided that administrative due process of law was not included in the standard of universal protection covered by *jus cogens*.

an evolving norm of customary law,[56] this is not the line of reasoning that is being advanced here. My argument is, rather, that administrative due process must be viewed as a general principle of law. As a result, neither the express consent of all States nor a general practice, in the sense indicated before, is required for its recognition. However, not only is evidence of its acceptance important, but it is also argued that this theory explains evidence more persuasively than others.

Evidence from State practice: Parallel developments and cross-fertilization

In the light of the preceding discussion an attempt will be made to assess the significance of the developments that have been analysed in more detail in the first parts of this inquiry. Coherently with the methodology followed in this inquiry,[57] I will begin by considering the law that must be observed. In this respect, a twofold trend has emerged. First, several constitutions, not only in Europe and the Americas but also in Commonwealth countries such as South Africa, as well as in East Asian countries such as Japan and South Korea, lay down principles of procedural fairness. The existence of a constitutional provision serves to reinforce the elaboration of due process requirements by the courts and their generalization.

A second trend, which has a growing importance and reach, concerns legislation.[58] In the last twenty-five years, State after State has enacted legislation regarding administrative procedure. All of the codes set out procedural requirements for adjudication; some do so for administrative rulemaking, which would otherwise be the object of guidance to public officers. Considered as a whole, these provisions of hard law and soft law strengthen the fundamental requirement to respect pre-established procedure or, if it does not exist, to adhere to practice. The underlying rationales may vary, but the effects are very similar. Another common feature of codes of procedure is the importance that is assigned to general principles of law. Sometimes they are considered as a whole, either in a preamble or in an ad hoc article, sometimes there is a list of general principles. Included among these are very broad principles such as equality and the Rule of Law, and general principles of law such as due process of law, proportionality, and transparency.

Two further points should be borne in mind when considering the codification of administrative procedure: the importance of regional practice and cross-fertilization. There are regions of the world, including Europe and the Americas, where there is virtually no State that has failed to enact legislation of this type. It can thus be argued that a regional custom exists. Equally important is the time element.

[56] See Theodor Meron, *Human Rights and Humanitarian Norms as Customary Law* (Clarendon Press, 1989) 96 (arguing, in light of the International Covenant on Civil and Political Rights, that judicial due process of law has attained this status); Wolfgang Friedmann, 'The Uses of "General Principles" in the Development of International Law' (1963) 57 Am J Int'l L 279, 290 (same thesis, based on both the Universal Declaration and the similar rules enacted by Western countries and the USSR).

[57] See above, Chapter 1, Section 2, p. 13.

[58] See Jack Goldsmith and Eric Posner, 'A Theory of Customary International Law', 1117 (noting that national legislation is one of the 'least controversial sources').

Almost always legislation codifies established government practices and standards elaborated and imposed by the courts. It can thus be argued that at least some requirements of procedural due process are long established, an aspect that has particular relevance for the formation of custom.[59] In another region of the globe, East Asia, the trend has emerged more recently, but is extending rapidly. Even a country with a distinct and long-consolidated legal tradition such as China is not immune from this trend. This can be explained in more than one way. Although in some instances the possibility of autonomous or parallel developments cannot be excluded, there is evidence that in many others this is not the case, the Austrian model being perhaps the best example in central Europe, while the influence of the US Administrative Procedure Act (APA) has spread over the years in other regions.

All of this not only substantiates my claim that an increasingly general practice exists, but also that it contradicts one of the central claims of Alvarez's thesis, originalism. In fact, the history of due process, now entrenched as a fundamental requirement of justice, is one of judicial lawmaking, transplants, and unfaithfulness to the legal texts revered by originalists. Even those who proclaim their fidelity to originalist dogma, Justice Scalia for example, have acknowledged that the correct interpretation of the Due Process Clause of the Fifth Amendment to the US Constitution involves a boundary crossing, the importation of the 'old English law' in this case.[60] Regressing further, the roots of this old English law were also a transplant. In the famous *Bagg*'s case, Sir Edward Coke, Chief Justice of the King's Bench, referred to procedures that were required 'by the law of the land' in order to introduce a new and original principle, the maxim *audiatur et altera pars*, in the context of the unfair dismissal of a civil servant. Although Coke referred to the *Magna Carta*, he relied much more on Seneca's *Medea* to anchor the 'new' principle to the rule of reason more generally.[61]

Originalism and strict adherence to the text are also contradicted by the evolution of due process in a non-Western state, India. This example is of particular importance because Alvarez, in other sets of arguments, claims that scholarship and practice on matters of general principles are limited to considerations of Western liberal democracies.[62] By design, the framers of Article 21 of the Indian Constitution had expressly rejected including a provision akin to the Due Process Clause of the Fifth Amendment of the US Constitution. They chose instead a more modest obligation, focused on the requirement to respect the 'procedure established by law'. But in the course of the following three decades, the conception of procedural fairness adopted by the Court went well beyond the 'procedure established by law'. The

[59] Vaughan Lowe, *International Law*, 41.

[60] 'A conversation between US Supreme Court Justices: Antonin Scalia and Stephen Breyer' (2005) 3 I-CON 519, 535 (Justice Scalia affirming '[I]f you have that philosophy, obviously foreign law is irrelevant with one exception: old English law—because phrases like 'due process' and the 'right to confrontation' were taken from English law, and were understood to mean what they meant there'). See also Sanford L Kadish, 'Methodology and Criteria in Due Process Adjudication: A Survey and Criticism' (1956) 66 Yale LJ 319, 328 (referring to the opinions of 'other countries in the Anglo-Saxon tradition').

[61] See above, Chapter 3, Section 1, p. 41.

[62] José Alvarez, 'Boundary Crossings', 40–2.

Court increasingly stated not only that a statute authorized governmental interference with liberty, but also that it prescribed a procedure for so doing and even that the procedure was fair.

If in India procedural fairness developed in contrast with doctrines of strict adherence to the text, in France it was entirely developed by the administrative court, the *Conseil d'État*. Two aspects of this praetorian construction are particularly interesting. First, it accentuated the distinctiveness of public law, in contrast with doctrines of legal positivism that prevailed in the field of private law.[63] Second, as Réné Cassin, the vice-president of the *Conseil d'État*—writing extrajudicially—expressly observed, after 1945 judicial activism was justified, or reinforced, by the necessity to reinterpret legislation that had been enacted under the influence of Nazi forces and had endangered fundamental liberties.[64]

More generally, the history of due process, now entrenched as a fundamental requirement of justice, is one of judicial lawmaking, transplants, and unfaithfulness to the legal texts revered by originalists. In contrast with their doctrines, judges have built the effectiveness and legitimacy of their respective legal systems through the development of general principles. Most judges had little choice, since States and national officials rarely provide much guidance in that area. But the spread of codification is likely to provide new impulse to the uses of comparative legal analysis.

Evidence from State practice: Bilateral and multilateral treaties

The second answer to the question concerning the possibility that due process is viewed as a global principle of law rests on a process of induction and generalization from existing treaties. In this respect, the findings made in Parts I and II are very helpful. Three developments are discernible and meaningful.

The first is the broadened interpretation of procedural requirements laid down by regional charters of fundamental rights. Both Article 6 of the European Convention on Human Rights (ECHR) and Article 8 of the American Convention of Human Rights are concerned with due process rights in the context of the judicial process. This might have induced the courts that are entrusted with the task of ensuring their observance to take a narrow view of what constitutes a judicial decision and to require only that the procedure established by law be respected and that a hearing be provided. But this is not what the courts did. In fact, Article 6 ECHR has been applied in a number of areas that can properly be called administrative, such as disciplinary procedures and those for issuing sanctions to businesses. Interestingly, this broad conception of due process has been imposed on supranational authorities when exercising not only regulatory powers in the economic sphere but also powers aimed at combatting transnational terrorism.

[63] François Geny, *De la méthode et de la technique du droit privé positif à celle du droit administratif*, in *Le Conseil d'État. Livre jubilaire* (Sirey, 1952) 290; Yves Gaudemet, *Les méthodes du juge administratif* (L.G.D.J., 1972).

[64] Réné Cassin, 'Introduction' (1951) 10 Etudes et documents du Conseil d'État 11.

Similarly, Article 8 of the American Convention of Human Rights has been said to be applicable to the unfair dismissal of public employees, thus confirming the global reach of the hearing requirement.[65]

The second trend is the emergence of autonomous requirements of due process. For instance, in addition to the general requirement established by the Agreement on Trade-Related Aspects of Intellectual Property Rights (TRIPS Agreement) that procedures concerning the enforcement of intellectual property rights be 'fair and equitable', there is the more specific requirement that intellectual rights holders be provided with due process safeguards including notice and comment.[66] Similarly, in *Shrimp* the Appellate Body (AB) imposed the respect of basic requirements of due process, including the duty to provide a hearing and that to state reasons. Other institutions issue soft law rules for the same purpose. For instance, the Council of Europe's Committee of Ministers recommended that, for any measure adversely affecting individuals, reasons be given either directly or when the affected party so requests. Duties of procedural fairness are imposed also on non-State authorities, for instance, within the framework of the assignment of domain names, where notice and comment is assured to affected parties.[67]

The third trend concerns a particular area that is of remarkable relevance from a global viewpoint, that of direct foreign investment. Its importance can be easily justified on the following grounds: the number of BITs has dramatically increased, from a few dozen to more than 3,000;[68] almost 200 countries are parties to one or more treaties on investment;[69] in the last twenty years 'the majority of cases in investment arbitration have been based' on BITs.[70] It is in this context that a two-fold change has emerged. One is the diffusion of general standards of conduct, the most important of which is the FET standard. The other is the provision of a due process clause in respect of direct and indirect expropriation.

Specialists point out that, despite their differences, 'certain general features … characterize virtually all BITs'.[71] Each BIT puts some emphasis on the parties' commitment, generally expressed in the preamble of the treaty, to ensure 'a stable

[65] Inter-American Court of Human Rights, *Baena et al. v Panama* (2001) Inter-Am Ct HR (ser C) No 72, paragraph 126 ('the discretionality of the administration has boundaries that may not be surpassed, one such boundary being respect … for the guarantee of due process').

[66] See above, Chapter 3, Section 2, p. 49.

[67] See Sabino Cassese, *Global Standards for National Administrative Procedure* (2005) 68 Law & Cont Probl 109–10.

[68] The UNCTAD website lists 2816 BITs (2116 of which are in force) and 345 other international treaties (274 of which are in force). See Stephen M Schwebel, 'Investor-State Disputes and the Development of International Law' (2004) 98 Am Soc'y Int'l L Proc 27 (for the thesis that treaties contribute to custom); José Alvarez, 'A Bit on Custom' (2009) 42 NYU J Int'l L & Pol 17 (for the contrary thesis).

[69] Cristopher F Dugan et al., *Investor-State Arbitration* (Oxford University Press, 2008) 51.

[70] Christoph Schreuer, 'Travelling the BIT Route—Of Waiting Periods, Umbrella Clauses and Forks in the Road' (2004) 5 J World Inv & Trade 231.

[71] W Michael Reisman and Robert D Sloane, 'Indirect Expropriation and its Valuation in the BIT Generation' (2004) 74 British Ybk Int'l L 115; Federico Ortino, 'Redefining the Content and Role of "Rules" and "Standards": A New Approach to International Investment Treaty Making' (2013) 28 ICSID Review 152.

framework for investment [that] will maximize effective utilization of economic resources and improve living standards'[72] or, within its operational provisions, clarifies that the treaty serves to 'provide and maintain a favorable environment for investments in this territory by nationals and companies of the other Party'. Moreover, in order to achieve these goals, the contracting parties agree on some broad clauses, including full protection and security, the constant protection of the law, and the FET standard. It is used by most of the main Model BITs, such as those of Germany, India, and the US, and it is referred to by more than ninety per cent of existing BITs.[73] The FET standard thus appears to be quantitatively and qualitatively the most important standard of conduct that governments must respect[74] and that which comes closer than others to national concepts of justice, such as the *traitement juste et équitable* in France or the Takings Clause of the Fifth Amendment.[75]

This brings us to the more particular provisions governing expropriation. BITs are increasingly more demanding in this respect. While less recent treaties simply enshrined the obligation not to affect foreign investments without paying compensation for them, BITs express a more sophisticated approach, by focusing on a variety of conditions, including 'due process of law'. Interestingly, the scope of application of such clauses does not cover only the traditional form of expropriation, often qualified as 'direct', but also a variety of measures that 'indirectly' affect the exercise of the right to property. Especially when BITs use broad concepts such as that of the 'measures having effect equivalent to nationalization or expropriation', they include both regulation (eg urban plans that prohibit certain uses of land or buildings and 'regulatory takings') and adjudication (eg withdrawal of authorization or licences). This applies to both traditional and new important capital-exporting countries, such as Germany[76] and China.[77] This regulation of due process is thus of increasing significance in relation to my claim that this is a principle of global law. The wide acceptance of the clause concerning expropriation, broadly intended, and the even wider acceptance of the FET standard show that these are not an imposition by Western countries.[78]

[72] US 2012 Model BIT; Indian Model Text of Bilateral Investment Promotion and Protection Agreement (BIPA); Canada 2004 Model BIT.

[73] Jonathan Coe, 'Fair and Equitable Treatment under Bilateral Investment Treaties' (2002) 96 Am Soc Int'l LP 9, 18 found that the FET standard was adopted by 90% of the more than 500 BITs examined. A few years later, Ioana Tudor, *The Fair and Equitable Treatment Standard in the International Law of Foreign Investment* (Oxford University Press, 2008), after examining more than 350 BITs, found that 95% of them adopted this standard. See also Rudolf Dolzer and Cristoph Schreuer, *Principles on International Investment Law*, 130 (defining FET as a 'single unified standard').

[74] Campbell McLachlan, Laurence Shore, and Matthew Weiniger, *International Investment Law. Substantive Principles* (Oxford University Press, 2007) 11.

[75] Stephan W Schill, 'Fair and Equitable Treatment, the Rule of Law, and Comparative Public Law', in Stephan W Schill (ed), *International Investment Law and Comparative Public Law* (Cambridge University Press, 2010) 153.

[76] See the German Model BIT (Article 4(2).

[77] China's BITs often refer to due process in the context of expropriation, see p. 147.

[78] Campbell McLachlan, Laurence Shore, and Matthew Weiniger, *International Investment Arbitration* (Oxford University Press, 2007) 219.

An emerging *jurisprudence constante*

Once it has been clarified that the rules that must be respected by public authorities include certain requirements of procedural due process of law, it is, of course, important to see how judges and arbitrators adjust treaty provisions to the facts before them[79]. The analysis begins with an overview of two scholarly findings that appear to relativize the importance of general principles of law in contemporary judicial and arbitral practice. The focus then shifts to the two options that are available to judges and arbitrators and to their respective importance in such practice.

Scholarly literature concerning general principles of law has observed, first, that not all general principles that are valid *in foro domestico* are suitable for transposition into the international arena[80] and, second, that despite a large amount of legal literature on principles there are not a lot of cases in which judges and arbitrators have referred to general principles of law as intended by Article 38(1)(c) of the ICJ Statute.[81] This finding has been confirmed by an accurate and recent study concerning arbitral practice within the framework of ICSID.[82] What might be inferred from this is that the potentialities inherent in the provision laid down have not been converted into reality. The scarcity of references to the third category of norms laid down by Article 38(1) is obviously an important element of fact. However, rarely are facts themselves meaningful. On the one hand, the meaning that is ascribed to certain facts can be objectionable, for instance, if one thinks that arbitral practice simply has subsidiary importance; that is, it does not attract the relevance of treaty provisions.

On the other hand, the significance of such facts can be discussed in the light of other facts, which allegedly are likely to support a different view of reality. I will begin from this latter viewpoint.

As observed in the first part of this inquiry, due process of law emerged in the UK not as a matter of legal philosophy, but as a moral requisite that any judicial or quasi-judicial authority must respect; then as a constitutional principle in the US Bill of Rights in the late eighteenth century; and in continental Europe and Latin America as a judge-made, unwritten principle of administrative law between the end of the nineteenth century and the first half of the twentieth. Lawyers trained in these jurisdictions have not been reluctant to acknowledge the importance of due process in the international arena. A clear example is provided by the French

79 See W Michael Reisman, *The Quest for World Order and Human Dignity in the Twenty-first century* (The Hague Academy of International Law, 2012) 180 (arguing that arbitrators must engage in actualization).

80 Michael Akehurst, 'The Hierarchy of Sources in International Law' (1975) 47 Br Ybk Int'l L 273, 278.

81 Wolfgang Friedmann, 'The Uses of "General Principles"', 280. For the same remark, as regards the Permanent Court, see Cherif Bassiouni, 'A Functional Approach to "General Principles"', 791 (referring to the opinions of Hudson and Lauterpacht).

82 Ole K Fauchald, 'The Legal Reasoning of ICSID Tribunals—an Empirical Analysis' (2008) 19 Eur J Int'l L 301, 312 (observing that general principles were referred to in eight out of the 98 decisions considered).

magistrates who worked as Advocate General in the EC/EU. They deployed a method of interpreting EC law that was directly inspired by the jurisprudence of the French *Conseil d'État*, in particular by the doctrine of general principles of law, with or without an express textual basis. Another major international court-like body that has included administrative due process within the principles which it must observe, is the Appellate Body of the World Trade Organization (WTO), which did so without explicit justification or citation to authority. Another major international court, the European Court of Human Rights (ECtHR), broadly interpreted Article 6 ECHR with a view to enforcing due process in the context of quasi-judicial procedure. Other international courts have enforced due process with regard to particular forms of administrative action, for instance, International Tribunal for the Law of the Sea (ITLOS) did so in cases concerning the confiscation of vessels. It can be argued, therefore, that administrative due process has a fundamental importance for all these courts. It is not simply a pan-European general principle of law, but a principle that is referred to by a variety of international courts and tribunals for its advantages. Due process of law is a perfect 'variable standard' from a Hartian perspective, being a standard that entrusts judges with a considerable margin of discretion in considering issues of fact and law.

There is also another trend that is emerging: in addition to being a sort of model for other courts, Article 6 ECHR serves as a common framework for discourses regarding both due process and substantive interests protected by human rights. For instance, EU courts refer to Article 6 and its interpretation even in 'hard' cases, such as those concerning the antiterrorism measures taken by the institutions of the EU in cooperation with the UN. This is not an isolated trend. Indeed, in the context of ICSID arbitral procedures, the ECHR has been taken into account, though not as a binding legal source, but as a persuasive authority. For instance, when assessing the impact of regulatory measures on investors' rights, an arbitral tribunal assessed the significance of the impact of the measures on foreign investment by using the proportionality test developed by the ECtHR.[83] An important process of cross-fertilization has thus begun.

ICSID arbitral tribunals have also sought to ensure that 'justice' is rendered to individuals and businesses, drawing on BITs. There is not simply a growing predisposition of judges and arbitrators to refer to due process of law, but also to give weight to a series of factors or indicators of procedural fairness.[84] In the last twenty years arbitral tribunals have developed standards of due process that would be recognizable to any comparative administrative lawyer as general principles of law.[85]

[83] *Técnicas Medioambientales Tecmed, S.A. v United Mexican States* (ICSID Case No ARB(AF)/00/2), Award of 29 May 2003 (*Tecmed*), paragraphs 121–2.

[84] There is a debate as to whether decisions by arbitral tribunals constitute, if not precedents, a *jurisprudence constante*: for a positive answer, see Andrea K Bjorklund, 'Investment Treaty Arbitral Decisions as Jurisprudence Constante' (2010) 10 Transn Dispute Management 1.

[85] See Thomas Wälde, 'The Specific Nature of Investment Arbitration', in Philippe Kahn—Thomas W Wälde (eds), *Les aspects nouveaux du droit des investissements internationaux—New Aspects of International Investment Law* (Brill/Nijhoff, 2004) 100 (arguing that general principles comprise both international law and comparative law).

Arbitrators not only regularly refer to due process, they also give negative weight to facts concerning State treatment of investors that mirror the types of procedural dysfunctions and anomalies that are censurable in the major legal systems of the world. In some cases, arbitrators endorse the claimants' argument that the decisions taken by the State were based upon evidence not in the record, or upon evidence which the recipient had no opportunity to test by cross-examination (or that was even undisclosed).[86] In other cases, they criticize governments for giving no reason at all.[87] Such indicators manifestly correspond to the types of procedural dysfunctions and anomalies that have been elaborated in the major legal systems of the world.

Obviously, judges and arbitrators react to the arguments put forward by claimants. A particularly significant line of argument is that followed by Professor Reisman, an expert in a dispute concerning the Guatemalan regime for expropriation: the lack of any opportunity for the private party to be heard was regarded as one of the main drawbacks of such an 'idiosyncratic ... regime'.[88] But several other cases examined in this inquiry show the predisposition of arbitrators to pursue the elaboration of procedural constraints on government, though they do so without referring to the 'general principles'. A particularly important development in this respect is the use of the FET standard. Today the FET standard is treated by many arbitrators as a repository of general principles, precisely because arbitrators have interpreted it broadly in light of principles that are common to other legal systems.

Two conclusions follow from this. The lack of explicit references to the third category of norms that the ICJ has the power to apply should not be interpreted as meaning that arbitrators do not pay attention to the standards that govern the conduct of public authorities within domestic legal systems. In fact, arbitrators have refrained from referring to that category, but they have used indicators of due process (a procedure must exist and be respected, affected parties must be provided with a reasonable opportunity to be heard within such procedure, and the decision-maker must give reasons) that reflect general principles of law that are shared by most, if not all, legal systems of the world and that are applied by other international courts and tribunals such as the ECJ and the AB.

A synthesis

Thus, in the end, my argument comes down to these two points related to legal realities and legal theories. First, a growing body of legal principles, both written and unwritten, has emerged and due process, viewed as a general principle of law, plays a 'foundational' role in this respect, in the sense that it contributes to shaping the foundations of a legal order as such. This body of legal principles is not only

[86] See *Joseph Charles Lemire v Ukraine*, ICSID Case No ARB/06/18, Award of 28 March 2011.

[87] *Marion Unglaube v Republic of Costa Rica*, ICSID Case No ARB/08/1, Award of 16 May 2012, § 246.

[88] W Michael Reisman, *Expert Opinion* in *Railroad Development Corporation v Guatemala*, ICSID Case No 07/ARB/23, Award of 11 June 2009.

common because principles such as due process of law and proportionality are general to different areas; it is also common to national and international courts to the extent that the latter have developed the same principle in ways that have made it normal and legitimate for use by all courts.

Second, it can be noted that such developments are in contrast with both arguments used by those who express scepticism about general principles and warn against unauthorized boundary crossings. The first is the argument of original intent, in the sense that a treaty, for instance a BIT, operates as a strict constraint on dispute resolution under that treaty. The second is the argument of design: boundary crossings, it is asserted, are only defensible in cases where there exists sufficient institutional 'fit' between the source legal system (from which one imports the principle) and the target legal system (the new host for the principle).[89] Neither comparative legal analysis nor inter-judicial dialogues are regarded as being important, though the latter are growing in intensity and often give rise to debates within judicial institutions about the uses of the former. However, both arguments are questionable on normative grounds and do not provide accurate descriptions of what judges and arbitrators have actually done, and continue to do, when they develop general principles. The greatest significance of the operation of similar legal institutions, with regard to State and non-State entities, is that it undermines the old model of separation.

3. Two Objections Refuted

Having argued for the view that administrative due process is a general principle of global law, I now wish to consider two objections. First, thus far I have intentionally left one important question unanswered. Neither the ideas and thoughts about due process of law nor the indicators of procedural fairness and propriety examined in this inquiry come out of the blue. The question thus arises of whence they originate. Less recent legal theories often neglected this question. They did so partly due to the conviction that the issue of origin was a philosophical one or, in any event, of little legal importance if compared with the legal source of principles.[90] But they also did so because of the existence of a set of shared beliefs about the law that made it easier to identify general principles. Nobody doubts that this task increasingly became more difficult during the second half of the last century. Some commentators take this remark further, contesting not simply the usefulness, but also the possibility of identifying shared ideas about due process or other general principles of law. Because their objection focuses on culture, I will call it the cultural objection. It must be kept distinct from another objection, which concerns the significance of

[89] See José Alvarez, 'Boundary Crossings', 37 (contending that the first flaw of public law theories is to neglect that each treaty 'reflects the preferences of those who design it').

[90] Norberto Bobbio, 'Principi generali di diritto', in *Novissimo Digesto Italiano* (CEDAM, 1966) XII, 892.

the standards agreed by the States within regional and global regulatory regimes. Unlike the other objection, this one does not focus on the origin of general principles of law. It focuses, rather, on the significance of their acceptance by the States in the context of global regulatory regimes. Because such regimes are generally set up by groups of countries that are led by the West, so the argument goes, newcomers are obliged to accept standards which they have not contributed to. To the extent to which the argument that is thus made against global standards draws on moral grounds, I will call this the moral objection. These objections cannot simply be dismissed as isolated or eccentric. They are raised by several commentators. The questions that they pose are both questions of value and questions of technique, for instance, with regard to the complacency with which some recent studies deal with general principles such as participation and transparency. Not infrequently policy-makers raise the same objections, either tactically or from a true belief, calling into question the legitimacy of regional and global regulatory regimes. However, these objections do not succeed, for the reasons that will be presented.

Normative and descriptive elements

Before I say what is wrong with the objections raised against the global reach of due process, I will first observe that they are characterized by both descriptive and normative elements.

In descriptive terms, proponents of the second objection, that which draws on moral grounds, acknowledge that there are not only scholarly attempts—in particular, those made by the proponents of 'global administrative law'[91]—that point out the importance of procedural standards, but also legal institutions and mechanisms relating to legality, fairness, and participation. They contest, however, the unequal participation in the elaboration of such global standards. Their argument is, in essence, a prescriptive one. Once a global regulatory regime has been created and its standards have been set out, newcomers must accept the standards that have been previously set out and have few possibilities to change them, due to institutional mechanisms and the difficulty that all proponents of change inevitably face. In this sense, the argument that is made denies neither the existence of legal institutions and processes that favour the emergence of procedural standards, nor their legal relevance. However, it asserts that, since there is unequal participation by incumbent States and newcomers in their elaboration, this undermines the significance of such procedural requirements.[92]

Descriptive and prescriptive elements also inform the cultural objection. This view does not simply reiterate the usual remark that the distinction between process and substance is objectionable. It is argued that procedural safeguards are not

[91] Benedict Kingsbury, Nico Krisch, and Richard B Stewart, 'The Emergence of Global Administrative Law', 15.

[92] Bhupinder Chimni, 'Co-option and Resistance: Two Faces of Global Administrative Law' (2005) 37 NYU LS J Int'l L & Pol 799; Ugo Mattei and Laura Nader, *Plunder: Why the Rule of Law is Illegal* (Wiley, 2008) 137 (discussing 'international imperial law').

at all neutral; they reveal strong connections with value judgments, which can be shared within certain 'clubs' of nations, but not in the global arena. In other legal cultures of the world, it is asserted, procedural rules are not disconnected from issues of substance.[93] An emphasis on due process and fair procedures is simply a manifestation of a new type of imperialism, a cultural imperialism, due especially to the dominance of American law.[94] Insisting on this is also misleading because it obscures the real problem; that is, the necessity to achieve peace and prosperity for all. In a similar vein, it has been argued that the overemphasis on the Rule of Law has the effect, if not the purpose, of hiding increasing plunder at the expense of less-favoured nations.[95]

The case against the cultural objection

In this section, I will show two flaws in the cultural objection. The first flaw is that the historic origins of a certain principle, in our case due process of law, must not be confused with their significance in the present. Nor is the assertion that process values are an exclusive patrimony of Western legal cultures sustainable.

The merit system offers a very good example of the undue confusion between the origins of a principle and its validity in the public sphere. Contrary to what some opine, the merit system is not a Western idea. It was elaborated in a non-Western and authoritarian institutional framework, the Chinese Empire. Though it was functional to the preservation and exercise of authority, it also had an important function in terms of openness to talents, wherever they came from socially. Both rationales, sound administration and openness, justified its gradual introduction by Western countries.[96] It was simply greatly preferred to the purchase of public offices and political patronage.[97] The introduction of a new system of administrative justice within the Ottoman Empire constitutes another example, and one that goes in the opposite direction, from West to East. Since 1850 the ruling élite thought that the decline of the Empire depended not only on technology and military power, but also on legal and administrative factors. They thus decided to introduce changes in the administration of justice, setting up judicial institutions based on the French model.[98] Such institutions were thus closely connected with executive power. But this did not prevent Turkish administrative courts from developing standards of

[93] Bhupinder Chimni, 'Co-option and Resistance: Two Faces of Global Administrative Law' (2005) 37 NYU LSJ Int'l L & Pol 799.

[94] Ugo Mattei, 'A Theory of Imperial Law: A Study on U.S. Hegemony and the Latin Resistance' (2002) 10 Indiana J Global L St 383.

[95] Ugo Mattei and Laura Nader, *Plunder*, 2 ('the transnational rule of law, as a deeply Western idea, has led incrementally to patterns of global plunder').

[96] Sabino Cassese and Jill Pellew (eds), *The Merit System, Le système du merite* (Institut international d'administration publique, 1987).

[97] On political patronage, see Henry Parris, *Constitutional Bureaucracy* (Allen & Unwin, 1969).

[98] Sami Omar, 'Des rapports et des resemblances existant entre les Conseils d'Etat turc et français', in Conseil d'État, *Livre jubilaire pour le cent cinquantieme anniversaire* (1952) 555.

justice. As the discussion of *Taskhin* illustrated, the Supreme Administrative Court has shown its allegiance to due process and the underlying value of the Rule of Law, which is not perceived as a 'foreign' value.[99] It can also be said that the consolidation of the administrative court was—together with the creation of the Constitutional Court—an important element in the strategy of judicial empowerment in Turkey.[100]

Those who criticize the global reach of due process might perhaps respond to this first argument by saying that it fits perfectly with their assertion, in the sense that it demonstrates that certain legal institutions originated in the Western legal tradition, though they can be, and have been, accepted by other nations. However, this response fails for it does not pay enough attention to two dimensions. The first is time. Certain minimum procedural safeguards might have been virtually absent in a legal culture because of the dominance of certain ideas and thoughts about government and law. However, this does not exclude the possibility that the subsequent development of such safeguards is regarded as being consistent with the necessities felt at the time. This highlights the other dimension that must be taken into account; that is, political preferences.

The biggest problem with the cultural objection resides, however, in its claim that process values are simply Western constructs. That there are dissimilar principles and institutions in different legal orders is certainly possible and even frequent, but it cannot be viewed as an axiom. As Amartya Sen has convincingly argued, this way of looking at principles and values is vitiated by a half-hidden form of racism; this becomes visible when it is affirmed, as if it were evident, that some values, such as democracy, are an exclusive patrimony of only some nations of the world. The least that can be said is that this way of looking at modern cultures rests on a selection of non-Western cultures, which is debatable.[101] Moreover, as argued by Sen, empirical analysis may reveal that sometimes local or regional customs are more similar to those of other parts of the world than was expected. His argument is confirmed by the empirical findings presented in this inquiry with regard to administrative procedure. Consider South Africa, which did not simply keep the requirements of natural justice that it inherited from British law, but codified them. Consider also India. Whatever the intent of the framers of the Indian Constitution, through a gradual but continuous process of evolution, the requirement that the 'procedure provided by law' be respected has evolved into a broader and more complex requirement. A procedure must be provided and it must be fair.[102] The cultural objection is, therefore, not only questionable normatively, but also empirically weak.

[99] See above, Chapter 7, paragraph 1, p. 123.

[100] Hooten Shambayati and Esen Kirdig, 'In Pursuit of "Contemporary Civilization": Judicial Empowerment in Turkey' (2009) 62 Pol Research Quart 767, 771.

[101] Amartya Sen, 'Democracy as a Universal Value' (1999) 10 J of Democracy 3.

[102] Another case, discussed by Mosler in the light of Judge Tarazi's dissenting opinion in the ICJ ruling concerning American hostages in Iran, is that of inviolability of foreigners: Hermann Mosler, 'To What Extent does the Variety of Legal Systems of the World Influence the Application of the General Principles of Law Within the Meaning of Article 38 (1) (c) of the Statute of the International Court of Justice', in *International Law and the Grotian Heritage* (Asser Institute, 1985) 175, 181.

The case against the moral objection

After having responded to the cultural objection, the focus in this section will be on the moral objection. As noted before, at the heart of the moral objection there is the assertion that the significance of due process and other general principles of law is undermined by the fact that newcomers must accept them in order to be accepted within existing global regulatory regimes. I will proffer three arguments by way of response. My first argument is that, whatever the questions of value and technique that policymakers pose about administrative due process of law, a distinction ought to be made between those who govern and those who are governed.[103] My second argument is that, even for policymakers who regard due process as inconsistent with the basic principles of their form of government, a 'thin' conception of procedural fairness and propriety is far from being unacceptable. Thirdly, because the objection that is being refuted draws on moral grounds, it will be argued that such objection is hardly acceptable if it is made by policymakers who seek to ensure that due process of law is observed by their partners.

To begin with, it has been seen from the preceding argument in this book that an increasing number of nations have set out procedural due process requirements. However, someone might object that this trend does not affect a certain type of polity, which is not a despotic one, but one in which those who govern take care of the public interest without recognizing the value of due process. History and comparison provide several examples of this. For instance, Otto Mayer argued that in Germany at the end of the nineteenth century due process was a constant and necessary element (an invariant, in our terminology) for trials, but not for administrative procedures.[104] The same might be said for an authoritarian government of our epoch.

However, a distinction must be made between those who govern and those who are governed. Two cases discussed before, *Kadi* and *Mumbai traders*, provide the focus for our discussion. What was at stake in *Kadi* was the legitimacy of the measures taken by UN institutions, including the freezing of funds of suspected terrorists or supporters of terrorist groups. Initially, such measures were taken without any sort of procedural constraint, such as prior notice and comment. The only protection that was provided to targeted persons was that their national authorities could submit their cases to the Sanctions Committee for re-examination. However, when Kadi asked his permanent representative to the UN to assert his rights, that governmental body simply failed to reply.[105] It can be reasonably argued, therefore, that if he had had some sort of procedural protection against this exercise of power, he would have used it. There is a stronger case for arguing that, whatever local or national authorities thought about it, procedural fairness and participation were invoked by the artisans and traders who were affected by the building of an

[103] For this distinction, see Norberto Bobbio, *The Age of Rights* (first published 1991; Allan Cameron (tr), Polity Press, 1996) 5.

[104] Otto Mayer, *Droit administratif allemand* (1904; CPSA, 2011) 29.

[105] CFI, Case T-315/01, *Kadi v Council and Commission*, paragraph 271.

infrastructure in Mumbai.[106] This case is of interest for an additional reason, for it was undisputed that local and national authorities possessed their own procedural norms. The dispute was, rather, about the respect of procedural norms by those who managed the project. A demand for greater openness and participation thus had a substantial effect on procedural due process of law, without undermining local or national norms. The Mumbai traders' case also provides an interesting refutation of another objection that is sometimes raised against due process; that is, it favours the wealthy. This case thus holds out the prospect of confining due process values within the family of individualistic concerns that are so often criticized by the advocates of Asian values.

Thus far I have considered the moral objection from the viewpoint of citizens (*ex parte populi*). It will be now be assessed from the viewpoint of those who govern (*ex parte principis*). It might be argued that a government can legitimately abstain from acknowledging any kind of process rights for its citizens because its political philosophy is that which Rawls defines as a benevolent absolutism.[107] However, that being the case, political control of bureaucrats would be a major concern. 'Control', in this sense, refers to the way in which those who rule the country—whose legitimacy rests either on some kind of election or on allegiance to certain moral or religious views—may influence or, better, direct agencies and other public bodies. It may, for example, be desirable to set out the procedures that public administrators must follow in order to ensure that fixed policies are constantly and rigidly applied. According to some commentators, this instrumental rationale underpinned the codes of administrative procedure enacted by some countries that were under the Soviet rule, such as Hungary after 1956. Consider also probity, viewed as a principle of procurement procedures, in the sense that there should be neither corruption nor improper use of government supplies.[108] Although this a principle underpinning procurement reform promoted by global bodies, it is not necessarily in contrast with the concerns of an authoritarian government, maybe even of a government led by religious beliefs. If a government of this type were to set out a requirement to follow a pre-defined procedure, in our case to avoid corruption, then the rulers could not reasonably argue that there is no such thing as a global concept of procedural propriety, if not of fairness.

Finally, the plausibility of the moral objection is questionable for a reason concerning membership of regulatory regimes. The critical remark that is made is that newcomers are obliged to accept such standards if they want to obtain membership. There are, however, two difficulties with this argument. First, it is not easy to understand why the government of the day might legitimately take a certain measure, as with certain treaty provisions that open up new markets to its products,

[106] See above, Chapter 6, Section 3, p. 113.

[107] See John Rawls, *The Law of Peoples* (Harvard University Press, 1999) 4.

[108] Christopher McCrudden and Stuart G Gross, 'WTO Government Procurement Rules and the Local Dynamics of Procurement Policies: A Malaysian Case Study' (2006) 17 Eur J Int'l L 151, 161. For a discussion of judicial review in authoritarian regimes, see Peter H Solomon, 'Courts and Judges in Authoritarian Regimes' (2007) 2007 World Politics 122.

encapsulating the logic of free trade, while a requirement to give reasons for measures that affect free trade, such as subsidies to national producers, would be intolerable. The implausibility of the moral objection becomes even more evident when looking at bilateral relations, in particular BITs. It is easy to understand, for instance, why the government of the People's Republic of China constantly inserts a due process clause in the provisions of its BITs regarding expropriation. In this respect, there is no Chinese Wall.[109] The reason is that in promising greater advantages to their partners, government negotiators are concerned to avoid unjustified harm to the capital that is provided to them. But the reverse side of the coin is the weakening of the argument that due process values are alien to its own culture. On the one hand, a concern for due process against direct and indirect expropriation by the public authorities of other States signals awareness that it is intrinsically important. On the other hand, as for the principle of reciprocity, the State is bound by the clauses it has agreed to. It becomes more difficult, therefore, to justify its refusal to respect the same procedural requirements when dealing with its own citizens.

4. Implications for Legal Interpretation

The objections just considered do not therefore rebut the argument that I have made concerning the global reach of administrative due process of law, a general principle that has emerged from existing norms, as well as from judicial and arbitral practice. Hence we should reject the case against it. The argument was nevertheless based upon an important premise that deserves some further thought. Being a global principle, administrative due process of law is of fundamental importance for government, in the sense that it provides standards of conduct for public authorities. However, this does not mean that there is a sort of 'global Fifth Amendment'. It can be helpful though to begin from this.

Reasons against a 'global Fifth Amendment'

The expression just used requires a quick clarification. A recent and accurate academic work that discusses the implications of investment arbitration awards concerning North American Free Trade Agreement (NAFTA) Article 1110 has raised the question whether a 'global Fifth Amendment' exists.[110] This provision requires host governments to compensate foreign investors not only for traditional expropriation, but also for measures tantamount to expropriation, in particular 'regulatory takings'. The authors reject the idea that NAFTA simply

[109] Stephen W Schill, 'Tearing Down the Great Wall—the New Generation Investment Treaties of the People's Republic of China' (2007) 15 Cardozo J Int'l & Comp L 73.

[110] Vicki Been and Joel C Beauvais, 'The Global Fifth Amendment: NAFTA's Investment Protection and the Misguided Quest for International "Regulatory Takings" Doctrine' (2003) 78 NYU L Rev 30, 83.

imports the US takings standard, and contend that the quest for an international doctrine of this kind is 'misguided'. Because the question that they pose is distinct from the question that is central to this inquiry, there is no need to take sides in this discussion.

Their approach is nevertheless helpful for present purposes in two respects. First, they present a convincing case that, while other commentators have argued that NAFTA is but a sort of legal transplant of the US regulatory takings standard into the investment field, NAFTA tribunal decisions exceed US takings protections.[111] This confirms the observation that legal transplants often lead to outcomes that differ from expectations. Second, and *a fortiori*, even though judicial and arbitral decisions are replete with mention of 'due process of law', the Fifth Amendment must not be viewed as a model for other domestic legal systems. The reason is, on the one hand, that in US public law due process is associated with theories of fundamental rights that are not necessarily shared by other legal cultures, even within the common law. On the other hand, while the US Supreme Court has traditionally used due process of law in constitutional litigation involving statutes, this is not the case elsewhere. For these reasons, the legal realities examined in this inquiry are not susceptible of being conceptualized as if they were manifestations of a sort of 'global Fifth Amendment'.

A duty of consistent interpretation

With this necessary caveat, the conclusions reached before—administrative due process is a term of art, it must be viewed as a general principle of law, and has a global reach—have certain implications that should be made explicit.

First, because it is a general principle of law, administrators, judges, and arbitrators should take it into account when adjudicating disputes across all policy areas, especially if there are no particular provisions dealing with issues of procedure.[112] Individuals and businesses should, other things being equal, be able to expect that similar, if not the same, requirements of administrative procedure be respected coherently with the principle of consistency.

Secondly, a theoretical perspective that emphasizes the autonomy of existing legal orders, whilst recognizing the importance of general principles of law, implies a prima facie argument based on the global reach of due process. This argument suggests that, coherently with a basic hermeneutical canon, among the various possible interpretations of existing legal provisions, some are to be preferred. A preference must be given to those interpretations that are coherent with due process of law, and are thus more consistent with the changed perception of the importance of transnational processes in the world we live in.[113]

111 Vicki Been and Joel C Beauvais, 'The Global Fifth Amendment', 37.

112 Benoît Jeanneau, *Les Principes généraux du droit dans la jurisprudence*, 143.

113 For a similar line of reasoning, see Jenny Martinez, 'Towards an International Judicial System' (2003) 56 Stanford L Rev 429, 529 (arguing that courts should apply a sort of 'antiparochialism' canon) and Stephen Breyer, *The Court and the World* (Alfred Knopf, 2015) 7.

Thirdly, although this inquiry is concerned with the role that administrative due process of law can play in the transnational arena, there is a corollary to what was just said: spillover effects cannot be excluded.[114] At least in all legal systems that assign an important role to equality, viewed as a principle that requires treating like cases alike and reasonably differentiating the cases that differ, the recognition of administrative due process of law is susceptible of having an impact on purely national legal relations. Courts and other public institutions might face a growing demand that existing administrative procedures be respected, that some kind of hearing be provided and that reasons are stated. That being the case, it might be increasingly difficult for them to dismiss such claims about administrative due process.

[114] See Paul Craig, *Administrative Law* (5th edn, Sweet & Maxwell, 2003) 209 (pointing out spillover effects).

Index

Administrative procedure
  advantages and costs 20, 112, 135
  codification 23–25, 190–92
  commencement 134
  concept 21–22
  consultation v. participation 111
  within international authorities 6, 31
Allan, Trevor 178
Alvarez, Josè 191
Alvis case 54, 165
Amco case 51, 165, 171
Amicus curiae briefs 116
Aristotle 8
Audi alteram partem (or *audiatur et altera pars*)
  as a principle of international law 159, 187
  as a requirement of administrative due process 38–50
  content 44, 49, 53, 59, 145
  cross-examination 197
  origins and meaning 35, 89, 191

Bagg's Case 36
Barak, Aharon 162
Basel Committee 113, 128
Bentham, Jeremy 90
Bermann, George 23
Black, Hugo 92
Blackstone, William 36
Borges, Jorge-Luis 12
Brennan, William 92
Burke, Edmund 10

Cassese, Sabino 22
Cheng, Bin 159
Coke, Edward 35–36, 191
Comparative legal analysis
  and international law 159, 184
  uses of 12
Cooperation between public authorities
  and *raison d'état* 133
  as distinct from coexistence 126
  principle of comity 129
  in standard-setting 127
  within administrative procedure 128

Damaska, Mirjan 42
Dignity
  as inherent to human persons 105
  as a rationale for due process requirements 106
Discretion
  as distinct from arbitrariness 145
  judicial 11

Due process of law
  administrative and judicial process 1, 151
  administrative adjudication and regulation 42
  and legality 146
  and terrorism 5, 45, 57, 78, 192, 202
  as a variable standard 56, 196
  as distinct from denial of justice 150
  as distinct from non-arbitrariness 143, 169
  as a general principle of law 163, 190, 197
  complementary and corrective role 170
  Due Process Clause 191
  essential v. non-essential requirements 167
  foundational role 174, 196
  global Fifth Amendment 38, 204
  global reach 178, 200–01
  models of 92–94
  moral roots of 36, 88, 185, 195
  origins of 37, 199
  practical advantages of 8, 130, 147
  procedural 145, 148, 191
  process v. substance 7, 199
  rationales for 88–92, 103, 121, 133, 164
  wilful disregard of 142
Duty to give reasons, *see* giving reasons requirement

ELSI case 2, 141–42
Estoppel 122
EU law
  essential procedural requirements 105, 168
  sources of 133
Expropriation 194

Fair and equitable treatment
  as a source of due process requirements 197
  as an autonomous standard 167
  as a broad standard 175
  as a standard of BITs 193–94
  importance of 165–67, 194
Ferrecchia case 55, 165
Frankfurter, Felix 38
Fuller, Lon 109, 184

General principles of law
  as distinct from equity 161
  as norms of conduct 163
  fairness 130
  good faith 130
  res judicata 151
  complementary and corrective role 160
  foundational role 163

General principles of law (*cont.*):
  implications for legal interpretation 172, 206
  in international law 157–59, 189
  in EU law 177, 189
  recognized by civilized nations 157, 188
  Statute of the ICJ 150
Giving reasons requirement
  advantages 62–63
  minimum standard 65
  per relationem 69, 169
  variety of 64
Global administrative law 95
  and international law 96
  critique of 199
Globalization
  and cultural imperialism 200
  critics 6, 112, 129, 198–99
  spillover effects 81, 206
Grotius 181

Harlow, Carol 164
Hart, Herbert L. 11, 161–62, 165
Hauriou, Maurice 18
Hearing
  essence 145
  right to be heard 109
Hegel, Georg 182–83

Inspection Panel 115, 122
Interest balancing 110, 131, 144
International law
  as *jus gentium* 181
  custom 161, 187
  domestic law and international law 182–83
  sources of 157, 161
International Civil Aviation Authority 113

Judicial review
  foundations of 185
  idea of bounded judicial discretion 162
  non liquet 156
  principled approach 119
Juno Trader case 96, 104
Justice
  as protection from injury 103
  theories of 95
Jus cogens 100, 189

Kadi case 5, 57–58, 144, 202
Kant, Immanuel 89, 182
Koskenniemi, Martti 186–87

Laferrière, Eduard 40
Lagrange, Maurice 54
Law
  'general common law' 181
  legal positivism 174
  natural law and positive law 155
  principles v. rules 162
  public law and private bodies 8, 186
  public law values 87
Luhmann, Niklas 112

Maduro, Miguel 57
Magna Carta 191
Margin of appreciation 107
Marlin Mining case 97, 114
Mashaw, Jerry 92–94
Mayer, Otto 17, 36, 43, 202
McIlwain, Charles 100
Montesquieu 180
Mumbai case 115–16, 203

Natural justice 31, 36–38, 145
Nature of things 180–81, 185–86
Nemo judex in re propria
  as a principle of international law 156
  origins 89
Non liquet 41, 72, 158, 172

OECD, guidance for Member States 129

Perelman, Chaim 174
Procedural protection
  dignitarian value of 106
  and process values 119, 200–01
  specific procedural norms 79, 164
Procedural fairness or justice 44, 145, 164, 189, 193
Proportionality 47, 175, 189
Puchta, Georg-Friedrich 181

Raison d'état 100
Rawlings, Richard 164
Rawls, John 95, 203
Reisman, Michael W. 160, 197
Right
  of defence 103
  human rights 144
Romano, Santi 12
Rule of Law
  and *Rechtsstaat* 24, 63, 89, 146
  as a value of the EU 81
  critique of 200
  ideals 148
  theories of 86–87

Savigny, Carl-Friedrich 181–82
Scalia, Antonin 191
Schlesinger Rudolf 184
Schmitt, Carl 181, 183
Schwebel, Stephen 141
Sen, Amartya 201
Seneca 36, 191
Shapiro, Martin 12
Shrimps and turtles case 52, 71, 99, 116, 129, 144, 149, 175
Smith, Adam 103, 181

Sound administration 121
  as compliance with predefined rules 121
  as consistency 122
  as scientific or technical accuracy 124
Southern Bluefin Tuna Case 98, 125
Standards
  global standards 114, 184, 199
  of civilization 188
  variable v. non-variable standards 162, 165
Stewart, Richard 111

Taskin case 123, 201
Terlizzi case 153, 177
Tizzano, Antonio 33
Transocean Marine Paint Association case 56, 105, 176
Triepel, Heinrich 182–83
Tysiac case 107, 149

Values
  concept of 85–86
  as distinct from principles 87, 162
  as distinct from rationales 88–89
  as distinct from rights 42
  dignitary 93, 106
  in public law 1, 7, 9, 63
  shared by all legal systems 163, 183
  social importance of 162
Vattel, Emmerich 2, 52, 180
Venire contra factum proprium 108

Wälde, Thomas 160
Warner, Jean-Pierre 55, 105, 177
World Bank
  as employer 75
  guidelines 98
  Inspection Panel 115–16, 122

The manufacturer's authorised representative in the EU for product safety is Oxford University Press España S.A. of el Parque Empresarial San Fernando de Henares, Avenida de Castilla, 2 – 28830 Madrid (www.oup.es/en or product.safety@oup.com). OUP España S.A. also acts as importer into Spain of products made by the manufacturer.

www.ingramcontent.com/pod-product-compliance
Lightning Source LLC
LaVergne TN
LVHW011800200926
848484LV00003B/744
* 9 7 8 0 1 9 8 7 8 8 3 8 6 *